AF560103

PROBLEMS IN TEACHING AND LEARNING MATHEMATICS

By

Dr. R. YASODA

Assistant Professor

School of Education & HRD

Dravidian University

Kuppam – 517 425

DISCOVERY PUBLISHING HOUSE PVT. LTD.

NEW DELHI-110 002

First Published - 2009

Reprinted - 2017

ISBN: 978-81-8356-378-9

Problems in Teaching and Learning Mathematics

Published by:

DISCOVERY PUBLISHING HOUSE PVT. LTD.

4383/4B, Ansari Road, Darya Ganj

New Delhi-110 002 (India)

Phone: +91-11-23279245, 43596064-65

Fax: +91-11-23253475

E-mail: discoverypublishinghouse@gmail.com

sales@discoverypublishinggroup.com

web: www.discoverypublishinggroup.com

Printed at:

Infinity Imaging Systems

Delhi

Preface

Teachers play an important role in any educational system. Mathematics occupies a key place in the curriculum of our educational system. In the present age of automation and Computers, it is a vital subject, in the sense that it aids in learning of other school subjects as well as remains very necessary and useful for the adult life. Students who had difficulty in learning mathematics are likely to have negative attitudes towards it. A good teacher should possess knowledge about the nature and types of learning difficulties or problems in children. This knowledge will promote better awareness on the concept of learning difficulties of students and development of positive attitudes towards students with learning problems. Attitudes, beliefs and motivation play an important role in the learning of mathematics. Teacher is an artist who moulds and shapes physical, mental and moral power of the mind. To accomplish their task effectively, a teacher should be highly competent. To become a competent teacher one should possess thorough understanding about various aspects of difficulties in students. Intensive training and education help the teacher to perform the diversified role more effectively.

The present investigation is aimed to identify the difficulty areas in secondary school level mathematics, teaching and learning problems and attitude of teachers and students towards mathematics. For this, the author of the book developed rating scales to identify the difficulty areas in secondary level mathematics and also the level of difficulty as perceived by teachers and students. Checklists to assess the problems of teachers in teaching mathematics and problems of students in learning mathematics are also developed.

Similarly, attitude scales were developed to assess the attitudes of teachers towards teaching mathematics and attitudes of students towards learning mathematics. The focus of attention is also to find out the effect of independent variables of teachers on their attitude (sex, age, general qualification, professional qualification, teaching experience, locality and management) and the effect of independent variables of students on their attitudes (class, sex, age, locality, management, father's occupation, family literacy index and family income). Further, the study aimed at predicting to what extent and how far the independent variables influence the dependent variables (difficulties, attitudes and problems).

The study covered three districts i.e. Chittoor, Kadapa and Nellore. From each district, 20 schools were selected. The total number of schools covered in the three districts is 60. All the teachers working in these schools (161) and dealing VIII, IX and X class mathematics form the sample of the study. Eight to ten students covering VIII, IX and X classes are randomly selected from each school consisting a total of 644 students. Overall, 644 students and 161 teachers are the sample of the study.

The report is presented in 7 chapters. Chapter – I brings out the theoretical framework. In chapter – II the review of literature is presented under the heads, research studies on maths education, studies on mathematics curriculum and textbooks, studies on teaching of mathematics and problems solving, studies on problems faced by students and teachers, studies on attitudes of students and teachers and studies on the effect of personal and demographic variables of the students and teachers in learning and teaching mathematics respectively. Chapter – III describes the statement of the problem, objectives, hypotheses and variables. Chapter – IV describes the development of the tools. Chapter – V deals with the analysis of data and discussion. Chapter – VI discusses the summary and conclusions. Finally, in the last chapter the educational implications of the study, limitations and suggestions for further research are presented.

I am ever thankful to my guide Prof. S. Padmanabhaiah for his valuable guidance and constructive suggestions throughout this scientific piece of research work. I also sincerely acknowledge the contribution of the mathematics teachers and secondary school students who served as the subjects of this study. I am confident that the contents of the book will be of much useful to the students learning mathematics and teachers teaching mathematics at school and collegiate levels. This book will be of an immense help to the researchers and students working in the area of learning difficulties in mathematics. It is a modest attempt to make the field practitioners to understand the concept of learning difficulties in mathematics and any suggestions to improve the quality or to cover the other areas in improving learning in mathematics are wholeheartedly welcome.

Author

Contents

1

Introduction

IMPORTANCE OF EDUCATION

The overall development of a nation depends on the proper utilisation of its natural as well as human resources. The opinion of the Planning Commission in the 7th Five Year Plan (1985-90) may be mentioned in this context: "Human resources development has necessarily to be assigned a key role in any development strategy, particularly in a country with a large population. Trained and educated on sound lines, a large population can itself become an asset in accelerating economic growth and in ensuring social change in desired directions. Education develops basic skills and abilities and fosters a value system conducive to, and in support of national development goals both long term and immediate."

Hence the development of human resource is a must for any modern society. As M.S. Swaminathan remarks "Human resource is the most valuable global resource and any short or long term development strategy should be oriented towards the continued well being of the human race."

Human resource development is the development of all sections of people in the society. Harbison and Myers define it as " the process of increasing the knowledge, skill and the capacities of all the people in a society."

Education plays a significant role in the development of human resources. The report of the Education Commission (1964-66) states:

" If this change on a grand scale is to be achieved without violent revolution, there is one instrument, and one instrument only that can be used: EDUCATION. Other agencies may help, and indeed sometimes have a more apparent impact. But the national system of education is the only instrument that can reach all the people".

The school can help in manpower planning though it has no direct role in the matter. It is a social agency and it has social accountability. Education is a social process and so it has a significant role in manpower planning in the light of individual as well as social needs.

According to the Rigveda, Education is " a force which makes an individual self-reliant as well as self-less". The Upanishads consider that the result of Education is more important than its Nature as the end-product of Education, is ' salvation `. Panini, the Scholar and Grammarian views Education as the training one obtains from Nature, while Kanada, the ancient philosopher calls it a means of developing self-contentment. Sankaracharya regards Education to be synonymous with self-realisation.

Swami Vivekananda remarks " Education is the manifestation of divine perfection, already existing in man ". According to Mahatma Gandhi " Education is the drawing out of the best in child and man – body, mind and spirit."

The purpose of education is manifold: to quote John Dewey " What nutrition and reproduction are to physiological life, education is to social life."

In all the countries of the world, it may be seen that high per-capita incomes are associated with high rates of literacy. Education is valued because it contributes to a better life. Alfred Marshall emphasised the importance of Education as a national investment, it is the most valuable of all capital, invested in human beings.

According to McClelland (1961), "Economic growth in any society is dependent on the existence of a high level of need for achievement among people in that society."

In a democratic country, Education can be used for giving training in good citizenship. It can produce leaders who are capable of independent thought, judgement, self-expression, originality and initiative. Emphasising the importance of education, the Kothari

Commission's report on Indian Education (1964-66) says "In a world based on science and technology, it is the education that determines the level of prosperity, welfare and security of the people and the quality and number of persons coming out of our schools and colleges will depend on our success in a great enterprise of national reconstruction whose principle objective is to raise the standard of living of our people".

Indian Education Commission (1964-66) states: Education ought to be related to life, needs and aspirations of the people so as to be a powerful instrument of social, economic and cultural transformation.

Education is the process by which an individual is enabled to function according to the expectations of the society as well as according to his capabilities. Locke (1969) states " Plants are developed by cultivation and men by education." To Pestalozi " It is natural, harmonious and progressive development of man's innate powers." Rousseau recognises education as " A process of development. It is the natural development of humanity, the spontaneous development of all our innate nature and faculties."

According to Smt. Indira Gandhi, the late Prime Minister of India, "Education is a lifelong process by which the man's inherent qualities of excellence, creativity and receptivity would be developed to the maximum possible extent and makes him a real human being. "Education is a liberating force, and in our age it is also a democratising force, cutting across the barriers of caste and class, smoothing out inequalities imposed by birth and other circumstances".

The development of a country is primarily determined by the quality of its human resources, which depend on the level of knowledge, skills and attitudes. Therefore, creating the right minds through the right process of education requires the top-most priority.

Education in recent years has been regarded as the greatest and most effective instrument of human resource development. The Ministry of Education in India has been re-christened as the Ministry of Human Resource Development.

From this discussion it is clear that education leads to the overall personality development (spiritual, moral, cultural, social, mental and economic). Therefore education is a must for any country for its development and it has no alternative.

IMPORTANCE OF MATHEMATICS IN HUMAN LIFE

Mathematics has always been regarded as a tool for sharpening the intellect. For this purpose one has to think systematically, logically and precisely.

Brahmagupta, the great Indian mathematician of the eighth century said, " If you want to shine in the company of the learned, propose mathematical problems and solve them."

As we move into the 21st century, there is consensus among the experts about the necessity for all students to have string mathematical ability. Majority of eminent educationists of the past as well as of the present, including Herbert, Froebel, Pestolozzi, Dr. Maria Montissori, Sri. T.P. Nunn etc. have advocated the importance of mathematics. In their opinion, the intellectual and cultural development of a person is not possible without the study of mathematics.

In several fields centered round human activity such as Accountancy, Banking, Shop-keeping business, Tailoring, Carpentry, Taxation, Insurance, Post and Telegraphs and so on there is the use of mathematics. It has become the basis of the world's entire business and commercial system. Thus mathematics has been an inseparable part of human activity.

Mathematics is the logical study of shape, size and situation and it is mainly based upon the concepts of numbers and geometry of figures. It has come to play a remarkable role in the engineering of highways, the search for energy, the design for TV sets, the study of epidemics, and the navigation of ships. The career and financial prospects of every individual depend heavily on his mathematical knowledge and learning. Consequently, from social and scientific points of view there has developed a growing interest in how one learns mathematics, and how one's mind works in the analysis of a mathematical problem.

Many a phenomenon of the universe can be predicted through mathematical calculations. For instance on 24th october, 1995, people watched the solar eclipse and the 'Diamond Ring' during its totality, which dazzled the eclipse gazers. But the exact date and time of the eclipse was calculated much earlier by the solar scientists, using mathematical calculations. Actually, mathematics is the science of reasoning. It enables an individual to know the laws of nature. Plato once rightly remarked, "Let none ignorant of Geometry enter my door, to pray, Bless us, Oh Divine numbers."

There has been explosion of knowledge in every field of human endeavour including science and technology. Extension research in science and technology resulting in several discoveries and inventions has changed the face of human society by providing things that make modern life happier and more comfortable than ever before. At the root of all these, we cannot ignore the role of mathematics. Mathematics is the mother of sciences and as Compte (1964) has rightly said "All scientific education which does not commence with mathematics is, of necessity, defective at its foundation".

Hence it is imperative that our educational environment provides opportunities to all students to do worthwhile and purposeful mathematical work.

PLACE OF MATHEMATICS IN SECONDARY SCHOOL CURRICULUM

Mathematics occupies an important place in the school curriculum. It has been its inseparable part of school curriculum ever since the beginning of formal education and it continues to be so. Its curriculum has undergone various changes from time to time in accordance with the changing needs of the society. Realising its social relevance, the Education Commission set up in 1964 recommended that Mathematics should be taught as a compulsory subject of general education upto Class X. Since general education envisages Mathematics for all, the selection of content should be relevant to the practical needs of everyday life. Hence the load of Mathematics curriculum should be realistic.

Mathematics at the Secondary school level is the basic structure on which the whole super structure of mathematics, mathematical sciences, physical sciences, social sciences and technology in the universities and technical institutions rests. To quote professor

K.E.Brown "Mathematics has become the basic fabric of our social order. The strength of that fabric, in fact the very survival of our nation— may well depend upon the amount and kind of mathematics taught in our secondary schools. This is a great sobering responsibility for those who design and administer the programmes. If we take the responsibility lightly, our children will suffer the consequences of our foolish action."

But as observed by J.N. Kapoor(1993) in his book "Some Aspects of school Mathematics" school mathematics in India today is at the crossroads. Many students find mathematics a difficult subject. Even most of the teachers express difficulty in understanding some of the newly introduced topics in the mathematics curriculum. At this stage, a great deal of clear thinking and careful planning is necessary in which school teachers, university professors, educational administrators and even the general public have a significant role to play. Our object should be not to change the curriculum; but to improve it significantly. The way the students learn school mathematics and the habits they form now while learning it, will, to some extent, determine the future pattern of intellectual activity in the country.

TEACHING OF MATHEMATICS AT SECONDARY SCHOOL LEVEL

It is generally felt that improvement in the teaching process is of paramount importance. If the teacher teaches in a planned methodical way, it is expected that the achievement of the children is certainly going to be satisfactory.

Teacher's awareness of the teaching methodologies and techniques of testing are vital not only for an effective transaction of curriculum in the classroom but also for improvement in the standards of achievement of children. The Delors' International Commission on Education for the 21st century stated in its Report, "Improving the quality of education depends on first improving the recruitment, training, social status and conditions of work of teachers. They need the appropriate knowledge and skills, personal characteristics, professional prospects and motivation if they are to meet the expectations placed upon them." (Delors, 1996:142).

In the study of mathematics the emphasis should be more on the development of a general problem-solving ability rather than on finding a solution to a particular problem.

Knowledge is useful only when one is able to apply it effectively. The ability to apply it in turn needs power to think effectively. Therefore the teacher of mathematics should not insist the pupils to cram or memorise the mathematical facts. The pupil should attack problems logically in the spirit of a discoverer.

Mathematics should not be taught as a set of isolated facts and formulas. It has to be taught as a science in which the relationship of facts is as important as the facts themselves and wherein facts are arranged in sequences.

The teachers have to learn mathematics as an organised structure, otherwise they would themselves teach it as a mass of unrelated facts. They have to learn each fact as it is related to the whole. The big ideas have to be stressed.

The teachers have to know not only the contents of the new mathematics, they have to know something of the spirit, the nature, the abstractions and the generalisations of mathematics. They have to know substantially more than what they are expected to teach. They have to have greater insight into mathematics than what they are expected to communicate to their children.

Mathematics, as it is taught today in most of the schools, appears to be a fragmental collection of facts, techniques and theorems that bear little relation to each other. Moreover, these topics are taught as if they have no connection with real life. Thus the student fails to have the necessary motivation to learn mathematics. He begins to look at mathematics as a bag of tricks which have to be learnt for the examination purpose alone but which are otherwise meaningless.

It can be seen that on an average three to four problems are taught in a normal class period. More than two-thirds of the problems taught are completely solved and the teacher writes synthetic solutions on the blackboard. Most of the remaining incomplete problems are left initiated or partially solved due to lack of time or other external factors. Mention should be made of just a few teachers who leave some problems, strategically, unsolved leaving the rest of the work to students to do so in the classroom.

Mathematics has too long been taught by rule-of-thumb methods. It has almost been taught as mechanics is taught to an uneducated person in a motor workshop. Certain rules are given to the students very often without proofs or with 'proofs by intimidation' or with 'proofs by waving of hands' or with 'proofs resting on the authority of the teacher'. The students are expected to apply these rules to numerous examples and they have to go on applying these rules till they are completely 'brainwashed' and forget their initial objections to the rules.

By and large, it can be generalised that the comprehensive teacher behaviour in a mathematics class room has been that of presenting solutions to problems by themselves giving little or no scope for the students to attempt to learn any skill individually or independently. The usual 'class work', in solving problems from the given mathematics textbook exercises is very much minimal. Most times, teachers resort to the synthetic process of displaying the solution of a problem, though elegantly, ignoring the analytical thinking that has to take place in the process.

PROBLEMS OF STUDENTS AND TEACHERS IN MATHEMATICS EDUCATION

The observation of a classroom reveals pathetic conditions prevailing in the field. Most of the schools lack even basic infrastructural facilities like Mathematics laboratory/ workroom. The present educational system loaded with rhetorical teaching lessons and examination oriented values, gives the teacher no scope for fostering creativity. In the mass education system, that prevails now-a-days, their enrgies are spent to maintain discipline in the classroom and to finish the syllabus in time.

Many pupils perform poorly in mathematics and find the subject very difficult and uninteresting. The probable reasons may be some socio-economic factors which have a bearing on the performance of such pupils and existing school conditions etc., One major factor related to the school is perhaps the heavy curriculum load in mathematics.

Many changes are being made in the mathematics curriculum. There may be certain new topics, which have been included in the present curriculum, with which the teachers are not familiar. Even in other topics, there could be some points about which the teachers have some doubts.

To enable the teachers to handle the difficult topics effectively, they must be provided with self-learning materials like teachers' handbooks etc. To help students understand the more abstract concepts easily and meaningfully, the schools must be provided with necessary audio-visual aids like models, charts, and different types of boards etc.

But contrary to these components, no teacher's guides are available in mathematics. Individual teachers are left completely to fend for themselves. They even do not read the textbooks. Textbooks are used for their collection of problems. Teachers know some standard techniques for solving standard type problems. They repeat them year after year. The concepts are never emphasised.

There are no charts, models and films for illustrating mathematical concepts. This is not surprising, since for 'drill', audio-visual aids are not needed. The need for such aids is very urgent for the improvement of conditions conducive for effective teaching-learning process.

Apart from these problems, heavy syllabus is one of the major problems of both teachers and students of mathematics. The authorities force the teachers to complete the syllabus in the stipulated time frame, and also expect cent per cent results in the subject, which is a hard task for the teachers. In the light of the speedy, and examination-oriented teaching, students find it very difficult to understand the subject without any logic. This in turn leads to more number of failures in the mathematics subject.

One more problem expressed by the mathematics teachers of secondary schools is that their students are not thorough with primary level mathematics. They lack even the knowledge of four fundamental operations, etc.

What are the causes for these problems? How to overcome these problems? How to achieve the objectives of teaching mathematics effectively at secondary school level? etc, are the areas to be investigated.

ATTITUDES OF STUDENTS AND TEACHERS TOWARDS MATHEMATICS EDUCATION

Why do students dislike mathematics? Is it because of apathy, frustration, lack of motivation or aptitude, hostility, scare due to the difficulty and abstraction of this subject?

Obviously different factors such as physiological, social, emotional, intellectual and pedagogical may cause 'maths-aversion' in different students and it is the duty of the mathematics teacher to identify and isolate these factors. Once the disease is diagnosed, the remedy might be easy and often it may require lot of effort on the part of the teacher. Every teacher should see that the message is carried to the student whether he is willing or not. He should be made to cooperate, to get motivated and feel important by getting involved in the learning process. The teacher should throw him a challenge in order to make the subject fascinating, provide him with intellectual food to satisfy his curiosity and induce him to develop the habit of thinking which is very essential for problem solving in his future life. Solving problems through mathematical games could be helpful in this area.

It is sad to observe that even today, the educational system in India remains essentially examination oriented. Under this system, learners do not receive mathematics education. They mostly prepare themselves for passing examinations. Such a situation not only damages the purpose of all education but also proves ruinous for mathematical education. Learners memorise important results and proofs in order to be able to reproduce them in examinations. The result is that success in examinations has become the all-important objective of mathematical education. If we want to make mathematical education more meaningful, this situation will have to be changed and the entire system of education will have to be reviewed and reoriented.

If we observe carefully mathematics classes we find that the rate of progress is decreasing at all the stages of school education. Mathematics is also presented from a wrong point of view. It is presented as a matter of learning dead facts and techniques and not in terms of its true nature, which involves processes that demand thought and creativity. Today's method of teaching is traditional where chalk and duster are used by the teachers and pen and paper by students.

Making students aware of the strategies, or principles, relevant to problem solving is one of the goals of the standards of the National Council of Teachers of Mathematics (NCTM). This can best be noticed while observing students do proofs in Geometry. Typically, students observe the model proofs presented by the teacher and then try to copy their example. Often, this is done with little or no thinking on the part of the student.

It is therefore necessary that only correct mathematics should be taught correctly at the secondary school stage.

The syllabi and method should be tailored to project at least a reasonably correct picture of mathematics in the minds of the students.

To provide complete and wide knowledge in the subject, the textbook should contain appropriate and adequate number of chapters, exercises, problems, and worked-out examples.

The progress and improvement of scientific method and Mathematics are linked to the prosperity of the whole human civilisation. To arouse and maintain the interest of the students in Mathematics, therefore, the elements of curiosity, motivation, imagination, novelty, originality, newness and usefulness are required. Actually, interest is a motivating force that arouses, sustains and regulates concentrated effort. It is a dynamic system of human personality in action; and is responsible for the persistent and consistent behaviour of an individual. Sawherey and Telford define interest as "favourable attitude towards objects." In the structural sense interest is an element or item in an individual's make up, either congenial or acquired, because of which he tends to have the feeling of 'worth-whileness' in connection with certain objects or matters relating to particular subject or a particular field of knowledge, particularly scientific method and Mathematics.

It is observed that the teachers and students show a lot of indifference to their own responsibilities and duties. This is the time teachers working at school level and authorities concerned should rethink about the existing practices in the class room and appraisal mechanism for the same. There is a need for transparency and accountability on the part of the teacher.

There are some adverse comments on mathematics as follows:

- "It is too remote from life to interest the student".
- "Mathematics has outlived its usefulness as a subject of secondary school instruction".
- "Mathematics is completely taught on theoretical grounds".
- "It is more abstract in its nature".
- "Teaching is confined to the classroom and not related to pupils life".

Obviously, the teachers assume a monopolised responsibility to solve problems, one after the other and as many as one could, in order to complete or 'cover' the heavy syllabus and examination requirements.

A dominant trend of 'haste' to proceed as fast as, or as much as they could has been quite transparent and evident. Such an accelerated style would, by implication, hamper sustained effort on the problem-solving stages and processes. With the result, the students would acquire rapid, but, mechanical drill type skills resulting in the total loss of the thrill and the ecstasy of creative problem-solving processes.

Mathematics is not merely a 'product', but a process. It is not only a 'knowledge'; it is an activity also. Its 'static' part is important, its 'dynamic' part is even more vital. Not only mathematical facts are to be taught, methods of arriving at these facts are also to be communicated. All these require a rethinking about the goals of mathematics education.

The need for unifying concepts for simplifying teaching of mathematics itself stresses the need for thinking about objectives and curriculum. The new curricula have to place more emphasis on thinking and less on memory. How this can be achieved requires a great deal of thinking.

What are the causes for this situation? How to overcome this situation in the study of mathematics? In these circumstances, how to develop positive attitudes among the teachers and the students?

THE PRESENT STUDY

The observations made in the foregoing pages demand an indepth study of the field of mathematics education. The discussion reveals that knowledge of mathematics is inevitable for human beings. It also reveals that there are major drawbacks in the study of mathematics at the secondary school stage. Therefore, it is proposed to conduct a thorough investigation to identify the difficulties faced by teachers in teaching mathematics, and by students in learning mathematics, and to study their attitudes towards mathematics education which probably reveal the route cause for all the problems listed above and of course it is proposed to study the variations in the problems and attitudes faced by students and teachers among different sub groups basing on personal and demographic variables to make the study of mathematics more meaningful, easy and enjoyable at the secondary school level.

Schunerts (1951) study gives credibility to the present research as he has found that possible factors for promoting mathematics abilities are 'resident in the teacher, in the teaching, in the pupil, and in the school'.

Accordingly the investigator is interested in collecting all the relevant literature available on mathematics education including the research already done in this field, to get sufficient insight for suggesting remedial measures to overcome the deficiencies in the present system and to suggest suitable strategies to improve the situation. Further, the researcher is also interested in procuring empirical evidence on the basis of the opinions or attitudes obtained from the students and teachers of mathematics in secondary schools to analyse whether their views are in line with the insight obtained by the researcher. The exact problem with its objectives will be listed out only after getting a thorough review of related literature.

RESUME OF SUCCEEDING CHAPTERS

The next chapter i.e., Chapter 2 gives an analytical presentation of the research work conducted so far in the area in which the investigator is interested to investigate further.

It is natural that anybody after having obtained complete information about the status of research could be in a position to state the problem for investigation with its objectives, hypothesis, variables, scope and limitations. These aspects are presented in Chapter 3.

The fourth chapter describes the methodology of investigation-methods of measuring variables, methods of sampling, methods employed in the collection of data, methods of quantifying the responses of the subjects to different tools and finally methods of analysing the data obtained to draw dependable, meaningful and useful conclusions.

The fifth chapter is exclusively meant for analysis of the data and discussions thereon.

There are two more concluding chapters in the thesis—one provides the summary and conclusions or major findings and the other one describes the educational implications of the study and suggestions for further research in this area.

2

Review of Related Literature

CONCEPTUALISATION OF THE PROBLEM

An objective of teaching of mathematics should be to make clear the nature of mathematics itself as reflected in the following characteristics:

1. *Mathematics is a Dynamic Intellectual Enterprise.* Mathematics is primarily an intellectual subject. It should not be presented as a collection of rules, which have to be applied mechanically to a large number of examples. The whole curriculum should be built round interesting and intellectually challenging problems. The student of mathematics is not simply a verifier of results but an explorer of new vistas of knowledge.

   Locke (S.K.Mangal, 1990) said:

   Mathematics is the mirror of civilisation. In the modern world as we make larger use of quantitative terms, we have to be accurate to a split second. Modern civilisation stands on a foundation of applied mathematics.

   It is indispensable to each and every minute of man's life. It is considered the Science of Sciences and Art of all Arts. Almost all the subjects require mathematical knowledge to a greater extent.

2. *Mathematics is Logical.* Logic is the essence of mathematics. Mathematics draws necessary conclusions from explicitly stated assumptions. The student must study a number of axiomatic systems. These may not be deep, but they must be logically correct. He must understand the nature of proof. After a good mathematical training, the student must be able to detect faulty deductive reasoning, and to differentiate between definitions, axioms and postulates and validly – drawn theorems deduced from axioms.

   Locke strongly endorses this view in the following statement:

   "Mathematics is a way to settle in the mind a habit of reasoning."

   "Mathematics in its widest significance is the development of all types of formal deductive reasoning" —*Whitehead*

   "Mathematics is the science which draws necessary conclusions" —*Pierce*

3. *Mathematics is a study of sets with structures.* Sets and Structures are the basic unifying concepts in mathematics. At the school stage, mostly algebraic and order structures are studied. The student must be clear about these structures for natural numbers, for integers, for rational numbers, for real numbers and for complex numbers.

   Poincare accepts this view when he says:

   "Mathematicians do not study objects, but the relations between them. Matter does not engage their attention. They are interested in form alone".

4. *Mathematics is a study of patterns in number and space.* The student must develop a sense for noticing patterns when he comes across these. Number and space intuitions have to be strongly built. A student must be able to exploit symmetries in number and geometrical patterns.

   As mathematics is defined as " the science of number and space", there is no exaggeration in saying that it is the creator as well as the nourisher and superior of all the arts.

Mathematical regularity, symmetry, order and arrangement play a leading part in beautifying and organising the work of these arts.

5. *Mathematics deals with general structures.* By seeing carefully a number of particular structures, the student should be able to perceive a general structure with his intuition. He must feel how the certainty of scientific results depends to a great extent on the use of the mathematical methods.

Courant and Robbins (1941) voice the same opinion when they say:

Mathematics as an expression of human mind reflects the active will, the contemplative reason and the desire for aesthetic perfection. Its basic elements are logic and intuition, analysis and construction, generality and individuality.

6. *Mathematics deals with abstract structures.* Abstraction is essential in mathematics. The school curriculum must be motivated by very concrete situations, however, the goal of abstraction must however not be given up and must ensure that the children can see the point of abstraction.

Hilbert endorses the same in his statement :

"Mathematics is nothing more than a game played according to certain simple rules with meaningless marks on paper".

7. *Mathematics deals with precise and elegant structures.* The student must be able to make precise statements and should be able to detect loose statements when these are made.

Mathematics is the numerical and calculative part of man's life and knowledge. It helps man give exact interpretation of his ideas and conclusions. In the form of a mathematical equation, on the other hand, describing the relationship between the quantified aspects of a phenomenon is not only exact but also brief.

8. *Mathematics deals with deep structures.* The student must build up an ambition to study deep structures and derive pleasure out of them. The primary aim of teaching mathematics is to enable the student develop understanding and skills related

to mathematical concepts, principles, formulas, and operations and to develop abilities to apply them to problem-solving situations.

Rosenbloom (1966) stresses that problem-solving is a basic mathematical activity.

Thus, mathematics, is especially a programme of education, which fosters a very high order of mental processes of questioning, reasoning, analysing, inducting and logical thinking.

Hence how should the subject be handled to achieve the objectives of teaching mathematics at school level? The following discussion gives the details.

A mathematical concept is a mental construct, based on abstracting a common response to the sets of apparently different stimuli through interaction; elements of each set are identical and related to each other by the rules of relations. This mental construct of abstracted response is given a universally accepted name and symbol. One concept is distinguishable from another. These concepts are hierarchically related. The process of concept acquisition involves the process of associating understanding gained from real or partly real experiences with the words. Mathematical symbols and words play an important role in the understanding of Mathematics. The child may not be able to communicate his thoughts and his concepts, not due to lack of understanding of concepts but due to lack of vocabulary.

According to Campbell (1956), a teacher's confidence in his/her ability to execute appropriate teacher behaviours to positively effect student outcomes or teacher efficacy as it is known, is an essential aspect of teaching.

Sax and Ottina (1958) found it advantageous to have the development of concepts precede the learning of computational skills.

Ausubel, D.(1960) in the study "The use of advance organisers in the learning and retention of meaningful verbal learning" emphasised that an advance organiser outline of what the teacher is going to cover is to be put on the blackboard before beginning a lesson. This is a clever method of teaching the theorems in geometry.

Chase (1960) found the knowledge of concept necessary in learning problem solving skills. He also found it necessary for children to learn computational skills and to learn to observe details.

According to Lovell (1961) the two important factors likely to affect the learning of mathematical concepts are; the mathematical understanding of the teacher and the home environment in which the child is reared.

Supples and Macknight (1961) and Supples and Ginsbeg (1962) have shown that incidental learning of mathematical concepts is not effective and that the prior learning of one concept does not facilitate the acquisition of a related concept.

Sloan and Pate (1969) revealed striking differences in question — asking behaviours between the traditional mathematics teachers and those from the school mathematics study group (SMSG). S.M.S.G. teachers asked more and more questions at interpretation and evaluation levels resulting in the increase of student cognitive levels of thinking in problem-solving settings.

V.N. Wanchoo (1974) in his article "Survey and development of research in science and mathematics education" concluded that: (i) The quantum of research done at the primary level was meager; (ii) The research work done in the area of evaluation was mostly confined to test constructions; (iii) The work done in the area of concept development was practically negligible.

Shukla (1981) in his study 'Identification of major skills involved in mathematics teaching at secondary school stage' found that mathematical problem-solving can be best achieved when students:

- are exposed to the problem properly;
- are made to recollect known relationships;
- are made to find out the necessities required for the solution; and
- are made to analyse the given data in the light of the relationship and necessities.

Mainka (1983) found that mathematical concepts developed better in pupils who were good at language and did not develop to their fullest form in pupils who were poor at language.

With the help of these observations, Miss. M. Kumar in her article entitled "Language ability and acquisition of mathematics concepts at primary school level" (1985) concludes that the pupil is unable to analyse the problem or stimuli presented to him in reversible way due to lack of knowledge of language. He is unable to abstract relevant information from the data presented and finds it difficult to interpret results. A child good at Mathematics is always good at English while the converse is not always true. The author opines that language barrier is overcome by presenting concrete experiences, like diagrams, geo-boards, geometrical blocks etc., The use of these aids is stressed till the pupil acquires mastery over language.

McIntosh, W. (1986) in the study "The effect of imagery generation on science rule learning" stated that Creating and using mental images about rules could help students solve problems. A study was conducted with 52 ninth grade students who were assigned to one of the two groups. Both groups were given information on Boyle's law, Charles' law and Gay-Lussacs' law. One group of students was encouraged to create mental images of a typical gas as it responded to different amounts of pressure, temperature or volume. This group was also instructed to draw an image of this in their notebooks. Students of the other group were not instructed to make mental pictures or draw images in their notebooks. The result showed that the image group did better than the non-image group in solving the problems, but the non-image group did better than the image group on the memory part of the exam. Many other studies, however, have demonstrated that mental imagery can have a very beneficial impact on memory. This research has clear implications for mathematics instruction. For the solution of problems, which, by their very nature do not call for a diagram, it is sometimes quite helpful to visualise the situation being described. Visualisation can be in the form of sketches, diagrams or mental pictures. A mental picture is a thought diagram.

Zook, K.B., and Divesta, F.J.(1989) in their article "Effects of overt, controlled verbalisation and goal-specific search on acquisition of procedural knowledge in problem solving "says that thinking aloud helps students to become more systematic in their thinking while solving problems.

Vani R.H (1992) conducted research on "A study to identify the essential competencies in teaching mathematics as perceived by secondary teachers". The objectives of the study were:

- To identify the competencies essential to teach mathematics as perceived by school teachers teaching mathematics;
- To analyse and clarify the preferences of teachers under three domains viz., cognitive, affective, and psychomotor;
- To study the core competencies of teachers in teaching mathematics;

The major findings of the study were:

- There are at least 9 essential competencies found among the secondary school mathematics teachers;
- At least 21.4 per cent of total competencies are essential;
- Only one competency has been identified as essential under the affective domain.

Nagalakshmi (1995) studied the secondary school students of Hyderabad area on their performance in solving problems at the five stage of development, namely, comprehension, judging the adequacy of the data, given approximations and generalisations. She found that students were not aware of the various stages and processes and were mainly concentrating on arithmetic operations rather than on the understanding of the process as a whole.

Need for a Good Mathematics Foundation at the School Level

The country needs, today, effective and productive citizens who display scientific and constructive thinking and attitudes in all walks of life. This is possible, to a great extent, with carefully devised educational curricula, especially, on the school mathematics programme.

The Education Commission (1964-66) has recommended that "proper foundation in the knowledge of mathematics should be laid at the school". According to the commission "the advent of automation and cybernetics in this country marks the beginning of the new scientific industrial revolution and makes it all the imperative to devote special attention to the study of mathematics".

According to J.N Kapoor(1993) in his book, 'Some aspects of School Mathematics', Secondary school mathematics is the basic structure on which the whole super structure of mathematics, mathematical sciences, physical sciences, social sciences and technology in the universities and technical institutions rests. Weaknesses in the basic structure led in the past and can lead in future to considerable weaknesses in the super structure. To quote Prof. K.E. Brown, " Mathematics has become the basic fabric of our social order. The strength of that fabric, in fact the very survival of our Nation—may well depend upon the amount and kind of mathematics taught in our secondary schools. This is a great sobering responsibility for those who desire and administer the programmes. If we take the responsibility lightly, our children will suffer the consequences of our foolish action". Modern developments in science and technology require a new habit of original and critical thinking and the foundations of such a habit have to be laid in secondary school mathematics. Hence emphasis should be laid on the basic concepts instead of on the manipulational tricks. The teaching of secondary school mathematics should reflect something of its nature. It must bring out its chief characteristics such as abstractness, precision, generality, logical nature etc. and any topics, which do not satisfy these standards, have to go. Theorems in mathematics are as true today as they were yesterday but they can become obsolete in as much as more general or more interesting or more abstract or more useful theorems may be discovered.

At the university stage most of the physical and social sciences require the application of mathematics. Ignorance of mathematics will be a great handicap in the study of many other subjects.

First rate science and technology can be based only on first rate mathematics and whatever is not first rate has to be discarded. In science and technology if we are to catch up with advanced countries, we have to give considerable time, money and energy to improve our secondary school mathematics.

School mathematics curriculum has to be designed for four broad classes of persons:

(a) Those who are going ultimately to become professional creative mathematicians;

(b) Those who are going to use mathematics later as a tool (engineers, physicists, economists, industrial mathematicians, computer scientists etc.;

(c) those who are going to become teachers of mathematics; and

(d) The average citizen who needs it for his/her daily business and commerce, for its intellectual and cultural value and for its help in making him/her understand the discoveries of sciences.

Historical Development of Mathematics

Mathematics, is a study of relationships among quantities, magnitudes, and properties and of logical operations by which unknown quantities, magnitudes, and properties may be deduced. In the past mathematics was regarded as the science of quantity, whether of magnitudes, as in geometry, or of numbers, as in arithmetic, or the generalisation of these two fields, as in algebra. Towards the middle of the 19th century mathematics came to be regarded increasingly as the science of relations, or as the science that draws necessary conclusions. This latter view encompasses mathematical or symbolic logic— the science of using symbols to provide an exact theory of logical deduction and inference based on definitions, axioms, postulates, and rules for transforming primitive elements into more complex relations and theorems.

This brief survey of the history of mathematics traces the evolution of mathematical ideas and concepts, beginning in prehistory. Indeed, mathematics is nearly as old as humanity itself: evidence of a sense of geometry and interest in geometric pattern has been found in the designs of prehistoric pottery and textiles and in cave paintings. Primitive counting systems were almost certainly based on using the fingers of one or both hands, as evidenced by the predominance of the numbers 5 and 10 as the bases for most number systems today.

Throughout the centuries, mathematics has been recognised as one of the central strands of intellectual activity. From the very beginning, mathematics has been a living and growing intellectual pursuit. It has its roots in every day activities and forms the basic structure of our highly advanced technological developments.

Mathematics, like everything else that man has created, exists to fulfil certain human needs and desires. It is very difficult to say at what point of time in the history of mankind, and in which part of the world, mathematics had its birth. The fact that it has been steadily pursued for so many centuries, that it has attracted ever-increasing attention and that it is now the dominant intellectual interest of mankind shows that it appeals very powerfully, to mankind. This conclusion is borne out by everything that we know about the origin of mathematics. More than 2000 years before the beginning of the Christian era, both the Babylonians and the Egyptians were in possession of systematic methods of measuring space and time. They had the knowledge of rudimentary geometry and astronomy. This rudimentary mathematics was formulated to meet the practical needs of an agricultural population. Their geometry resulted from the measurements made necessary by problems of land surveying. Units of measurement, originally a stone or a vessel of water for weight eventually became uniform over considerable areas under names, which are now almost forgotten. Undoubtedly, similar efforts were made in early ages in the southern part of Central Asia along the Indus and Ganges rivers and in Eastern Asia. Projects related to Engineering, Financing, Irrigation, Flood Control and Navigation required mathematics. Again a usable calendar had to be developed to serve agricultural needs. Zero was defined and this at once led to positional notations for whole numbers and later to the same notation for fractions. The place value system, which eventually developed, was a gift of this period. These achievements and many more of a similar nature are the triumph of human spirit. They responded to the needs of the human society, as it became more complex. Primitive men could hardly be said to have invented or discovered their Arithmetic; they actually lived it. The men who shaped the stones in erecting the temple of mathematics were widely scattered, a few in Egypt, a few in India and yet some others in Babylon and China. These workmen confronted nature and worked in harmony with it. Their products, therefore, though scattered in time and space partook the unity of nature.

Mathematics is something that man himself created to meet the cultural demands of time. Nearly every primitive tribe invented words to represent numbers. But it was only when ancient civilisations such as the Summerian, Babylonian, the Chinese and the Mayon developed trade, architecture, taxation and other civilised contracts that the number systems were developed. Thus mathematics has grown into one of the most important cultural components of society. Our modern way of life would hardly have been possible without mathematics.

More recently mathematical growth has been in areas such as operational research, linear programming, system analysis, statistics, all involving processes to handle numerical information in an increasingly technologically advanced world.

Roger Bacon in the book 'Nature, Objectives and Approaches to Teaching of Mathematics' said, " Mathematics is the gate and key of sciences. Neglect of mathematics works injury to all knowledge, since he who is ignorant of it cannot view the other sciences or the things of the world. And what is worse, men who are thus ignorant are unable to perceive their own ignorance and so do not seek the remedy".

The history of mathematics is the story of the progress of civilisation and culture. Hindu civilisation climbed to lofty heights in the knowledge of mathematics but the path of ascent has not been traceable. Much of Hindu Mathematics remained merely a servant of Astronomy and it remained chiefly in the hands of the priests who put in verse from all the mathematical results, which therefore became unintelligible to the common man. While the Greek mind was pre-eminently geometrical, the Hindu mind was arithmetical. Numerical symbolism, the science of numbers and algebra attained far greater heights in India than they had previously reached in Greece. Hindu Geometry was merely Mensuration unaccompanied by demonstration.

Since time immemorial, Indians have made very significant contributions to mathematics. The system of numeration and the concept of zero are a gift of Indians to the world of mathematics.

The Recommendations of Various Committees and Commissions on Mathematics Education

In Indian schools, the present syllabus of mathematics has been modified in the light of changes suggested by Kothari Commission, and the guidelines suggested by the N.C.E.R.T. (J.N. Kapoor,1993).

The Commission has recommended that at the primary level, the courses in Arithmetic and Algebra be integrated and the emphasis be laid on the laws and principles of Mathematics and logical thinking. The syllabus should include the development of number system, systems of numeration and notation, equations, groups and functions. The Geometry course should be reorganised in a more rational manner.

At the high, and higher secondary level, the Mathematics syllabus, which at present, is divided in the traditional manner into Arithmetic, Geometry and Algebra. Trigonometry, Statistics, Calculus and Co-ordinate Geometry, need to be revitalised and brought up-to-date. The whole of Arithmetic course and also the basic operations in Algebra can be so arranged as to be completed by the end of the primary stage. Out-dated topics like simplification, factorisation, H.C.F., L.C.M., etc should be deleted. Trigonometry should be related to Algebra and then there will be no need to treat it as a separate subject. Much of the work on identities, solution of triangles, height and distances can be cut down. The emphasis on memorising of theorems and exercises in Geometry should be given up. The approach to the teaching of Geometry should be based on an axiomatic and systematic treatment.

Set language may be used in designing the basic terms in Geometry, and the difficult portions should be gradually taken up in the next grades.

Earlier the Indian Education Commission (1966) clearly pointed out: "We cannot overstress the importance of mathematics in relation to science, education and research. This has also been so, but at no time the significance of mathematics been greater than today...it is important that deliberate effort is made to place India in the world map of mathematics within the next two decades or so."

The National Policy on Education (1986) made the relevant observation as follows:

"Mathematics should be visualised as the vehicle to train a child to think, reason, analyse and articulate logically. Apart from being a specific subject, it should be treated as a concomitant to any subject involving analysis and reasoning. With the introduction of computers in schools, educational computing and emergence of learning through the understanding of cause-effect relationship and the interplay of variables, the teaching of mathematics will be suitably re-designed to bring it in line with modern technological devices."

In this context, NPE suggests that a multi-media approach for curriculum transaction should be adopted and Educational Technology should be extensively used. Accordingly, mathematics educators recommended the development of instructional packages comprising the following:

- The text book;
- The supplementary problem books, consisting of additional drill material plus some challenging mathematical problems for high achievers and the talented;
- Enrichment materials (including recreational mathematics) for high achievers and the talented for use in mathematics clubs in schools;
- Teacher's handbook based on the above materials;
- Models, charts, films etc.

According to experienced mathematics educators, the implication of the policy (NPE, 1986) statement for mathematics education is as follows:

At the upper primary stage, the pupil is not mature enough to appreciate mathematical proof. At this stage, the mathematics curriculum should be confined mostly to essential or functional mathematics required for day-to-day life needs. Therefore, the first step in the process of curriculum development is to identify the concepts/topics, which constitute essential mathematics and analyse them into specific learning points. Of these learning points there are some which are basic (they are of functional use and all further learning is based upon them) and should be acquired by all the pupils at mastery level i.e., learning must be more than 80 per cent, as far as these learning points are concerned. These learning points to be acquired at mastery level may be taken as the 'minimum level of learning' and we should ensure that every pupil 'succeeds' in attaining this minimum level of learning. The teacher should feel accountable for ensuring that the pupils attain that minimum level of learning.

At the secondary stage, a beginning will be made to teach mathematics as a discipline in a suitable manner. Even then the concepts of essential learning outcomes, minimum level of learning and mastery learning are relevant and valid.

The NCERT publication 'Position of Mathematics in India' has listed the following objectives in the Indian syllabi.(J.N.Kapoor,1993).

1. *Elementary level:* Ability to perform necessary computations; accuracy, precision, speed, neatness etc. Ability to represent verbal statements by diagrams and symbols; Ability for logical thinking, ability to estimate measurements and to conceive approximations to answers, ability to solve common problems related to home and social life: ability to develop interest in some vocation;
2. *Secondary level:* To develop understanding of those mathematical concepts, facts, terms, procedures, symbols, relationships and principles which are needed to solve every day problems, to develop such qualities as:
    (a) working with speed, precision, accuracy and neatness;
    (b) estimation and approximation; and
    (c) Capacity to apply mathematics to simple, concrete situations.

The UNESCO project lists the following objectives:

1. *Middle level:* To enable the pupils to understand and use mathematical concepts, principles, processes, skills in his day-to-day life activities; to meet the vocational needs of the pupils; to develop in the pupils a scientific outlook; to prepare the pupils for the secondary stage; to enable pupils to learn other sciences meaningfully and thoroughly; and to initiate the pupils into modern developments in mathematics;
2. *Secondary level:* To make the pupils learn the modern developments in mathematics; to prepare the pupils for advanced study of science and technology; to develop the

powers of logical thinking, abstract thinking and generalisation; to acquaint the pupils with a systematised knowledge of mathematics; to enable the pupils acquire techniques of problem solving; and to develop an attitude for investigation and critical analysis.

Thus mathematics is essentially a programme of education, which fosters mental processes of questioning, reasoning, analysing, inducting, logical and reflective thinking of a very high order. Hence, the teaching of mathematics is of utmost importance in any school curriculum.

RESEARCH ON MATHEMATICS EDUCATION

The Research studies are discussed in the following pages under 5 heads namely., studies on: (i) mathematics curriculum and textbooks; (ii) teaching of mathematics and problem-solving; (iii) problems faced by students and teachers; (iv) attitudes of students and teachers; and (v) personal and demographic variables.

Studies on Mathematics Curriculum and Textbooks

The way students learn school mathematics and the habits they form in the process, will, to some extent, determine the future pattern of intellectual activity in the country. The problems of school mathematics should therefore be of vital concern not only to professional mathematicians but also to everybody interested in the future of the nation. Hence a great deal of clear thinking and careful planning is necessary in which school teachers, university professors, educational administrators and even the general public have to contribute. Our object is not just to change the curriculum; it is to improve it significantly.

Some conceptual mistakes in mathematics are very dangerous for students and their future careers. It has been observed that many authors make these errors in writing the textbooks and the teachers and students become victims of these errors. Unfortunately, most teachers cannot detect these errors. All such conceptual mistakes in mathematics should be discussed in detail with teachers.

The textbook is one of the important aids in the teaching learning process and has occupied the pivotal role in educating the school children. "As the text book so the teaching and learning".

The National Board of School TextBooks, NCERT in its report of 3rd may, 1970 stated as follows:

"Text book is a tool for implementing the syllabi accepted for a state educational programme. Textbook is not just content or subject matter. It differs from an ordinary book by virtue of the principles which control its selective organisation of the subject matter, careful presentation of the materials for a selected group of students and techniques built into for helping the teacher as well as the learner".

It is probably the cheapest and most reliable source of information. It serves as a reference book for the teacher as well. It is a concise source of material for reviews. It enables the pupils to acquire the needed information speedily. At the revision stage, the student can work independently with the help of the textbook. When the topics are arranged from simple to complex then the students will grasp them in a very easy way. In mathematics logical sequence is a very important feature which has to be carefully followed while arranging the topics in the textbook. At the same time psychological sequence that is according to the abilities and interests of the students should be followed.

No programme of improvement of school mathematics can succeed without improvement in textbooks. Hence, the department of curriculum, methods and textbooks of the NCERT has carried out a number of studies on school mathematics. A conference on improvement on science and mathematics education in India was held on 21, 22 and 23 April at New Delhi under the joint auspicies of the NCERT and the UGC. It was decided that the first essential step was to be clear about the objectives of teaching mathematics and the detailed curriculum to be adopted.

Maharashtra State Bureau of Textbook Production and Curriculum Research (1974) made a survey of primary teachers' qualifications and their opinions regarding mathematics syllabus in Pune. The chief aim of the study was to find out the opinion of mathematics teachers regarding the new syllabus of mathematics for class I to VII. The important findings were: (1) Seven per cent of teachers who taught mathematics were B.Sc., Six per cent were B. A., Seventy two percent had got their S. S. C certificate, twelve per cent had passed the primary school certificate examination and three per cent were either F. Y. B. Sc. or F. Y. B. A; (2) Amongst the mathematics teachers of classes V, VI, VII, eighty per cent were trained, seventy two per cent had more than five years of teaching experience and forty seven per cent had undergone an orientation course in Mathematics; (3) ten per cent of the Mathematics teachers felt that the modern mathematics portion of the syllabus was very difficult for pupils, sixty three per cent felt that it was some what difficult and twenty seven felt that it was easy; (4) seventy four per cent teachers thought that modern Mathematics should not be kept optional but should made compulsory; (5) some teachers felt that to do justice to the portion of modern Mathematics , orientation courses of long duration should be organised for teachers, the Mathematics periods should be increased and new teaching aids should be provided.

Rajasekhara (1979) observed that one of the drawbacks in Mathematics teaching in rural areas is the wide communication gap between the urban planners of school Mathematics curricula and the conditions prevailing in rural schools and common curriculum designed for urban and rural students without taking into consideration the latter's environment.

According to A.D.C. Peterson (1986) the principle of 'learning through practice' asserts that every piece of Mathematics learnt by the pupil must be put to immediate use in the solution of a large number of exercises and problems. The extent, to which this principle is applied, distinctively characterises Mathematics textbooks and classroom activity. It is usual for each Mathematics lesson to contain an item of individual work by the pupils in which they apply the mathematics they have been taught to the solution of a sequence of exercises from the textbook. Teaching of this kind requires textbooks with a large number of examples, and the most popular textbooks provide them. This is the reason why there are more number of problems in the present day textbooks and less emphasis on concept teaching.

This way of teaching has certain considerable merits. Firstly, it gives each pupil a chance not only to know a set of mathematical techniques but also to become fluent in their performance. Secondly, it has a diagnostic function. It gives the teacher information, which he cannot always obtain by questioning about the progress of individual pupils. Thirdly, the pupil by repeating several times the techniques is given a better chance to discover the range of its application.

For this device to work effectively, the exercises must be graded from the easy to the difficult ones. The final exercises in each set are, where possible, less straight forward and demand an ability to modify the technique to suit a particular difficulty, or require the combination of the new technique with others in order to solve a complex problem.

The implication of this method of working is that children learn skills and acquire the ability to use them through considerable individual practice. It has had, and still has, considerable success in achieving certain aims.

Mohapatra(1990) has made critical appraisal of the secondary school mathematics curriculum of Orissa and found that: (1) the objectives of teaching mathematics are clearly defined; (2) the mathematics teachers are conservative; (3) the students realise the importance of mathematics; (4) geometry is better discussed than algebra; (5) teachers do not use the discussion method; (6) correct home assignments are not always given; (7) diagrams in textbooks are inadequate; and (8) there is a great need for in-service training of teachers.

Studies on Teaching of Mathematics and Problem Solving

Teaching of mathematics has utmost significance in the present day technological world. The teachers of mathematics, therefore, will have to make a sustained and conscious effort to help students develop; 'general and transferable skills of problem-solving'.

Development of intellectual abilities as the aim of teaching mathematics has been an issue of debate for mathematicians and mathematics educators, since the dawn of scientific and technological age. It has been desirable to determine which of the many intellectual abilities are involved in successful learning of a subject like mathematics.

The relative effect of the wanted-given approach with the action-sequence approach in mathematics problem-solving was studied by Wilson (1967) and he observe that Students who asked questions on 'What is given'? and 'What is wanted'? Performed well at higher levels.

Moore (1970) used the axiomatic method in 1903-1905 to create in the student a spirit of self-confidence and pleasure in personal creative endeavour. This method of teaching is called learner-oriented teaching. The most difficult aspect of the method is patience on the part of the teacher. He must not help, must not point out the obvious. He must be willing to wait until the student finds his way. Patience must be born out of the conviction that training a student to do problems is important—more important than conveying information. He must give the student puzzle after puzzle.

Rajendra Prasad (1975) studied junior high school mathematics teachers and found them to be very responsive to students' questions and statements in the problem-solving sessions. The teachers' positive intention to redirect student thinking to proceed reflectively on the problem solutions has shown better student performances. He found that student performance is a significant factor of teacher responding behaviour in the mathematics classroom.

Rajendra Prasad (1975) in his doctoral study found that Junior High School teachers were more fluent in asking probing questions in Arithmetic than in Geometry or Algebra. This differential finding on a group of junior high school mathematics teachers in Illinois reveals that the teachers themselves have an affinity towards a particular kind of problem. Problems in Arithmetic appear to be of greater interest than those in Algebra and Geometry.

Vygotsky, L. (1978) in the article " Mind in Society" has shown that students who cannot solve problems on their own can often solve them if they are given temporary supports or "scaffolds" from another person who is more competent in the particular area. Research studies suggest that the teacher should provide hints, clues, or ask "leading" questions when students need help in solving problems, instead of giving them the answers. Then also suggest that this support should be faced out to foster independent problem solving.

Barting's(1981) study of pupil's difficulties in problem solving lists out the following causes of inability to solve problems:

1. Lack of ability to perform accurate reading and the fundamental operations;
2. Failure to comprehend the problem as a whole or in part;
3. Lack of the knowledge of facts essential to the solution of a problem;
4. Lack of sufficient interest in the problem to inspire the required mental efforts;
5. Lack of ability to identify proper processes with the situations indicated in the problem;
6. Failure to form the habit of verifying the results;
7. The habit of being guided by some verbal sign instead of making an analysis of the problem;
8. Lack of ability or care to properly arrange the written work in orderly, logical form;
9. Habit of focussing the attention upon the numbers and being guided by them instead of by the conditions of the problem;
10. The pupil may fail because the problem requires exertion beyond the span of attention;
11. The failure to recognise the mathematical similarity to type problems which the pupils understand, because of some unusual situation in the problem in question;
12. The pupil may fail because of absolute inability to do reflective thinking;
13. Lack of ability to understand the problem.

Kirkire P.L. (1981) analysed classroom verbal interaction and related the same to students' achievement in mathematics. He found that creating interest by the teacher in the problems is the single most influential factor of student achievement.

Students often have difficulty in solving problems because they start working on a solution as soon as they finish reading a problem. Instead, they should try to understand the problem and then develop a problem-solving plan, as experts do. They should be taught the importance of planning the problem solving and be provided with time to practice planning their solution. Nickerson, R.S., Perkins, D.N., & Smith, E.E.(1985) in their study "The teaching of thinking" involved teaching a group of students to plan their problem solving in preparation for an exam they were going to take. Another group of students studied as they normally did for the exam. Students who were in the planning group performed better than those who used their traditional study methods, even though this group reported spending more time in studying than did the students in the planning group. Hence, the study suggests that students need time to practice planning their solutions to problems.

Studies on Problems Faced by Students and Teachers

Every teacher of mathematics, whose job is to learn teaching or to teach learning mathematics, is pretty well aware of one universal problem-students' apathy and hatred towards such an interesting and important subject. Every teacher of mathematics has either already faced or is bound to pause and consider the problem at some stage or the other.

Lynwood (1935) in his survey of 'Research in the Teaching of Secondary School Algebra' found that children encountered difficulties in comprehending 'what is given' and 'what is wanted'. He found that meaningful problems enhanced the interest of the children. He advocated the need for giving insufficient and superfluous data, at times, to increase student ability to choose the right elements for solving the problems.

Samant (1944) conducted a critical examination of the various practices of teaching mathematics in secondary schools. The study revealed that: 1. The analysis of the matriculation results showed that the percentage of failures in mathematics was very high; 2. Nearly 85 per cent at the matriculation level and 90 to 95 per cent at the annual examination level in schools invariably failed in more than one subject; 3. The percentage of failures in mathematics alone and mathematics plus other subjects was quite high; 4. Detention of the students in various classes did not help them improve in mathematics; 5. Liberal promotions helped to get better results in matriculation; 6. Student's dislike for mathematics was found to be one of the main causes for their failure in the subject; 7. The dislike for the subject was more noticed in the higher classes than in the lower classes; 8. The subject matter as presented and the poor quality of teaching were found to be the main causes for disliking the subject; 9. The homework in mathematics was poorly planned; 10. Private tuition did more harm than good; 11. Confusion in method and application of formulae, teachers' speed, the way of each step and lengthy calculations were some of the causes of poor performance in mathematics; 12. Nearly 46 per cent of the teachers were found to be qualified to teach mathematics; 13. The analysis of the instructional material revealed that there was a need for rearranging the topics with definite aims.

Jain D.K. (1979) studied the significant correlates of high school failures in mathematics and found that students lacked motivation for abstract reasoning. Most times, lack of knowledge of basic concepts and principles caused difficulties in problem solving.

Mohammad Miyan (1982) who examined the effectiveness of methods of the teaching mathematics found that for the ninth class students guided discovery method yielded remarkable results in promoting creative thinking. In other words, poor teaching led to increasing number of problems for children.

Shashikala.S.M (1985) conducted research on "An investigation into the learning difficulties in algebraic factorisation at VIII standard in some selected schools of Bangalore City and try out of a remedial approach"

The major findings of the study are as follows:

1. More than 70 per cent of the students were lagging behind in splitting the middle term in the factorisation chapter;
2. More than 65 per cent of the students were lagging behind in finding the common factors;
3. More than 60 per cent of the students were lagging behind in the basic fundamental operations;
4. There is a significant difference in the performance of pre-test and post-test.

Jain and Burad (1988) have found the following causes for poor results in secondary mathematics in Rajasthan: non-availability of mathematics teachers due to late appointments and frequent teacher transfers; lack of appropriate class rooms, black boards and other physical facilities: irregular attendance of students; low standard in the lower classes; non-availability of text books; lack of timely correction of home work ; overburdened and uninteresting curriculum: lack of child centred teaching; insufficient periods for teaching mathematics and lack of suitable teaching aids. They have, however, not analysed why these causes affect mathematics more than other subjects.

Chel (1990) examined the problem of under achievement in compulsory mathematics in the Madhyamic examination of West Bengal. He found the following causes for it:

- Gaps in the knowledge of concept;
- Difficulties in the understanding of mathematical knowledge;
- Lack of openness and flexibility in teaching;
- Difficulty in mathematisation of verbal problems and interpretation of mathematical results;
- The abstract nature of mathematics; and
- Fear and anxiety of students.

The study suggests greater motivation of the students for learning mathematics, removal of fear of mathematics and clear presentation of the subject as per the needs of the children.

Kasat (1991) made an indepth study of the causes of failures in the S.S.C.examination of Marathi-medium high school students in Palghat Tehsil . He examined 200 boys and girls who had failed and found that most of them had poor intelligence, poor numerical ability, poor comprehension and recall ability, no interest in mathematics, poor study habits, lack of help from parents and teachers, and difficulties in certain topics in the course. He did not suggest any steps to enable such students to do better in the examinations.

Iyer (1977), Iyer (1986), Jain (1986), Doshi(1989), Mohapatra (1990), Mishra(1991), Shah(1992) and Viswanadhan Nair (1998) also studied the factors responsible for high failure rates in mathematics.

Shiva Prasanna T.D (1993) conducted research on "A study of problems of mathematics teachers in Bangalore City in teaching mathematics at secondary level".

The major objectives of the study were:

1. To find out the exact problems faced by the teachers in teaching mathematics at secondary level;
2. To find out the different types of problems and to investigate these in different schools;
3. To suggest possible remedies in the light of the problems analysed.

Stratified Sampling Technique was employed in this Survey. The total number of teachers who participated in the study was 58 from 22 schools. The Investigator developed a questionnaire on the problems of teaching mathematics, which was validated by the experts. Percentile analysis was done to analyse the data collected.

Major findings of the study were:

1. Three main areas of the problems of teachers are personal, administrative and student related;
2. Understanding mathematics depends upon the ability of learners and the time taken to teach;
3. Sufficient drill work is necessary and good coverage of content for the examination is necessary;
4. Workload of mathematics teachers must be reduced;
5. Special classrooms with audio-visual facilities are to be provided;
6. Last periods to be avoided for teaching mathematics in the secondary schools.

G.L. Arora, Raj Rani, Saroj Pandey (2000) in their article "Training needs of primary school teachers" concluded that inadequate knowledge of teachers in the content and pedagogy of mathematics made it difficult to transact the curriculum in class room situation, and most of the schools lacked basic infrastructure facilities like chalk board, chalk and duster, toilets for girls and drinking water etc.

An attempt was made by Hukum Singh (2000) in his article "status of mathematics education – suggestions for improvement" to analyse the problems and highlight the present trends in mathematics education and then to suggest measures for its improvement. He observed that lack of real meaning, motivation and purpose cause widespread dislike among the students for the subject. He also emphasised that mathematics education is under tremendous pressure due to the explosion of knowledge represented by:

1. The change in mathematics;
2. The change in computer;
3. The change in the breadth and depth of applications of mathematics;
4. The change in the psychology of learning; and
5. The change in educational technology.

Studies on Attitudes of Students and Teachers

Mathematics is regarded as an important subject of study at the school stage. For qualitative improvement of mathematical knowledge and its application, it is of paramount importance to have information regarding the attitudes of teachers and pupils towards the subject. It is a common experience of all of us that many students consider Mathematics a dry and stuffy subject whereas many other consider it an interesting one.

Research workers studied the problem of the attitude of students toward Mathematics in the past, using Thurstone-type and Likert-type attitude scales. Both the scales have certain advantages and disadvantages.

Researchers on the subject in other directions have shown that some background variables play an important role in the development of attitude toward Mathematics. They are parents' qualifications, profession, income, family size, types of early institutions and reading facility etc.,

Newcomb, Murphy and others (1937) have classified the related variables, which are determinants of attitudes. Newcomb has dealt with the relationships between attitude and:

1. Individual characteristics;
2. Experimental variables;
3. Life experiences; and
4. Other attitudes.

Under the headings of individual characteristics are included sex, age, intelligence and some non-intellectual aspects. Here it seems proper for the respective teachers and researchers to conduct such studies, in which most effective factors for modifying attitudes can be identified, and, accordingly, they can adjust suitable teaching approaches to create interest, and to promote interest in learning a particular subject.

Patil (1966) hypothesised that the factors relating to mathematical backwardness are: 1. Private coaching; 2. Health; 3. Guidance from parents; 4. Quality of classroom teaching; 5. Interest in the subject; and 6. Economic conditions. His conclusion was that if students were interested in a particular subject, their achievement would be better in it and vice versa. The teachers are in a better position to stimulate the interest of students in mathematics than the parents. School management should appoint trained and efficient teachers in their schools and see that they adopt effective methods of teaching.

Husen (1967) conducted a study entitled "International study of achievement in mathematics: a comparison of twelve countries". He found that boys were on the whole superior to girls in mathematics in the countries studied. But the issue was complicated by differences in the performance of pupils attending co-educational or single sex schools and also by the possibility of dropping the subject at a later stage of secondary education in some countries. So far as attitudes were concerned, it appeared that in co-educational schools, the difference between the sexes was greater than in single sex schools. Boys were more favourably exposed to mathematics in co-educational schools than girls.

Yasui (1967) has reported in his study of an analysis of algebraic achievement and mathematical attitude between the modern and the traditional mathematics programmes in senior high schools (a longitudinal study) that the measures of student attitude towards Mathematics provided by the "Mathematical Inventory" showed no significant difference between groups.

Philips (1970) hypothesised that attitude towards mathematics has been developed over years. In his study comparing the attitudes and achievements of pupils with the attitude of their teachers in the previous three years, he found that the most recent teacher attitude towards mathematics teaching was significantly related to the pupil's achievement. Yadav, Chhangur Prasad (1988) also found similar results.

Guptha (1972) conducted an investigation on backwardness in mathematics and basic arithmetic skills. The hypotheses were: 1. Backwardness in mathematics is due to poor command over basic arithmetic skills; 2. Low achievers in mathematics have poor command over basic arithmetic skills, whereas high achievers have good command over it; 3. Backwardness is closely related to the attitude towards mathematics; 4. High achievers have more favourable attitudes than low achievers; and 5. Basic arithmetic skills can be mastered easily by means of a suitable remedial programme.

This study showed that:

1. Low achievers in mathematics had poor command and high achievers had good command over basic arithmetic skills;
2. Attitudes improved significantly when command over basic skills improved;
3. Low achievers in basic arithmetic skills had a negative attitude towards mathematics, while high achievers had a positive attitude.
4. There was a positive relationship between intelligence and basic arithmetic skills but attitude towards mathematics was significantly related to intelligence;
5. There was a significant positive correlation between intelligence and achievement in mathematics;
6. Basic arithmetic skills could be quickly and conveniently mastered by self-help in basic arithmetic skills. There was significant sex difference either in attitude towards mathematics or in achievement in mathematics.

As regards the income of the father and academic achievement Fraser (1959), Gorden and Will (1978) observed that income of the father is positively linked with their children's achievement in mathematics. Long and Resh (1976) could not find significant differences between father's income and child's level of abstract achievement.

Personality factors such as motivation, attitudes and cognitive styles affect students' performance in mathematics. Studies on students aged between 14 and 16 show that extravert boys and introvert girls do well within their own sex group when mathematics activities are given (Head, 1981).

Teachers are important in helping students to develop positive attitudes towards the subject. Students' perceptions of their mathematics teachers towards them as learners of mathematics relate strongly to students' anxiety (Morris, 1981).

A study on the liking or disliking for mathematics conducted by Virginia (1982) consists of two parts. One is assessing the feelings of pupils studying 5th and 6th classes towards mathematics and the other is to rank the subjects liked best to the least in September and again in May. He found that in grade 4 mathematics was a liked subject in both testings. Pupils in grade 5 indicated a positive attitude to mathematics and it ranked in top three subjects with little change from the beginning to the end of the year. In grade 6 pupils for the most part ranked mathematics as a liked subject in September but it was ranked lower in half the schools in May.

Gomathi Mani (1983) in her article "Motivation through mathematical games suggested that higher mental abilities such as translation, demonstration, illustration, comparison, verification, application, analysis, synthesis and evaluation should be developed through mathematical games. She also suggested that scientific attitude of accepting criticism and suspending judgements in addition to developing the personal mental tracts such as concentration, regular study habits, self confidence and systematic working can be developed through games. The most important value of a game vests in its power to create and sustain interest in mathematics, by involving the students in learning some mathematical principles. Thus mathematics can be made less abstract and more concrete through games, as they learn by doing through direct experience.

Likewise, Alvi (1986) of Cincinnati University has shown in his study of effects of individualised instruction on achievement and attitude in general Mathematics in the IX grade, that there was no significant difference between the attitude scores of the experimental group and those of the control group.

According to Foong (1987), college boys who dislike mathematics view their former teachers as impatient. Poor performance and negative attitude of students are found associated with restrictiveness and negative use of authority by teachers.

Parents can affect students' attitude to and performance in learning mathematics by their expectation of achievement, encouragement and attitude to the subject (Foong, 1987). Foong also postulates that students' attitude also depends on how they perceive the usefulness of a subject in terms of its attainment, intrinsic and utility values.

Foong (1987) used four scales (Father, Mother, Teacher, and Mathematics Usefulness) from the Fennema-Sherman Mathematics Attitude Scale to study the attitudes of 206 Female Secondary Four students in Singapore towards mathematics. The study reveals that higher achievers in mathematics have low mathematics anxiety but high positive perception of their teachers, and they perceive the subject as useful, and are able to handle high-test anxiety.

Neelima Kumari (1991) found that reasoning power, space visualisations and attitude towards mathematics were significantly related to mathematics achievement.

James T.F.Poon and T.J.Ng (1991) made an attempt to determine students' perceptions of Mathematics and Design and Technology. A questionnaire was administered to a sample of 37 secondary two students who had already completed one year of Design and Construction Studies at the secondary level. The instrument measures students' perception of usefulness of the subject; teachers' influence on them in terms of interest, encouragement and confidence in their work; and parents' encouragement, view of the subject, and emphasis on the subject.

The results from the three scales show that students perceived Mathematics more positively than Design and Technology. The greatest difference between their perceptions of the two subjects is from the subject usefulness scale. This undoubtedly shows that mathematics is considered to be a more useful subject.

It also reveals that students' perception of the usefulness of the subject relates more to the perceptions of their parents' rather than teachers' view on the usefulness of the subject. This adds to the evidence of parental influence on students' attitude and performance in learning as discussed by Foong (1987).

Attitude has been found to be one of the important correlates of achievement (Chopra, 1982; Sundararajan and Srinivasan, 1990) in Mathematics. Unless a student has a favourable attitude towards any subject of study, he may not achieve considerably in that subject and may not also like to study it at higher levels. With these observations in mind Dr. S. Sundararajan and Mr.B. Dhandapani (1991) conducted a study on "Attitude of the Higher Secondary Students of the Pondicherry Territory towards the Study of Mathematics and their Achievement in it". The important findings of the study are as follows:

1. A large number (97.29%) of students have a favourable attitude towards the study of mathematics;
2. The girls are better than the boys and the rural students are better than the urban students in their attitude towards the study of mathematics;
3. There is no significant difference between the Government and the Private school students in their attitude towards the study of Mathematics;
4. Only 60.61 per cent of the students have an optimum level of achievement in Mathematics;
5. Except in the case of Government and Private school Girls, in all others the difference is significant in respect of their achievement in Mathematics. Here the girls are better than boys, the private school students are better than the Government school students and the urban students are better than the rural students in respect of their achievement in Mathematics.

6. There is a positive relationship between the students' attitude towards the study of Mathematics and their achievement in it. However, the relationship is not significant at the 0.01 level, except in the case of girls.

Thomas (1991) revealed that high school students of Aizawl had positive attitude towards mathematics irrespective of sex and type of school in which they studied but their level of achievement in this subject was between 33 and 50 per cent only. There was a significant positive corelation between achievement in and attitude towards mathematics irrespective of sex. The sex differences in attitude towards mathematics were not statistically significant, as were the differences in their achievement in it.

Ram D. Singh, Sudarshan P. Ahluwalia and Sunil K. Verma (1994) studied the attitude of high school students towards mathematics. The findings of the study seem to agree with the findings of Sundararajan (1991) and Rajasekhar(1988) that girls do not have a more favourable attitude towards the study of physics than boys. It also reveals that the students of lower age show more favourable attitude towards Mathematics. This result tends to corroborate the finding of Metha(1979) that age is a significant factor and lower age groups prove to be much more progressive and liberal in attitudes.

Attitude was found to be significantly related to Academic Achievement in studies like that of Anttonen (1969), Kaul (1969), Jain (1979), Patel (1984), Bhudev (1990) and Tocci and Amgelhard (1991) whereas studies of Aitken (1970) and Behr (1973) reported otherwise.

Dr. V. Sumangala (1995) in her article "Some Psychological Variables Discriminating between High-and Low–Achievers in Mathematics" found that Achievement in mathematics is related not only to Cognitive Variables like Intelligence, Aptitude, etc., but also to the affective variables like Attitude towards Mathematics and Self-concept in Mathematics.

According to Krishnamurthi (2000) academic achievement depends on the number of variables. Important among them are: the students attitude towards the subject of study, their interest in it and their motivation for academic achievement.

Shukla (1981), Rao (1983), Chitkara (1985), Bhattacharya (1986), Patadia (1987), Bharadwaj (1987), Deshmukh (1988), Doshi (1989), Dutta (1990), Mishra (1991), Vasanthi (1991), Bhatia (1992), Dandapani (1992), Prabha (1992), Rosali (1992), Srivatsava (1992), Hazelbaker and Deborah jean (1997), Jackson and Jeanetha williams (1997), and Sumangala (1998) conducted research on the improvement of learning and teaching of school mathematics.

It is generally seen that less amount has been paid to student's attitude by the classroom teachers or researchers in comparison with considerable amount of attention given to the cognitive achievement. Mathematics, specially, can be quoted as an example in which very few attempts at measuring attitudes towards its study have been made. Mathematics is generally regarded as a difficult subject for study. It is not so popular even at the college level where less number of students offer it for their studies. Even now models of teaching, innovations and modern techniques of teaching the subject have not changed the situation.

Studies on Personal and Demographic Variables

Educational environment plays a significant role in promoting and achieving educational objectives. In its interaction with intellectual characteristics and personality factors of the students a particular educational institution could be stimulating, supporting, neutral, hostile or destructive to the academic performance of the students. This is more likely to be so in the Indian society where the physical, socio-cultural and educational environment of different schools shows very wide contrasts.

Schunert (1951) conducted a study to investigate: (1) The relationship between mathematical achievement and the training and experience of the teacher; (2) The relation between mathematical achievement and class size and the sex and organisation of the school; (3) The relation of mathematical achievement with twelve selected factors resident in the methods and materials of instruction.

He found that boys excelled girls in Geometry in pupils' factors. Teachers' factors were: (1) Classes taught by teachers with more than eight years of experience achieved better results than those taught by teachers of less experience. No significant difference was found between the achievement of the classes taught by teachers with less than two years experience and that of the classes taught by teachers with two to eight years of experience; (2) Classes handled by teachers who were graduates of state universities or private colleges formed better than those taught by teachers who graduated from teacher-colleges.

These comparisons show that results in algebra and geometry were consistent with respect of school enrolment size, supervised study practices, and with respect of lack of significant association between mathematical achievement and the three factors— amount of daily homework assigned, use of pupil leadership and the amount of college mathematics studied by the teacher.

Lovell (1961) concluded that the process of concept acquisition has three phases— perception, abstraction and generalisation and at each of these three phases variations in school environment in which the child studies are likely to influence his concept acquisition.

Husen (1967) in his study "International study of achievement in mathematics: a comparison of twelve countries" found that boys were on the whole superior to girls in mathematics.

Husten (1967), Dave and Dave (1971) found that poor academic achievement of their children was due to the low educational standard of their parents.

Callahan (1971) used the Dutton Attitude Scale to study the attitudes of 366 eighth graders in New York towards Mathematics, reasons for their likes or dislikes, and the time when such general feelings developed in schools. The results revealed that most students enjoy mathematics when they like the subject and perform well. Lasting attitudes are developed at each grade level but the late elementary grade levels, especially the VII grade level, are important in attitude development. The attitudes become firm between 12 and 13 years.

Guptha (1972) conducted an investigation into backwardness in mathematics and basic arithmetic skills. There was significant sex difference either in attitude or in achievement.

Fraser (1959), Gorden and Will (1978) observed that income of the father is positively linked with their children's achievement in mathematics. Long and Resh (1976) could not find significant differences between father's income and child's level of abstract achievement.

Santhanam (1972) in the study of sex differences across some behavioural dimensions of teaching mathematics found that female teachers asked more number of questions than male teachers. Also, there was an indication, although not significant, to believe that female teachers exhibit greater response than the male teachers.

H.G. Desai (1973) conducted a study on " the attitudes to mathematics of high school students of Saurashtra", to know if the students varied in attitude with respect to sex, grade and area in which they lived. The major findings of the study were as follows:

1. The pupil with favourable attitude to mathematics preferred to offer it at the S.S.C. examination;
2. The attitude of boys became more favourable as they moved from grade VIII to grade IX, their attitude was less favourable in grade X than in grade IX;
3. Girls in grade X had a more favourable attitude to mathematics than those in grades VIII and IX;
4. In general, pupils in grades IX and X had more favourable attitude to mathematics than those in grade VIII, their attitude being less favourable in grade X than grade IX;
5. The boys and girls of grade X had more or less similar attitude;
6. Boys in general, did not differ from girls in their attitude to mathematics;
7. Rural as well as urban children, as they advanced in their studies showed more favourable attitude to mathematics;
8. Urban children had more favourable attitude to mathematics than rural children.

Correlation between attitudes and achievement varies not only with grade level but also with the sex of the student and it is generally higher in girls than in boys (Behr, 1973).

Differences in both attitudes and achievement in mathematics are frequently found to favour boys more than girls at the junior high level and beyond (Hilton and Berglundd, 1974; Keeves, 1973; Nevin, 1973.)

K.N. Lalithamma (1975) conducted a study on "some factors affecting achievement of secondary school pupils in mathematics". It revealed that:

1. The average performance of pupils in mathematics was 23.14 with S.D of 8.20 and the distribution was negatively skewed;
2. There was significant difference in the performance of boys and girls in mathematics, the difference being in favour of boys;
3. The urban pupils were superior to rural pupils in mathematics;
4. Intelligence and interest in mathematics were higher in boys and urban pupils than in their respective counterparts;
5. The achievement in mathematics is positively related to intelligence, interest in mathematics, study habits and socio-economic status;
6. Studying lessons daily, studying mathematics by writing, repetition in learning, spaced learning, over learning etc. influenced the achievement in mathematics positively;
7. Private tuition, electric light facilities, radio, equipment for study etc. influenced the achievement in mathematics;
8. Achievement of the first borns was better than that of the last born; and
9. Achievement of the students of scheduled castes and tribes was lower than that of the total sample.

Sharma (1977) made an attempt to examine the achievement of children in relation to the school system. He found that children of the recognised private schools achieved higher scores in Arithmetic than those of the corporation schools. Hilde Brand and Patricia (1978) have shown positive relationship between educational environment and child's performance in mathematics.

Desai (1979) found that low achievers of high school had high ability in mathematics and less favourable attitude to the subject:

they came from families with very strict standards or discipline, they were kept very busy in domestic work and did not receive any outside help for the study.

Leder (1980) examines the relationship between the fear of success and self-differences in performance and participation in mathematics courses, and postulates that girls avoid success in mathematics because of society's expectancy that it is inappropriate for them to excel in the subject.

As no reliable and valid scale to measure the attitude towards Mathematics was available, Rajendra Mishra (1980) developed a Likert-type attitude scale in his study "A study of attitudes towards Mathematics of secondary school students".

Of all the variables studied it has been found that parents' qualifications influence boys but not girls in their attitude towards Mathematics. No strong evidence has been found to prove the influence of parents' profession, family size, parents' income and study room facility in this regard.

Sudha R. Sinha (1980) in the study " Effect of school system on the competence of secondary school students" investigated into the difference between the system of private and government schools and how it influenced the competence of its students. Three aspects of the system were examined—the material, organisational and human relations. The findings revealed that despite less physical facilities and higher workload, the private schools had better organisational structure and more competent students than the government schools.

Head (1981) found that extraverted boys and introverted girls did well within their own sex group when they were given mathematics activities.

Dr. S.C. Gakhar (1982) in his article "A study of acquisition of mathematical concepts among 8th graders of different types of schools" clearly demonstrates the differential effects of the type of the school on the acquisition of the mathematical concepts by the students. On the whole, students studying in private schools had better achievement than those studying in government schools.

This achievement was due to the strict supervision by the principal and managements of private schools, better teacher-pupil interaction, good educational environment, teacher's special care of the weak students, teacher's interest in the study of the children and sense of security and guidance and counselling in private schools.

Lalthanhawla(1983) studied the causes of failures in science and mathematics among high school students of the Mizoram state and found that general standard of achievement in science was 33.24 per cent as compared to 27.86 per cent in mathematics. Students from urban areas and from privately managed schools and older schools did better than those in rural areas and government schools and newly established schools. The provision of good library, laboratory, and special coaching classes are not related to the student's achievement in these subjects.

Pattison and Grieve (1984) studied whether sex differences contribute to spatial skills to tackle different types of mathematical problems. They found that boys excelled in problems related to measurement and proportion and in spatial problems, whereas girls performed better in more abstract deductive problems.

Dr. S.C. Gakhar (1986) in his article "Home variables as determinants of mathematical concepts learning" concluded that father's presence or absence, family size, and order of birth do not lead to significant variation in mathematical achievement, but the variables of parent's income and education are potentially effective in causing significant differences in the learning of concepts.

Iyer's study (1986) revealed that general anxiety, text anxiety, parental profession and parental education were factors responsible for under-achievement in mathematics. Menon (1986) found that higher occupational and educational level of father and mother, family income and parental attention were related to high achievement.

Padma and Chakravarthy (1990) have indicated in their study that a significant difference exists between the attitudes of boys and girls towards Computer Education at 0.01 level. They believe that this might be due to the fact that girls are more conscious about and aware of the technological progress of the country than boys. They have further concluded that no difference in attitude exists between tribal and non-tribal students towards Computer Education.

The study of M.B. Buch (1991), has confirmed that intelligence and socio-economic background are the major contributors to mathematics achievement. Apart from socio-economic status and intelligence, variables like teacher's qualifications, class size, encouragement to teachers by the head, use of audio-visual aids and feedback were found significantly related to the acquisition of mathematical relations.

Dr. S. Sundararajan and Mr. B. Dhandapani (1991) conducted a study on "Attitude of the Higher Secondary Students of the Pondicherry Territory towards the Study of Mathematics and their Achievement in it". The important findings of the study reveal the following:

- The girls are better than the boys and the rural students are better than the urban students in respect of their attitude towards the study of mathematics;
- There is no significant difference between the Government and the Private school students in respect of their attitude towards the study of Mathematics;
- Except in the case of Government and Private school Girls, in all others the difference is significant in respect of their achievement in Mathematics. Here the Girls are better than Boys, the private school students are better than the Government school students and the urban students are better than the rural students in respect of their achievement in Mathematics;
- There is a positive relationship between the students' attitude and their achievement. However, the relationship is not significant at the 0.01 level, except in the case of girls.

Thomas (1991) revealed that high school students of Aizawl had positive attitude towards mathematics irrespective of sex and type of school in which they studied. There was a significant positive correlation between achievement in and attitude irrespective of sex. The sex differences in attitude were not statistically significant, as were the differences in their achievement.

Singh (1992) compared the modern method of teaching mathematics with computer assistance with the conventional method of teaching. Computer-assisted instruction was always found superior. There was a definite positive change of attitude towards learning mathematics on the part of both boys and girls due to the use of computers.

Dr. R.D. Singh and Dr. S.C. Verma (1992) studied the attitudes of high school students towards Mathematics in relation to some individual characteristics like sex, age and intelligence. The important findings of the study are as follows:

1. The students of the high intelligence group have more favourable attitude towards Mathematics, than those of the average and low intelligence groups. This is more marked in the students of high intelligence than those of low intelligence.

2. The students of average intelligence have more favourable attitudes than those of low intelligence. On the whole, it may be concluded that attitude is based on intelligence.

3. As regards attitude towards Mathematics, males do not have a more favourable attitude than females. That is, attitude is independent of sex. This result contradicts the findings of Padma and Chakrabarty (1990). This may be because their findings are mainly related to the measurement of attitude towards computer education and not towards Mathematics. It may also be due to the difference in the social conditions of the subjects involved in the two studies. On the other hand, the findings of Singh and Verma seem to agree with the findings of Sundararajan and Rajasekhar (1988) that urban girls do not have a more favourable attitude towards the study of physics than urban boys. It is also observed that rural girls do not have a more favourable attitude towards the study of Physics than rural boys.

The students of the age 13 + show a more favourable attitude towards mathematics in comparison with the students of the ages 14 + and 15+, but the students of 14 + do not have a similar attitude in comparison with the students of the age of 15 +.

Ram D. Singh, Sudarshan P. Ahluwalia and Sunil K. Verma (1994) studied the attitude of high school students towards mathematics. The findings of the study seem to agree with the findings of Sundararajan (1991) and Rajasekhar (1988) that girls do not have a more favourable attitude than boys towards the study of physics. It also reveals that the students of lower age show more favourable attitude towards Mathematics. This result tends to corroborate the finding of Metha (1979) that age is a significant factor and lower age groups prove to be much more progressive and liberal in attitudes.

According to Alfred S. Posamentier, Hope J. Hartman, and Constanze Kaiser (1988), research has demonstrated that computer-aided geometry lessons improve students' spatial abilities, especially those of girls. Reiss, K., and Albrecht,A (1994) conducted a study to know whether there is a difference between girls and boys concerning learning of geometry with and without computer? The sample for the study was 25 girls and 21 boys in two parallel eighth grade classes. Students completed 10 lessons on "special points and lines at the triangle". Although most recent research shows less difference based on sex in cognitive aspects of mathematical competence than in past research, spatial ability is an exception. Comparable research in 20 countries has shown sex differences related to geometry and measuring. Although there is no empirical proof of a causal relationship between good spatial ability and good performance in mathematics, it is evident that spatial abilities are an important factor.

Dr. Santhamma Raju and Sri Prakash (1996) conducted a study on " Mathematical aptitude in relation to socio-familial variables" to find out the relationship between nine socio-familial variables and mathematical aptitudes of secondary school pupils. The results show that out of the nine variables considered, except the family environment index, other variables have marked a slight relationship with the mathematical aptitude. There is no difference based on gender (except for family acceptance of education), locale (rural-urban) and caste (forward and backward) in the relationship between socio-familial variables and mathematical aptitude. But, there exists a significant difference in the mean socio-familial variables except family environment, high-average and low-mathematical aptitude.

Khalid (1997) focussed his research on factors affecting mathematics achievement and found that confidence, socio-economic status, gender beliefs, peers, location of school, school environment, ethnic beliefs and previous achievement in mathematics contributed significantly for achievement in Malaysian schools.

Dr. R.S. Patel (1997) in his article "An investigation into the causes of under-achievement in mathematics of eighth grade pupils having high numerical ability" found that low intelligence, problems of pupils, low socio-economic status of parents, poor achievement motivation, poor aspiration level, poor study habits, long absence from school, high anxiety level, little time devoted for practice work, etc were the real causes for the poor achievement among pupils possessing higher numerical ability.

Dr. R. Vasanthi and Ms. Bama Lalithambika (1997) in their article "Interest of the high school students in mathematics" concluded that there is significant difference in the interest between the students of:

1. Private schools and government schools;
2. private schools and government aided schools;
3. private schools and corporation schools and there is no significant difference between the students of;
4. government schools and government aided schools;
5. government schools and corporation schools;
6. government aided schools and corporation schools.

It also shows that the educational qualification of parents has a powerful bearing on the interest of students in mathematics.

Dr. V. Sumangala (1998) in her article 'Effect of Tutoring on Achievement in Mathematics of Secondary School Pupils' found that home-tutoring in mathematics, whether by parents or by siblings, has significant, positive but low effect on achievement in mathematics. Beryl (1981) study also revealed that in the absence of home stimulation and parental support it is very difficult to attain higher educational achievement.

Dr. Marlo Ediger (1999) in his article 'Parents, the teacher and mathematics' suggested the following for the good of the child in mathematics achievement:

1. Having quality parent/teacher conferences;
2. Meeting parents at PTO meetings;
3. Initiating an introduction to New School Year time with parents;
4. Implementing an invigorating Introduction to the New School Year meeting;
5. Using educational psychology for providing a model to parents in assisting their offspring in homework;
6. Trying to initiate parental education classes in Teacher Education programmes at colleges and universities;
7. Integrating human relations and curricular improvement in teaching and learning situations.

Shakuntala Devi (2002) in her book "Mathability: Awaken the math genius in your child" states that the negative approach of a parent or teacher with high expectations, without the element of fun, drives the child away from what is really an interesting subjects (Maths).

Hiroshi Isero, (2003) in the article "Positive Attitude for Learning" suggests that by taking appropriate measures and developing the right attitudes both in the family and this school setting, it is possible to enhance children's egresses to learn.

Dr. Sunil Sumar Singh, Shaheen Malik, Dr.A.K.Singh (2003) in the article "Achievement Difference of Class II students in Maths, with regard to Area, Gender and Social Groups, during B.A.S. and M.A.S. in Gonda District" reveals locality affects on achievement of students i.e., urban students found better than rural students whereas sex would not affect the achievement in Mathematics.

Dr. Thilaka Suresh and C. Geetha, (2003) in this study "Mathematics Anxiety Among High School Students" found that there is gender difference in Mathematics Anxiety among the students. Girls are more anxious than boys in Mathematics except in numerical ability. High School students from government aided,

Corporation and Matriculation Schools differ significantly in mathematics and anxiety. Students from Government Schools are found more anxious than the other students in mathematics.

The studies available on the problems of students and teachers in particular areas, of curriculum and textbooks in mathematics, teaching and problem solving, problems faced by students and teachers in mathematics education, attitudes of students and teachers towards mathematics education, and personal and demographic variables etc. have been reviewed. These studies reveal to us the salient features required for a good mathematics textbook, effective mathematics teaching, process of problem solving, and good learning of mathematics etc.

The present study concerns itself with an analysis of difficulties regarding the contents prescribed in the secondary school mathematics textbooks, problems and the attitudes of students and teachers reflected on the basis of their experience in teaching and learning the subject. To this extent the present study is an extension of the previous studies reviewed and extremely relevant to the present day teaching and learning of mathematics in our area. At the same time the present study fills up the gaps in the different aspects like difficulty analysis of contents in the textbooks, problems of students and teachers in teaching and learning mathematics, and attitudes of students and teachers, which indeed would contribute much for the improvement of teaching and learning mathematics among students and teachers in the secondary schools.

3

Statement of the Problem

Its Objectives, Hypotheses and Variables

Based on the observations in the earlier chapter, the researcher is in a position to state the problem with its significance, objectives, hypotheses, variables and operational definitions of terms and explanation of concepts.

SIGNIFICANCE OF THE STUDY

The development of a country is primarily determined by the quality of its human resources. India needs today, effective and productive citizens with scientific and constructive thinking and positive attitudes. This need can be met by well-planned educational curricula, including a systematic mathematics programme at the school level.

There is a specific mention in the National Policy on Education 1986 (NPE) about mathematics education in the following words: "Mathematics should be visualised as the vehicle to train a child to think, reason, analyse and articulate logically. Apart from being a specific subject, it should be treated as a concomitant to any subject involving analysis and reasoning."

The teaching of mathematics should be rewarding experience. Teachers must be trained to generate a healthy intellectual environment and encourage students to participate and express their views through open discussions on creative problems of mathematics.

Research in psychology has shown that 'almost any subject can be taught in some intellectually honest form to any child at any stage of development, if it is properly taught' (Bruner). The limitations are set not so much by the capacity of children to learn, as by the capacity of teachers to communicate.

"No system of education, no methodology, no text book can rise above the level of its teachers. If a country wants to have quality education it must have quality teachers." —*V.S. Matthews*

Whether the students learn or not will depend upon many factors, probably the chief of which are:

1. His motivation and readiness to learn;
2. His maturity level in relation to the task to be learned;
3. His relation to the teacher;
4. His ability to learn through words;
5. The degree of his freedom from fear; and
6. the teachers skill in communication.

If these conditions are reasonably favourable, the student can learn much that is significant.

But the present state of teaching mathematics in the majority of our schools is far from satisfactory. The rate of failures in mathematics is considerably higher than in any other subject. Many pupils find mathematics a difficult subject. For most of them mathematics has been a meaningless group of symbols and problems or at best, combinations to be memorised.

Moreover, many changes have been carried out in the mathematics curriculum. There are certain new topics, included in the present curriculum, but the teachers are not familiar with them. Completion of syllabus has become a subject of concern for the teachers and students. Hence, the teaching community generally feels that it is time consuming and also burdensome for them to adopt new strategies to teach mathematics in tune with the changing trends and demands.

Most of the teachers very frequently air their feelings as follows:

"Mathematics is a difficult subject for students"

"Teaching Geometry is very difficult"

"Mathematics can`t be taught meaningfully"

"Mathematics is a dry subject" etc.

This attitude of the teachers' lead to the development of negative attitude in the students and they voice it by saying:

" Mathematics is difficult to learn"

"I am afraid of mathematics"

"I am afraid of Algebra"

"I dislike mathematics"

"Geometry is very difficult"

"How to get through the mathematics examination?" etc.

These attitudes and circumstances raise certain pertinent questions—How to make teaching and learning mathematics easy and more meaningful? What are the main reasons for these difficulties, problems, and for such attitudes in the students and teachers? What exactly is needed now to overcome these difficulties, problems and to improve the present situation?

It is against this backdrop that a comprehensive and constructive research work is felt necessary relating to mathematics education so as to get a better picture of the situation and to identify means and ways to improve the teaching- learning process.

STATEMENT OF THE PROBLEM

Based on the above observations, the problem for the present investigation is as follows:

"An Investigation into the Problems relating to Teaching-Learning Mathematics at secondary level".

OBJECTIVES OF THE STUDY

The main objectives of the study are:

1. To identify the difficult areas in secondary level mathematics as perceived by the pupils and teachers;
2. To identify the problems faced by the pupils in learning mathematics and by the teachers in teaching the subject;
3. To study the attitudes of pupils towards learning mathematics and of teachers towards teaching it;
4. To study the variations in the problems and attitudes of pupils of different sub groups depending upon their personal and demographic variables;
5. To study the variations in the problems and attitudes of teachers of different sub groups depending upon their personal and demographic variables;
6. To suggest the suitable strategies for the improvement of teaching –learning mathematics at the secondary level.

HYPOTHESES

To realise the objectives stated above, the following descriptive and statistical hypotheses were formulated in null form for the purpose of testing:

1. The pupils in general do not feel that studying mathematics at the secondary level is an easy task;
2. The teachers in general do not feel that teaching of mathematics at the Secondary level is an easy and pleasant job;
3. There would not be any significant problems faced by students in learning mathematics;
4. There would not be any significant problems faced by teachers in teaching mathematics;
5. Pupils in general do not possess positive attitudes towards learning mathematics;
6. Teachers in general do not possess positive attitudes towards teaching mathematics;
7. Personal and demographic variables of pupils would not significantly influence the intensity of problems faced by them

in learning mathematics. (This major hypothesis will be divided into minor hypotheses separately for each independent variable for testing);

8. Personal and demographic variables of teachers do not significantly influence the intensity of problems faced by them in teaching mathematics. (This major hypothesis will be divided into minor hypotheses separately for each independent variable for testing);
9. Personal and demographic variables of students do not significantly influence their attitudes toward learning mathematics. (This major hypothesis will be divided into minor hypotheses separately for each independent variable for testing);
10. The personal and demographic variables of teachers do not significantly influence their attitudes toward teaching mathematics. (This major hypothesis will be divided into minor hypotheses separately for each independent variable for testing);

VARIABLES STUDIED

As the present study envisages an investigation into the problems relating to teaching-learning mathematics at the secondary level on the basis of the difficulties (in content, teaching and learning), problems, and attitudes of students and teachers, the dependent variables are as follows:

Dependent Variables

1. Difficulty level of different chapters (in content, teaching and learning) as perceived by students and teachers in secondary level mathematics.
2. Problems of teachers and students in teaching and learning mathematics respectively.
3. Attitudes of students and teachers towards mathematics education.

Independent Variables

The independent variables considered in the investigation are: (i) Two kinds, namely, student related personal and demographic variables and teacher related personal and demographic variables. The student related independent variables are class, sex, age, locality, management of school, father's occupation, family literacy index, and annual income of the family etc. The teacher related independent variables are sex, age, educational qualifications) general and ii) professional, experience, locality, and management of the school etc. A brief description of these variables is given as follows:

Variables Related to Students

- ***Class***

Students studying VIII, IX, and X classes are considered in the study to find the differences among the classes.

- ***Sex***

Male and female students (boys and girls) are considered as sub-samples to carry on the differential analysis.

- ***Age***

The chronological age of the students as reported by them through the personal data sheet is considered, to divide the sample into three subgroups to study the variations in their problems and attitudes toward learning mathematics.

- ***Locality***

The entire sample of the subjects is classified into three groups the urban, semi-urban, and rural, depending upon their residential status, i.e., those who reside in the municipal towns and cities as urban, those who reside within the area of 20 km from town as semi-urban and those who reside in panchayat area as rural groups.

- ***Management***

The schools included in the study are categorised into four types viz., government schools, zilla parishad schools, Municipal schools, and private schools to find the variations in the problems and attitudes of their learners.

- ***Father's Occupation***

The occupational status of the parents may have its bearing on the problems and attitudes of students towards mathematics education. However, the occupation of father alone is considered in this investigation. Based on the occupations the sample is divided into three sub groups.

- ***Family Literacy Index***

The educational level of the family is estimated by collecting information about the number of years of study by all individual members of the family and dividing the total by number of persons in the family which gives the family literacy index. Thus, the family literacy index reflects the educational status of the family and it may have its influence on the problems and attitudes of students in learning mathematics.

- ***Family Income***

The annual income of the family as reported by the student is considered for making three sub groups of the sample of subjects. The economic status of the family may have its influence on the problems and attitudes of students in learning mathematics.

Variables Related to Teachers

- ***Sex***

The male and female teachers of mathematics of the secondary school are included in the study and there may exist difference between them in teaching the subject.

- ***Age***

The age of the teachers may influence their problems in teaching and their attitude towards teaching mathematics. Therefore, the chronological age of the teachers as reported by them through personal data sheet is considered as a variable for the study. The sample is divided into four sub groups.

- ***General Qualification***

The general qualification of the teachers of mathematics may influence the problems in the field. Therefore, the general education possessed by them is considered as one of the personal and demographic variables in the study. The sample is divided into three sub groups based on the *experience*.

- ***Professional Qualification***

The professional qualification of the teachers of mathematics may exercise a great influence on their problems in mathematics education. Therefore, it is taken as one of the personal and demographic variables in the study. The sample is divided into three sub groups based on the *experience*.

- ***Teaching Experience***

The experience in years (length of service) in the field of teaching mathematics may influence more the problems they face in teaching mathematics and their attitudes towards mathematics education. Therefore, teacher's service is included as a variable in the study. The sample is divided into four sub groups based on the experience.

- ***Locality***

Mathematics teachers working in urban, semi-urban and rural areas may have differences in the problems they face in teaching mathematics and in their attitudes towards mathematics education. Therefore, all such teachers are regarded as criterion groups for the investigation.

- ***Management***

For the present study as in the case of students, teachers are classified into four categories: Teachers of government schools, of zilla parishad schools, of municipal schools and of private schools.

OPERATIONAL DEFINITIONS OF TERMS AND EXPLANATION OF CONCEPTS

The following definitions and descriptions are operationalised for the purpose of measuring the variables in study:

- ***Mathematics***

"Mathematics is the science of number and space"

"Mathematics is the science of measurement, quantity and magnitude".

"Mathematics is the science which draws necessary conclusions"

"Mathematics is a way to settle in the mind a habit of reasoning."

- ***Mathematics Education***

The study of how one studies Mathematics is often called Mathematics Education. Usually a person studying mathematics is at least partly interested in the question of how anyone would ever think of that in the first place.

- ***Class***

A group of pupils or students scheduled to report regularly at a particular time to a particular teacher (Good,1973)

- ***Secondary School or High School***

Schools with classes VI to X are called high schools or secondary schools in the state of Andhra Pradesh in India. There will be public examination at the end of VII class and X class in these Schools.

- ***Content***

The ideas, meanings, concepts, explanations, etc., presented in the form of lessons/chapters in the textbook.

- ***Teaching***

B.O. Smith(1963): Teaching is a system of actions involving an agent, an end in view, and a situation including two sets of factors—those over which the agent has no control (class size, size of classroom, physical characteristics of pupils etc.) and those that he can modify (ways of asking questions, instructions and way of structuring information or ideas gleaned.)

Yoakm and Simpson: Teaching is a means whereby society trains the young in a selected environment as quickly as possible to adjust themselves to the world in which they live.

Learning

The dictionary of C. V. Good (1973) defines it as "Change in response or behaviour(such as innovation, elimination or modification of responses, involving some degree of performance)caused partly or wholly by experience, such experience being in the main conscious, but sometimes including significant unconscious components, as is common in motor learning or in reaction to unrecognised or subliminal stimuli; includes behaviour changes in the emotional sphere, but more commonly refers to the acquisition of symbolic knowledge or motor skills, does not include psychological changes, such as fatigue or temporary sensory resistance or non-functioning after conditioned stimulus."

Gates and others define it as "the progressive change in behaviour which is associated on the one hand with successive presentation of a situation, and on the other, with repeated efforts of the individual to react to it effectively."

Teaching-Learning Process

Teaching—Learning process is a means by which the teacher, the learner, the curriculum and other variables are organised in a systematic manner to attain pre- determined goals and objectives.

Difficulty Level

An approximation is made in order to fit the content of reading materials into the reading ability of the child by different testing procedures. The difficulty level of chapters included in the textbooks of mathematics for VIII, IX and X classes is considered in this study.

Content Difficulty

Some of the topics included in the prescribed textbook would be above the ability levels of students studying that particular class. Such topics are treated as difficult to the students content-wise. Teachers also find difficult in handling the contents, which are newly introduced and with which they are not aware of.

Teaching Difficulty

Teachers may find difficulty in transmitting the difficult and some of the newly introduced lessons effectively and meaningfully to the students. It has been treated as teaching difficulty.

Learning Difficulty

Students find difficulty in understanding some of the contents given in the textbook, even if the teacher presents them effectively. It has been taken as learning difficulty.

- ***Problem(s)***

Any significant, perplexing and challenging situation, real or artificial, the solution of which requires reflective thinking.

The term 'problems' refers to those difficulties of the secondary school teachers in teaching and of the pupils of VIII, IX, X classes in learning mathematics syllabus.

- ***Attitudes***

Guilford (1954) defined attitude as " A personal disposition common to indivisual but possessed to different degrees which implies to react to object situations or positions in ways that can be called favourable or unfavourable."

According to Bogardus (1931) "Attitude is a tendency to act toward or against something in the environment which becomes thereby, a positive or a negative value."

4

Methods of Investigation

This chapter deals with the design of the study, the different procedures followed in the construction and development of data—gathering instruments on different variables which are included in the study and the methods adopted for the selection of the samples, collection of data, scoring and analysis.

DESIGN OF THE STUDY

The present study is essentially a survey with descriptive and explorative objectives. It is undertaken to describe the present status and therefore it is called as descriptive survey. It is exploratory since it is also proposed to improve the situation by exploring the possible means and ways.

Moulay (1964) observed " No category of educational research is more widely used than the survey type. Educational surveys are particularly versatile and practical in that they identify the present conditions and point to the present needs. Descriptive surveys are oriented towards the description of the present status of a given phenomenon".

MEASUREMENT OF VARIABLES AND DEVELOPMENT OF THE TOOLS

As it has been described earlier, it is proposed to study the difficulties, problems and attitudes of students and teachers on different aspects such as content, teaching and learning mathematics at the secondary school level. Therefore, a rating scale to obtain the difficulty level of each chapter in mathematics at VIII, IX and X grades on content difficulty, teaching difficulty and learning difficulty is developed. Two problem checklists to study the problems faced by the students and the teachers in teaching-learning mathematics and two check lists-cum-rating scales to study the intensity of the problems faced by them are developed. The other tools developed are in the area of attitudes. The Likert type of summated ratings to measure attitudes is employed. The two attitude scales on five- point scale—one to study the attitudes of students and the other to study the attitudes of teachers towards mathematics education are also developed. Of course to collect the data pertinent to personal and demographic variables of students and teachers personal data sheets are also developed. Thus the seven tools that are required to measure the variables included in the study are described one by one in the following pages.

Description of the Rating Scales to Measure Difficulty Level of the Chapters

As envisaged earlier it is proposed to study the difficulty level felt by both students and teachers on different chapters of VIII, IX and X class textbooks. For this purpose, a rating scale for each class is developed which will be administered on the students of the respective grades. The rating scale contains 11 columns—first column is for serial number, second column contains title of the chapter, third, fourth and fifth columns are meant for the content difficulty (at three levels: less difficulty, moderate difficulty and more difficulty); columns six, seven and eight are meant for teaching difficulty at three levels and columns nine, ten and eleven are meant for the learning difficulty at three levels. However, with the same columns as described above a separate rating scale is also prepared to study the difficulty faced by the teachers on different chapters included in the text books of three grades—eighth, ninth and tenth, as any teacher of mathematics in the secondary school normally teaches all the three classes.

The rating scales developed are self-explanatory. Suitable instructions are incorporated in the beginning itself. These tools were administered to a small group of teachers and students to study whether there was any ambiguity, whether the respondents raised any doubts while answering the tools and whether the responses made by the subjects were proper. No queries and deficiencies were noticed in the tools. Therefore, the tools are treated as they are in the final investigation, taking them as valid and reliable.

Description of Problem Check List–cum–Rating Scales

The checklist is a simple device, consisting of a prepared list of items. It is a type of questionnaire in the form of a set of categories for the respondent to check. It is used to record the presence or absence of the phenomenon under study. Responses to the checklist are thus a matter of fact, not of judgement. This tool has the advantages of systematising and facilitating the recording of observations and of helping to assure the consideration of all-important aspects of the object or act observed. It is an important tool for gathering facts for educational service. It may also be used as a form of recording for observational studies of behaviour and educational appraisal studies of school textbooks, instructional procedures and outcomes etc.

Collection of Items

The relevant literature on the problems faced by the teachers and students regarding the content, textbook, learning and the teaching was thoroughly examined for the selection of the items. Experienced teachers teaching mathematics to VIII, IX and X classes and the students of these classes, school inspectors, teacher educators, parents and experts in the field were approached to list out the problems. Then a panel of experts were contacted with a request to suggest omissions and additions wherever necessary, to check the appropriateness of the items, and to suggest the better way of presentation of items, if any, in order to elicit information. Their suggestions were also carried out. All the items were rewritten incorporating the suggestions offered by the experts and again calculated for their scrutiny about clarity, simplicity and coverage of each item. The draft checklist at this stage consisted of 67 items for students and 46 items for teachers.

A four-column response pattern is appended to each item in the checklist. The first column is meant for checking whether they face the problem or not. If they feel the problem they have to put tick mark, if not they have to leave the column blank. Columns 2, 3 and 4 are for identifying the intensity level of the problem faced by them as less difficult, moderately difficult and more difficult.

To make these check lists – cum – rating scales self-explanatory, detailed instructions were given to both teachers and students.

Description of the Attitude Scales

"Attitude" is a familiar word and is used freely to express one's way of thinking, feeling or behaving. It has been used by psychologists in several connotations and there are a number of agreed definitions of the term.

Allport (1929) defined it as, "A mental or neural state of raciness, organised through experiences exerting a directive or dynamic influence upon the individual response to all the objects and situations with which it is related".

In the dictionary of psychology, Warren (1934) calls attitude "The specific mental disposition toward an incoming (or arising) experience, whereby that experience is modified or a condition of readiness for a certain type of activity."

According to Bogardus (1941) attitude is "A tendency to act toward or against something in the environment which becomes thereby a positive or negative value."

Thurstone (1944) defined attitude as " the degree of positive or negative effect associated with some psychological object".

To Guilford (1954) it is "A personal disposition common to individuals; but possessed to different degrees which impels them to react to objects, situations; or propositions in ways that can be called favourable or unfavourable".

According to Freeman (1968) "an attitude is a dispositional readiness to respond to certain situations, persons or objects in a constant manner which has been learned and has become one's typical mode of response".

Different Methods of Measuring Attitudes

Attitude can be measured in several ways. Attitudes are revealed in the behaviour of an individual. So, attitudes can be measured by direct observation of overt behaviour of the individual. Attitude can be inferred by one's unconscious responses to certain stimuli like paragraphs, cartoons etc. So, Projective techniques can also be used to assess an individual's attitude.

Assuming a positive correlation between what people say about a subject and what they will do about it, the most common method of estimating a person's attitude is through a questionnaire where, the individual expresses his/her opinion on several controversial statements on some psychological objects.

Among the techniques available for attitude scale construction, Thurston's equal appearing intervals and Likert's summated rating techniques are frequently used to check the effectiveness of education and teaching process. The Thurston technique makes use of objective judgement in the selection of items and requires a large number of judges and it is a time consuming process. The Likert's techniques obviate these difficulties. According to Shukla (1972) the advantages of the Likert's method is as follows: "The Likert's method of summated rating scale has been perceived significantly as relatively most reliable and valid, best understood and easiest to fill in".

In the present study, Likert's method of summated ratings has been used, because it yields scores very similar to those obtained by Thurston's method and at the same time it is less laborious than the latter. The coefficient of correlation between measures of attitude obtained by the two methods was as high as 0.92 (Edwards and Kenney, 1946).

Preparation of the Preliminary Form

Mathematics is an important subject of study at the school stage. For qualitative improvement of mathematical knowledge and its application, it is of paramount importance to have information regarding the attitudes of teachers and students towards the subject. As no reliable and valid scale to measure attitude towards mathematics was available for this study, it was decided to develop the attitude scales to measure the attitude towards teaching mathematics and the attitude towards learning mathematics.

For constructing the attitude scale opinions were collected about mathematics from students and teachers of secondary schools and they were converted into statements.

For the purpose of preparing the preliminary form, first, the nature and scope of the statements that have to be included in the proposed attitude scale have been examined in the light of the operational definition of the concept of the teacher's attitude towards teaching mathematics.

This has been presented to a panel of 20 experts with a request to suggesting improvements wherever necessary and the suggestions of the experts have been duly carried out. After this, in order to avoid ambiguity and overlapping all the statements have been reviewed and rewritten. The pilot form thus prepared consists of 49 statements of which 24 are supposed to represent the positive attitude and the remaining 25 the negative attitude of teachers towards teaching mathematics.

Pilot Study

The pilot forms of the attitude scales thus formulated have been administered to 150 students and 75 teachers selected at random in a way to examine whether the statements are easily understood by them or not and to ascertain whether they possess clarity or not. The responses are scored by giving appropriate weightage as described below:

The questionnaire uses a 5-point scale with responses ranging from Strongly Agree (1) to Strongly Disagree (5).

Item-wise Analysis

Item-wise analysis of the responses given by the teacher was carried out by the method of criterion of internal consistency suggested by Likert (1932). On the basis of weightages, total scores have been obtained on the scale to all the subjects (students and teachers). The top 27 per cent and the bottom 27 per cent of the subjects have been identified as criterion groups and mean scores obtained by these two groups have been calculated. On each item the difference between the mean scores is the discrimination value or item validity index, (Edward, 1969).

Preparation of the Final Form

Out of 49 items in the final form, only 43 (19 positive and 24 negative) have been selected for the inclusion in the final form of the attitude scale meant for teachers depending upon the discrimination value of the each item. Similarly, out of 44 items in the final form, only 42 have been selected for the inclusion in the final form of attitude scale meant for students depending upon the discrimination value of each item. Those items whose discrimination index is 0.3 and above has been selected for the inclusion in the final form of the scale.

Validity of the Attitude Scales

Content validity and intrinsic validity are established for both the attitude scales.

Content Validity

As described in the previous pages the statements, which reflect an attitude towards mathematics education, are collected from different sources—like literature, and experts on subjects (both students and teachers). They were carefully edited. An exhaustive list of item tool was developed. It was scrutinised by experts to avoid redundancy, ambiguity, overlàpping etc. and a representative sample of items has been retained in the pilot form. Therefore it can be concluded that there is substantial evidence to treat that the attitude scales have content validity.

Item Validity

The results of the item analysis reveal that poor items which could not discriminate between the two criterion groups having less than 0.3 discrimination value are not included in the final form. And hence it is concluded that all the items included in the final form are valid.

Intrinsic Validity

According to Guilford (1954), intrinsic validity indicates the degree to which the test measures what it purports to measure. In other words, this means verification of how well the obtained scores measure the test true score component. Intrinsic validity of a test is expressed in terms of the square root of its reliability value. Thus, the intrinsic validity of the attitude scales developed is square root of 0.802 = 0.896 for students' attitude scale and square root of 0.781 = 0.884 for teachers' attitude scale and it can be assumed as a highly satisfactory intrinsic validity.

Reliability of the Tools

Split-half reliability is calculated for the tool by considering all odd items as the first half and all the remaining even items as the second half. The split half reliability co-efficient of the half test or $r_{hh} = 0.64$ for teachers' attitude scale. The Spearman Broun Prophesy formula was employed to find out reliability of the full test and the value thus obtained was $r_w = 0.781$. Similar procedure is adopted to the other scale meant for students and the reliability of the full test obtained was $r_w = 0.802$ as the split-half reliability co-efficient of the tool $r_{hh} = 0.670$, which is also significant.

As the values are large and significant it is said that the attitude scales constructed for teachers and students are reliable.

Personal Data Sheet

Personal information regarding the students and teachers of secondary schools was collected through a well-planned personal data sheet meant for two types of subjects separately. Carefully worded personal data sheets were incorporated in the first page of rating scales meant for difficulty analysis of chapters for students and teachers.

SELECTION OF THE SAMPLE

The present investigation is aimed at identifying the existing problems of teaching and learning mathematics at the secondary school level. Hence, two categories of subjects namely students and teachers of the secondary schools, as the two sub-samples were selected as explained below.

At the first stage, three districts namely, Chittoor, Kadapa and Nellore were included in the study as these districts come under the jurisdiction of Sri Venkateswara University. 80 schools in total were selected at random from the three districts with not less than 20 from each district.

At the second stage, 8 to 10 students (covering 2 to 4 candidates from each class of VIII, IX and X) were selected at random from each one of the schools selected in the first stage so as to make the first sub sample of the students equal to 644. The second sub sample of teachers was identified by following the cluster sampling technique, that is by considering all the available teachers of mathematics from each one of the schools selected at the first stage. Thus, a total of 161 teachers formed the second sub sample of the survey. Thus, the sampling technique employed in the investigation may be called as a two stage random sampling technique.

COLLECTION OF DATA

The Investigator personally visited all the 80 schools and with the permission of the Head Masters of the schools, the self-explanatory instruments developed by the Investigator were administered to 644 students and 161 teachers. The students were given the instructions orally and were also asked to read the instructions given along with the instruments and motivated to respond genuinely to all the items given in the data gathering tools.

SCORING OF THE RESPONSES

As the instruments used in this investigation were rating scales, problem check list-cum-rating scales and attitude scales, they were scored by giving the following weightages. Rating scales were scored on a 3-point scale by giving weightages 3, 2 and 1 to the three alternatives viz, maximum extent, moderate extent and least extent respectively.

The problems were scored on a 3-point scale by giving weightages 1, 2 and 3 to the three alternatives viz, least extent, moderate extent and maximum extent. The grand total (frequencies and intensity scores) for each individual on the entire scale was obtained by adding the weightages on all the items.

The Likert's type of attitude scales were scored on a 5-point scale by giving weightages 5, 4, 3, 2 and 1 in the case of positive items and 1, 2, 3, 4, and 5 in the case of negative items respectively. The grand total for each individual on the entire scale was obtained by adding the weightages on all the statements.

ANALYSIS OF THE DATA

As the data collected through the different statements in the tool from different subjects are basically qualitative in nature, item-wise analysis was carried out to identify the specific deficiencies in different aspects of teaching-learning mathematics in secondary schools. Statistics such as frequencies, percentages and chi-square were employed to make the description more precise.

The total scores (problem intensity scores and attitude scores) obtained by all subjects on all the variables were computed. The data were carefully analysed employing appropriate statistical techniques. Descriptive statistics such as Mean, Median, Mode, Quartile Deviation, Standard Deviation, Skewness and Kurtosis were used to describe the distribution of scores. The inferential statistics such as 't' test (critical-ratio) and 'F' test were employed to test different hypothesis. The numerical results obtained were interpreted numerically to draw conclusions and thereby educational implications.

A detailed analysis of the data and a discussion on the results are presented in the succeeding chapter.

5

Analysis of the Data and Discussion

This chapter is presented under four sections. The first section deals with content analysis—content difficulties, teaching difficulties and learning difficulties—as perceived by students and teachers of mathematics. The second section depicts an analysis of the problems faced by students and teachers in teaching-learning mathematics. The attitude of students and teachers towards mathematics education is presented in section 3. Section 4 describes the distribution of problem intensity scores and attitude scores of both students and teachers and the differential analysis due to the different personal and demographic variables included in the study.

CONTENT ANALYSIS

As envisaged earlier, it is aimed at identifying the most difficult chapters included in the syllabi of secondary school mathematics (the prescribed textbooks of VIII, IX and X classes). For this purpose a content difficulty intensity scale (a 3- point scale) was used covering contents, difficulty in teaching the contents and difficulty in learning the contents as perceived by teachers and the taught. Thus there are three sub sections:

(i) content difficulty analysis as perceived by students and teachers of VIII class;

(ii) content difficulty analysis as perceived by students and teachers of IX class; and

(iii) content difficulty analysis as perceived by students and teachers of X class

Content Difficulty Analysis as Perceived by Students and Teachers of—VIII Class

The VIII class Mathematics textbook has 15 chapters. The responses of students and teachers in respect of each chapter have been obtained on a 3-point scale, namely, less difficult, moderately difficult and highly difficult, on the three aspects namely content difficulty, teaching difficulty and learning difficulty. These responses have been aggregated for total samples (students 227 and teachers 161) and presented in the following tables:

It would be interesting to see the perceptions of students and teachers on the difficulty level of each chapter. The following is the description in that direction.

The first chapter deals with Real Numbers. It covers the Rational numbers, operations on real numbers, properties of rational numbers, decimals, irrational numbers denoting the rational and irrational numbers on the number line and finding square roots using factorisation method.

The following table 5.1 presents a numerical picture regarding difficulties of students and teachers in content, teaching and learning at different levels.

Out of 227 students, 96 (about 42.3%) perceived that the contents of the chapter ' Real Numbers' are difficult at the low intensity level whereas 88 out of 161 (about 54.7%) teachers perceived that the contents of this chapter are difficult at the less intensity level.

At the moderate level of difficulty, 44 out of 227 (about 19.4%) students and 25 out of 161 (15.5%) teachers perceived content difficulty in chapter 1. Interestingly, only 2 per cent of students and 2 per cent of teachers felt that the contents of this chapter are highly difficult, this percentage need not be taken into account, as it is negligible.

Table 5.1: Frequencies and difficulty intensity scores of Chapter I

	STUDENTS					TEACHERS				
	L	*M*	*H*	*T*	*INT*	*L*	*M*	*H*	*T*	*INT*
C	96	44	5	145	199	88	25	3	116	147
T	42	16	6	64	94	89	16	3	108	130
L	53	15	5	73	98	72	40	9	121	179

Note: C: Content difficulty, T: Teaching difficulty, L: Learning difficulty,
L: Frequency at low level, M: Frequency at moderate level,
H: Frequency at high level, T: Total frequency, I: Intensity Score
(These symbols are followed throughout the thesis)

In so far as the teaching difficulty is concerned, about 19 per cent, 7 per cent, and only 2 per cent of students and about 55 per cent, 9 per cent, and only 2 per cent of teachers perceived teaching this chapter as difficult at the low, moderate, and high intensity levels respectively.

Similarly, learning this chapter is perceived as easy by majority of students of about 68 per cent but about 75 per cent of the teachers regarded it as difficult even in learning by their students on the basis of total frequencies.

However the difficulty intensity as perceived by students is 46 per cent, 49 per cent, and 45 per cent regarding content, teaching and learning respectively whereas it is 42 per cent, 40 per cent, and 49 per cent as perceived by teachers. Therefore it is a less difficult chapter as the difficulty intensity lies between 40 per cent to 49 per cent.

The second chapter is titled as Commercial Mathematics. *It elucidates the* Ratio, Proportion, Percentage, Simple Interest, Compound Interest, Partnership, Time-Work, Time-Distance etc. In fact the basic concepts of ratio, proportion, percentage and simple interest are introduced in the VI class itself. Again in VIII class, these topics are reviewed and extended up to the applications of compound interest, partnership, Time-work, Time-distance.

Table 5.2: Frequencies and difficulty intensity scores of Chapter II

	STUDENTS					TEACHERS				
	L	*M*	*H*	*T*	*INT*	*L*	*M*	*H*	*T*	*INT*
C	31	59	19	109	206	23	62	40	125	267
T	13	42	20	75	157	38	48	37	123	235
L	38	45	13	101	182	16	54	61	131	307

The data of the table given above presents a clear picture of the difficulties of students and teachers in three aspects namely content, teaching and learning.

31 out of 227 (about 14%) students and 23 out of 161(about 14%) teachers perceived that the contents of Commercial mathematics were difficult at the less intensity level.

At the moderate level of difficulty, 59 out of 227 (about 26%) students and 62 out of 161 (39%) teachers perceived content difficulty in chapter 2. But at the high intensity level 19 students (about 8%) and 40 teachers (about 25%) perceived content difficulty in it.

As far as teaching difficulty is concerned, about 55,19%, and 9 per cent of students perceived it in chapter 2 for their teachers at the low, moderate, and high intensity levels whereas about 24 per cent, 30 per cent, and 23 per cent teachers perceived it at the low, moderate, and high intensity level respectively.

On the basis of the total frequencies, about 48 per cent of the students and 78 per cent of the teachers perceived content difficulty, about 33 per cent of students and 76 per cent of teachers perceived teaching difficulty, whereas about 45 per cent of students and about 81 per cent of the teachers perceived learning difficulty.

Even the difficulty intensity scores reveal that the chapter 'Commercial Mathematics' is very difficult for the students and teachers as the difficulty intensity lies between 60 per cent to 70 per cent for students and 64 per cent to 78 per cent for teachers.

The results categorically show that 75 to 80 per cent of teachers and 45 to 50 per cent of students expressed their difficulty in all the three aspects, namely, content, teaching and learning this chapter.

Therefore some urgent steps must be taken to remedy the situation.

The third chapter in VIII class textbook is 'Mensuration'. It deals with the lengths, areas and volumes of geometrical figures. Here pupils study the areas of different triangles, different quadrilaterals, ring and sector. In the earlier classes, they studied plain circles. Here is a continuation of those lessons.

Table 5.3: Frequencies and difficulty intensity scores of Chapter III

	STUDENTS					*TEACHERS*				
	L	*M*	*H*	*T*	*INT*	*L*	*M*	*H*	*T*	*INT*
C	45	49	14	108	185	35	56	27	118	228
T	33	25	7	65	104	48	44	20	112	196
L	47	37	6	90	139	24	58	36	118	248

This table gives an idea of the difficulties expressed by the students and teachers regarding the content, teaching and learning of chapter III.

At the less intensity level 45 out of 227 (about 20 per cent) students as well as 35 out of 161(about 22%) teachers perceived that the contents of this chapter are difficult. At the moderate level of difficulty, 49 out of 227 (about 22%) students and 56 out of 161 (35%) teachers felt content difficulty in chapter 3.But at the high intensity level 14 students (about 6%) and 27 teachers (about 17%) perceived content difficulty in chapter 3.

As far as teaching difficulty is concerned, about 15 per cent, 11 per cent, 3 per cent of students and about 30 per cent, 27 per cent, 12 per cent of teachers experienced difficulty in teaching the chapter Mensuration at the low, moderate, and high intensity levels.

About 40 per cent of students and about 73 per cent of the teachers considered it difficult for learning.

The total intensity scores make it clear that Mensuration is moderately difficult for students and highly difficult for teachers as the intensity scores lie between 51 per cent to 57 per cent for students and 58 per cent to 70 per cent for teachers.

The IV chapter is 'Sets and Relations'. It is a newly introduced concept in this class. The theory of sets developed by the German scientist George Cantor (1885-1915) has an important role in modern mathematics. The set concept and set language unifies different branches and enriches every branch of mathematics.

Table 5.4: Frequencies and difficulty intensity scores of Chapter IV

	STUDENTS					*TEACHERS*				
	L	*M*	*H*	*T*	*INT*	*L*	*M*	*H*	*T*	*INT*
C	68	25	16	109	166	97	12	3	112	130
T	40	18	12	70	112	91	18	2	111	133
L	49	14	11	74	110	89	18	5	112	140

The table familiarises the difficulties expressed by the students and teachers in respect of the content, teaching and learning of chapter IV.

At the less intensity level 68 out of 227 (about 30%) students and 97 out of 161(about 60%) teachers perceived that the contents of this chapter are difficult. At the moderate level of difficulty, 25 out of 227 (about 11%) students and 12 out of 161 (7%) teachers perceived content difficulty in chapter 4. But at the high intensity level 16 students (about 7%) and 3 teachers (about 2 %) experienced the same.

Both at the moderate and high intensity levels, majority of the teachers and students regarded this chapter as easy for teaching and learning respectively.

Similarly, based on the total frequencies, learning this chapter is perceived as easy by majority of students (about 67%) whereas about 70 per cent of the teachers felt it difficult for their students.

But based on the intensity scores, students perceived it as less moderately difficult chapter whereas teachers perceived it as easy chapter as the intensity lies between 41 per cent to 53 per cent for students and 39 per cent to 42 per cent for teachers.

Majority of the teachers and students consider the chapter easy. But some teachers find it difficult in understanding the concepts like Sub set, Proper sub set and power set etc.

If these concepts are explained clearly to the students by adopting inductive method through concrete examples, this chapter can be made easy.

The V Chapter in the textbook is 'Elementary Number Theory'. It carefully orchestrates with even numbers, prime numbers, composite numbers, twin primes, factors and multiples, unique factorisation theorem, finding G.C.D by division method, L.C.M, relatively prime numbers and theorem of Gauss.

In this Chapter an attempt is made to enable the student to comprehend the properties of numbers, to solve life problems using the concepts of L.C.M, G.C.F and Gauss theorem on co-primes. In fact, the basics of all the above concepts are introduced in the VI class itself and this is a continuation of them. Therefore teaching and learning this chapter is perceived easier than the other chapters by majority of teachers and students.

Table.5.5: Frequencies and difficulty intensity scores of Chapter V

	STUDENTS					*TEACHERS*				
	L	*M*	*H*	*T*	*INT*	*L*	*M*	*H*	*T*	*INT*
C	52	29	12	93	146	76	36	2	114	154
T	35	21	8	64	101	78	29	2	109	142
L	39	18	4	61	87	69	37	5	111	158

The table values reveal the details of content, teaching and learning difficulties of teachers and students. 52 (about 23%) out of 227 students and 76 out of 161 (about 47%) teachers perceived that the contents of this chapter are difficult at the low intensity level.

As regards the moderate level of intensity 29 out of 227 students (about 13%) and 36 out of 161 (about 22%) of teachers perceived that the contents of this chapter are difficult. The difficulty at the high intensity level is almost negligible.

35 students (about 15%) and 78 teachers (about 48%) experienced teaching difficulty at the low intensity level. At the moderate and high intensity levels, very few teachers and students felt any teaching difficulty in this chapter.

Regarding learning, about 17 per cent, 8 per cent of students and about 43 per cent, 23 per cent of teachers perceived difficulty at the low and moderate intensity levels. The difficulty expressed at the high level of intensity is of course negligible.

Based on the intensity scores, it is clear that the chapter is less moderately difficult for both students and teachers as the intensity lies between 48 per cent to 53 per cent for students and 43 per cent to 47 per cent for teachers.

The VI Chapter in the Textbook is 'Exponents'. In this Chapter a short hand notation called the Exponential Notation is introduced to indicate the products which contain two or more identical quantities. It describes the laws of exponents such as multiplication property, power of a power property, power of quotient property etc. As it is a continuation from the earlier classes, teaching and learning this chapter is taken as easy by most of the teachers and students.

Table.5.6: Frequencies and difficulty intensity scores of Chapter VI

	STUDENTS					*TEACHERS*				
	L	*M*	*H*	*T*	*INT*	*L*	*M*	*H*	*T*	*INT*
C	64	17	12	93	134	96	16	3	115	137
T	33	14	10	57	91	93	18	2	113	135
L	47	22	12	18	127	81	27	6	114	153

On the basis of total frequencies, about 41 per cent of students and about 71 per cent of teachers perceived the contents of this chapter as difficult.

As far as teaching is concerned, 57 out of 227 students (about 25%) and 113 (about 70%) teachers perceived this chapter as difficult.(on the basis of the total frequencies).

Based on the total frequencies 81 students (about 36%) and 114 teachers (about 71%) felt learning difficulty in chapter VI. In other words, while about 64 per cent of the students perceived learning this chapter as easy, about 71 per cent of teachers considered it as difficult for their students. However, the difficulty at moderate and high intensity levels cannot be accounted for, as it seems negligible.

But based on the intensity scores, this chapter is perceived as less moderately difficult both by students and teachers as the intensity lies between 24 per cent to 53 per cent for students and 40 per cent to 45 per cent for teachers.

Here the fundamental concepts are not dealt with meaningfully. Instead they are taught mechanically. This results in cramming the things blindly, which in turn leads to the development of a negative attitude towards the subject.

The VII chapter in VIII class textbook is 'Polynomials'. It enlists the multiplication of polynomials, division of polynomials and some special products. Primarily, the concept of Polynomials is introduced in VI class itself. In VII class students study algebraic expressions and polynomials in one variable and certain operations like + and ´ on. The following table elucidates the difficulties of students and teachers in content, teaching and learning of this chapter.

Table 5.7: Frequencies and difficulty intensity scores of Chapter VII

	STUDENTS					*TEACHERS*				
	L	*M*	*H*	*T*	*INT*	*L*	*M*	*H*	*T*	*INT*
C	42	24	25	91	165	64	40	9	113	171
T	31	12	10	53	85	69	32	7	108	154
L	40	17	12	69	110	52	47	13	112	185

42 (about 19%) out of 227 students and 64 out of 161 teachers (about 40%) perceived content difficulty of chapter VII at the low intensity level. Whereas 24 out of 227 students (about 11%) and 40 out of 161 teachers (about 25%) at the moderate intensity level, and 25 out of 227 students (about 11%) and 9 out of 161 teachers (about 6%) felt the same at the high intensity level.

About 14 per cent, 5 per cent, 4 per cent of the students and about 43 per cent, 20 per cent, 4 per cent of teachers perceived difficulty in teaching at the low, moderate, and high intensity level respectively.

Similarly, learning this chapter was perceived as easy by majority of students (about 70%) whereas the same percentage of teachers considered it the other way.

However, the intensity scores reveal that both the students and teachers felt the chapter as moderately difficult as the intensity ranges from 53 per cent to 60 per cent for students and from 48 per cent to 555 for teachers.

The VIII chapter is titled 'Factorisation'. A continuation of the previous chapter i.e, Polynomials. Students learn to divide the given polynomial into the product of different factors in this chapter. However, they face some difficulty because of the algebraic expressions involved here. The table given below gives the details in relation to the difficulties of students and teachers in respect of content, teaching and learning.

Table 5.8: Frequencies and difficulty intensity scores of Chapter VIII

	STUDENTS					*TEACHERS*				
	L	*M*	*H*	*T*	*INT*	*L*	*M*	*H*	*T*	*INT*
C	44	41	14	99	168	67	36	9	112	166
T	26	20	11	57	99	73	29	8	110	155
L	42	24	13	79	129	47	47	17	111	192

At the low intensity level, 44 out of 227 (about 19 per cent) students and 67 out 161 (about 42%) teachers perceived content difficulty of chapter VIII. On the other hand, 41 out of 227 (about 18%) students and 36 out of 161 (about 22%) teachers experienced the same at the moderate level of intensity. But at the high intensity level, only 14 students (about 6%) and only 9 teachers (about 6%) felt it difficult on the basis of total frequencies.

As far as teaching is concerned, 26 (about 11%), 20 (about 9%) and 11 (about 5%) of students and 73 (about 45%), 29 (about 18%)

and 8 (about 5%) teachers regarded teaching this chapter as difficult at the low, moderate and high intensity levels respectively.

The total results reveal that, 57 out of 227 students (about 25%) and 110 out of 161 (about 68%) teachers perceived teaching this chapter as difficult. In other words, when about 75 per cent of students perceived teaching this chapter as easy for their teachers, about 68 per cent of teachers perceived it as difficult.

Regarding learning aspect, 42 (about 19%), 24 (about 11%) and 13 (about 6%) of students considered this chapter difficult at the low, moderate and high intensity levels respectively while 47 (about 29%) at the low and moderate levels and 17 (about 11%) of teachers at the high intensity level viewed it difficult for their students.

On the basis of the total frequencies, 79 (about 35%) of the students and 111 (about 69%) teachers perceived this chapter as difficult for their students' learning. In other words, this chapter was easy for about 65% of students whereas it was difficult for about 69 per cent of the teachers.

Based on the difficulty intensity scores, students perceived the chapter as moderately difficult as the intensity scores range from 54 per cent to 58 per cent whereas teachers perceived it as less moderately difficult as the intensity scores range from 47 per cent to 58 per cent.

The IX chapter is on Linear Equations. It deals with the system of linear equations, method of substitution for solving them, dependent equations, linear equations and their graphs and linear functions.

The table 5.9 abundantly clarifies the difficulties of students and teachers regarding the content, teaching and learning of this chapter.

At the less intensity level, the content was difficult for about 22 per cent of the students and for about 32 per cent of teachers. At the moderate level of intensity, about 13 per cent of students and about 30 per cent of the teachers perceived content difficulty in this chapter. About 13 per cent of the students and about 8 per cent of the teachers experienced difficulty at the high level of intensity.

Table 5.9: Frequencies and difficulty intensity scores of Chapter IX

	STUDENTS					TEACHERS				
	L	*M*	*H*	*T*	*INT*	*L*	*M*	*H*	*T*	*INT*
C	50	29	30	109	198	52	48	13	113	187
T	30	22	11	63	107	66	39	11	116	177
L	39	21	3	68	105	37	55	24	116	219

As regards teaching about 13 per cent of students and about 41 per cent of teachers perceived this chapter as difficult at the less intensity level. At the moderate level of intensity, when about 10 per cent of students felt teaching this chapter as difficult for their teachers, about 24 per cent of the teachers perceived the difficulty. At the high intensity level, only about 5 per cent of the students and about 7 per cent of the teachers treated this chapter difficult.

In so far as learning difficulty is concerned, when about 17 per cent of students considered this chapter difficult and about 23 per cent of the teachers felt the same at the less intensity level. At the moderate level, about 9 per cent of the students and about 34 per cent of the teachers felt learning this chapter as difficult for their students. About 4 per cent of the students and about 15 per cent of the teachers expressed difficulty in learning this chapter for their students at the high intensity level.

On the basis of the total frequencies about 48 per cent of the students and about 70 per cent of the teachers found difficulty in the contents of chapter IX. When about 28 per cent of the students alone perceived teaching this chapter as difficult for their teachers, about 72 per cent of the teachers considered it difficult. About 30 per cent of the students and about 72 per cent of the teachers perceived learning this chapter as difficult for their students.

On the other hand, when about 52 per cent, about 72 per cent and about 70 per cent of the students perceived that the chapter is easy in respect of the content, teaching and learning, about 70 per cent, about 72 per cent and about the same 72 per cent of the teachers called it difficult respectively.

The difficulty intensity scores reveal that both students and teachers felt this chapter as moderately difficult as the intensity scores range from 51 per cent to 615 for students and from 51 per cent to 63 per cent for teachers.

Generally, students find difficulty in understanding the concepts like slope and its intercept form etc., in this chapter. This is because teachers, as far as possible, try to provide synthetic solutions to the students instead of adopting induction and analysis while teaching. When the students are taught without any reasoning and logic, they tend to find difficulty in understanding even the simple concepts. Hence, it is necessary to adopt inductive, analytic and laboratory methods in the beginning.

The 10th chapter deals with 'Linear inequations'. In fact, the linear inequations of the first degree in one variable and their solutions are studied by the pupils in VII class itself. In this chapter, they study about the linear inequations and their graphs, and systems of inequations. In the previous chapter the pupil studies to draw the graphs for linear equations in two variables and solve the simultaneous equations in two unknowns. If these aspects are studied properly by the pupils, then, learning the contents of this chapter becomes easy for them. But as it is observed in the earlier chapter itself that the contents, teaching and learning are difficult, the same difficulty continues in the present chapter also. The following table 5.10 reveals the details regarding the difficulties of students and teachers.

Out of 227 students, 42 (about 19%), 29 (about 13%), 28 (about 12%) perceived contents of this chapter as difficult at the low, moderate and high intensity levels, whereas out of 161 teachers 37 (about 23%), 45 (about 28%) and 27 (about 17%) experienced difficulty at the low, moderate and high intensity levels respectively.

Out of 227 students, 46 (about 20%) perceived teaching this chapter as difficult whereas out of 161 teachers, 106 (about 66%) regarded this chapter as difficult for teaching on the basis of the total frequencies.

In so far as the learning difficulty is concerned, about 74 per cent of students perceived it as easy whereas about 67 per cent of the teachers thought it difficult for their students on the basis of the total responses.

Table.5.10: Frequencies and difficulty intensity scores of Chapter X

	STUDENTS					TEACHERS				
	L	*M*	*H*	*T*	*INT*	*L*	*M*	*H*	*T*	*INT*
C	42	29	28	99	184	37	45	27	109	208
T	29	9	8	46	71	45	43	17	106	182
L	35	12	13	60	98	30	51	27	108	213

However, students perceived this chapter as moderately difficult as the intensity ranges from 51 per cent to 625 whereas teachers called it a more difficult chapter as the intensity ranges from 57 per cent to 66 per cent.

The XI chapter contains 'Introduction of Geometry'. In this chapter, the historical development of Geometry through centuries is given to facilitate the pupil to understand the various works of great mathematicians like Euclid, Bhaskara etc., and to encourage the pupil to study mathematics actively and interestingly.

But none looks up to it, as it is not considered important for the examinations. Unless and until the teachers have a positive attitude towards the subject, they will not be in a position to instil the same the students.

The following table reveals the details regarding the difficulties of teachers and students.

Table 5.11: Frequencies and difficulty intensity scores of Chapter XI

	STUDENTS					TEACHERS				
	L	*M*	*H*	*T*	*INT*	*L*	*M*	*H*	*T*	*INT*
C	39	21	18	76	135	49	46	21	116	204
T	23	15	9	47	80	53	42	21	116	200
L	26	22	9	57	97	47	37	29	113	208

It may be seen that out of 227 students 39 (about 17 per cent), 21 (about 9%), 18 (about 8%) perceived content difficulty in chapter XI at the low, moderate and high intensity levels whereas out of 161 teachers 49 (about 30%), 46 (about 29%) and 21 (about 13%) felt the same at the low, moderate and high intensity levels respectively.

At the teaching level, when about 79 per cent of the students perceived this chapter as easy for their teachers, about 72 per cent of the teachers experience difficulty on the basis of the total frequencies.

In so far as learning difficulty is concerned, out of 227 students 26 (about 11%) , 22 (about 10%) and 9 (about 4%) considered the chapter difficult at the low, moderate and high intensity levels respectively whereas out of 161 teachers 47 (about 29%), 37 (about 23%) and 29 (about 18%) perceived learning this chapter as difficult for their students at the low, moderate and high intensity levels respectively.

But as the difficulty intensity scores ranges from 57 per cent to 61 per cent, this chapter is moderately difficult for students and teachers.

In the general practical classroom situation, the formulae are taught by adopting dogmatic approach. For example:

1. The formula for area of the rectangle is l.b.
2. The formula for area of the triangle is (b.h) | 2
3. The formula for area of the parallelogram is b.h
4. The formula for area of the trapezium is h (a+b) | 2
5. The formula for area of rhombus is (d1.d2) | 2
6. The formula for area of the quadrilateral is (h_1+h_2).d | 2

If we look at the set of formulae given above, it is crystal clear that there is no relationship between them. Each formula is different from the other. Therefore the students find it very difficult to remember the formulae. They have no other way except by get them by heart.

The XII chapter in the text is 'Straight Lines'. It deals with basic axioms.

The following table gives details regarding the difficulties of students and teachers in content, teaching and learning in this chapter.

Table 5.12: Frequencies and difficulty intensity scores of Chapter XII

	STUDENTS					*TEACHERS*				
	L	*M*	*H*	*T*	*INT*	*L*	*M*	*H*	*T*	*INT*
C	47	29	24	100	177	51	47	11	109	178
T	24	20	10	54	94	47	47	9	103	168
L	37	14	9	60	92	39	44	23	106	196

47 out of 227 (about 21%) students and 51 out of 161 (about 32%) teachers perceived contents of this chapter as difficult at low intensity level whereas at the moderate level of intensity, 29 out of 227 (about 13%) students and 47 out of 161 (about 29%) teachers found the same. But, only about 11 per cent and about 7 per cent of students and teachers respectively perceived content difficulty in chapter XII at the high intensity level.

54 out of 227 (about 24%) students regarded teaching this chapter as difficult whereas 103 out of 161 (about 64%) teachers felt it difficult on the basis of the total frequencies.

Learning this chapter was considered difficult out of 227 students by 37 (about 16%) , 14 (about 6%) and 9 (about 4%) at the low, moderate and high intensity levels respectively whereas out of 161 teachers it was thought difficult for the students by 39 (about 24%), 44 (about 27%), 23 (about 9%) at the low, moderate and high intensity levels respectively.

But as per the difficulty intensity, the 12th chapter is moderately difficult as the intensity ranges from 51 per cent to 62 per cent for both students and teachers.

Though teaching of the axioms is essential to the students in the beginning, the teachers are not serious about this. Unless the students understand the basic axioms, they cannot learn the theorems based them. They can solve the riders based on them and so they fail utterly in doing geometrical constructions. Hence, emphasis must be laid on adoption of axiomatic approach while teaching geometry in the classroom.

Chapter XIII deals with Triangles and Polygons. The main objective of teaching Geometry at this stage is to develop intuition, induction and deduction, analytical thinking and logical reasoning.

This chapter consists of Congruency of Triangles, Similarity of Triangles, Polygons and geometric inequalities.

The table values give the details regarding the difficulties in content, teaching and learning in this chapter.

Table 5.13: Frequencies and difficulty intensity scores of Chapter XIII

	STUDENTS					*TEACHERS*				
	L	*M*	*H*	*T*	*INT*	*L*	*M*	*H*	*T*	*INT*
C	26	26	24	76	150	23	67	24	114	229
T	12	20	10	42	82	35	61	19	115	214
L	16	16	7	39	69	23	56	32	111	231

Regarding content, 26 out of 227 students (about 11%) and 23 out of 161 (about 14%) teachers perceived difficulty at the less intensity level. At the moderate level of intensity 26 out of 227 (about 11%) students and 67 out of 161 (about 42%) teachers experienced the same. 24 out of 227 (about 11%) students and 24 out 161 (about 15%) teachers found the contents of this chapter difficult at the high intensity level.

In so far as the teaching difficulty is concerned, about 81 per cent of the students perceived teaching this chapter as easy for their teachers whereas about 71 per cent of the teachers found it difficult on the basis of the total frequencies. About 83 per cent of the students viewed learning this chapter as easy whereas about 69 per cent of the teachers called difficult on the basis of total frequencies.

But based on the difficulty intensity scores, the chapter 'Triangles and Polygons' is highly difficult both for the students and teachers as the intensity lies between 59 per cent to 69 per cent.

This may be due to the presentation of solutions in the synthetic method in the textbook, which some teachers are not able to follow.

The XIV chapter is 'Circles and Concurrent lines in Triangles'. In this chapter students learn some important properties of circles and some basic theorems thereon.

Table.5.14: Frequencies and difficulty intensity scores of Chapter XIV

	STUDENTS					*TEACHERS*				
	L	*M*	*H*	*T*	*INT*	*L*	*M*	*H*	*T*	*INT*
C	30	20	19	69	127	30	51	35	116	237
T	10	8	8	26	50	35	58	20	113	211
L	10	7	6	23	42	24	46	50	120	266

The table values reveal that 30 out of 227 (about 13%) students perceived that the contents of this chapter are difficult whereas 30 out of 161 (about 19%) teachers alone felt the same difficult at the low intensity level. At the moderate level of intensity 20 out of 227 students (about 9%) and 51 out of 161 teachers (about 32%) perceived that the contents of this chapter are difficult. At the high intensity level, only 19 out of 227 (about 8%) students and 35 out of 161 (about 22%) teachers found the contents of this chapter difficult.

As regards the teaching difficulty, very few students perceived that teaching this chapter as difficult for their teachers whereas 113 out of 161 (about 70%) teachers considered teaching this chapter difficult on the basis of total frequencies. Regarding the learning difficulty when about 90 per cent of the students perceived learning this chapter as easy, about 75 per cent of the teachers felt it difficult for their students on the basis of total frequencies.

This chapter 'Circles and Concurrent lines in Triangles' is also a highly difficult chapter for students and teachers, as the intensity scores lie between 61 per cent to 74 per cent.

This chapter is supposed to be taught during February and March. By that time, the teachers will be busy conducting Unit tests, and doing Revision etc. Hence, most of the teachers do not find time to teach this particular chapter. Even if some of the teachers complete this chapter, most of the students find it very difficult to understand the logic behind the steps. While proving the theorems they cannot draw suitable figures to the given statement or rider.

Solving the riders is also very difficult for the students. Coming to the constructions, almost all the students are afraid of constructions. Ultimately, they are forced to learn by heart the selected theorems for the sake of examinations. As far as teaching part is considered, this aspect cannot be taught as other branches of mathematics. It requires deductive reasoning while presenting the things. Hence the teacher must be thorough with all the basic principles, axioms and theorems in Geometry. But this is not possible for a teacher because they have the habit of skipping this chapter right from the primary education with the assumption that learning Geometry is difficult for students. In fact, most of the teachers adopt Synthetic Method while teaching Geometry and it results in a lot of confusion among the students.

The last chapter in the text i.e. the 15th one is Symmetry. It deals with the concept of symmetry and the basic types of symmetry namely the line symmetry, the point symmetry and the image of a point or a set of points. Symmetry is introduced only with the primary aim of learning to understand the various symmetrical figures and objects in life situations and to appreciate the beauty in symmetry. The table given under scrutinises the perceptions of students and teachers regarding the contents, teaching and learning.

Table 5.15: Frequencies and difficulty intensity scores of Chapter XV

	STUDENTS					*TEACHERS*				
	L	*M*	*H*	*T*	*INT*	*L*	*M*	*H*	*T*	*INT*
C	22	12	15	49	91	63	28	22	113	185
T	9	7	4	20	35	69	29	15	113	172
L	10	2	4	16	26	62	28	24	114	190

It is obvious that about 10 per cent of the students and about 39 per cent of the teachers perceived content difficulty in chapter 15 at the low intensity level. About 5 per cent of the students and about 17 per cent of the teachers found the difficulty at the moderate level of intensity. And about 7 per cent of the students and about 14 per cent of teachers experienced difficulty of this chapter at the high intensity level.

As regards the teaching difficulty, when about only 9 per cent of the students perceived it for their teachers, about 70 per cent of teachers found it on the basis of the total responses. On the other way round, when about 91 per cent of the students perceived teaching this chapter as easy for their teachers, about 70 per cent of the teachers considered it difficult.

About 93 per cent of the students perceived learning this chapter as easy whereas about 71 per cent of the teachers felt it difficult for their students (on the basis of the total responses).

But this chapter can be treated as a moderately difficult chapter as the intensity scores ranges from 51 per cent to 62 per cent.

From the above discussions it is categorically observed that majority of the mathematics teachers working in secondary schools do not possess positive attitude towards the subject, their students and their profession. More vigorously, in almost all the chapters what draws the attention of the investigator is that, only the teachers expressed more difficulty than the students in all the three areas, namely, content, teaching and learning. It means, first of all the teachers are more worried than the students about the subject (facing so many problems) in teaching and learning mathematics.

Hence, the teachers must be provided with proper guidance and counselling to develop positive attitude towards the subject and build up confidence in their teaching and pupils' learning. It is high time we adopted a suitable strategy to cope with the situation, or else, the teachers will fall prey to fighting-shy attitude.

After having examined the perceptions of students and teachers on difficulty levels of content, teaching and learning of each chapter, it would be rather interesting to observe the relative difficulty levels of different chapters as perceived by both the groups on the three kinds of difficulties.

The following table depict the total number of subjects (frequencies) and the intensity of difficulty as expressed by the two groups on content, teaching and learning of all the chapters incorporated in VIII class mathematics text book.

Table 5.16: Table indicating the Content Difficulty of VIII Class as perceived by Students and Teachers

S.No.	*Chapter Name*	*Students*		*Teachers*	
		Frequencies	*Intensity Scores*	*Frequencies*	*Intensity Scores*
1.	**Real Numbers**	145 (1)	199 (2)	116 (4)	147 (13)
2.	Commercial Mathematics	109 (3)	206 (1)	125 (1)	267 (1)
3.	Mensuration	108 (5)	185 (4)	118 (2)	228 (4)
4.	Sets	109 (3)	166 (8)	112	130 (15)
5.	Elementary Number Theory	93	146 (11)	114	154 (12)
6.	Exponents	93	134 (13)	115	137 (14)
7.	Polynomials	91	165 9)	113	171 (10)
8.	Factorisation	99 (7.5)	168 (7)	112	166 (11)
9.	Linear Equations	109 (3)	198 (3)	113	187 (7)
10.	Linear Inequations	99 (7.5)	184 (5)	109	208 (5)
11.	Introduction to Geometry	78	135 (12)	116 (4)	204 (6)
12.	Straight lines	100 (6)	177 (6)	109	178 (9)
13.	Triangles and Polygons	76	150 (10)	114	229 (3)
14.	Circles andConcurrent Lines of Triangles	69	127 (14)	116 (4)	237 (2)
15.	Symmetry	49	91 (15)	113	185 (8)

From the table it is evident that chapters 1, 2, 3, 4 and 9 are relatively more difficult in contents as large number of students checked these chapters. However, by considering the intensity scores chapters 1, 2, 3, 9 and 10 stand as more difficult than the other chapters. So, the variation is observed in one chapter. Instead of chapter 4, chapter 10 appeared more difficult on the basis of intensity scores. It may be due to that large number of respondents who checked chapter 4 as difficult perceived it at the low intensity level.

On the other hand, the perceptions of teachers reveal that the chapters 1, 2, 3, 11 and 14 appear to be more difficult in content on the basis of frequencies and chapters 2, 3, 10, 13 and 14 as more difficult chapters as per the intensity scores. Three chapters are common in both the sets and the deviations observed in the sets are due to variations in the intensity level of difficulty as perceived by the teachers. Thus there are four sets of chapters, which are identified as more difficult chapters in VIII class textbook. Out of these four sets only chapters 2 and 3 are common. In other words, chapters Commercial Mathematics and Mensuration are the most difficult chapters in VIII class textbook for students and teachers content wise. Therefore, either the chapters have to be re-written or re-organised to suit the ability levels of students and teachers.

Similarly, an analysis of difficulties in teaching and learning as perceived by both students and teachers has been made and the results are presented in the following table 5.17.

From the table 5.17 it may be observed that chapters 1, 2, 3, 4 and 5 are the relatively more difficult in teaching as per the number of students who checked the chapters. But when the intensity of difficulty is considered chapters 2, 3, 4, 5 and 9 appear to be relatively more difficult. Chapter 9 replaced chapter 1 as more number of students rated the former as more difficult.

A study of the responses of teachers reveal that 2, 6, 9, 11, 13, 14 and 15 are the relatively more difficult chapters as per the frequencies. But the intensity scores of difficulty indicate chapters 2, 3, 11, 13 and 14 as the relatively more difficult.

Out of the four sets of relatively more difficult chapters only the 2nd chapter i.e, 'Commercial Mathematics' is common. In other words, Commercial Mathematics has been considered by both students and teachers as highly difficult chapter for teaching. This may be due to the fact that the basic concepts of Commercial Mathematics are introduced in the 6th class but not continued in the 7th class and all aspects corresponding to Commercial Mathematics are dumped in the VIII class itself without any reference to IX and X classes. This leads to make the chapter more cumbersome and tedious.

Table 5.17: Table indicating the Teaching Difficulty of VIII Class as perceived by Students and Teachers

S.No.	Chapter Name	Students		Teachers	
		Frequencies	Intensity Scores	Frequencies	Intensity Scores
1.	Real Numbers	64 (4.5)	94 (7.5)	108	130 (15)
2.	Commercial Mathematics	75 (1)	157 (1)	123 (1)	235 (1)
3.	Mensuration	65 (3)	104 (4)	112	196 (5)
4.	Sets	70 (2)	112 (2)	111	133 (14)
5.	Elementary Number Theory	64 (4.5)	101 (5)	109	142 (12)
6.	Exponents	57	91 (9)	113 (6)	135 (13)
7.	Polynomials	53	85 (10)	108	154 (11)
8.	Factorisation	57	99 (6)	110	155 (10)
9.	Linear Equations	63 (6)	107 (3)	116 (2.5)	177 (7)
10.	Linear Inequations	46	71 (13)	106	182 (6)
11.	Introduction to Geometry	47	80 (12)	116 (2.5)	200 (4)
12.	Straight lines	54	94 (7.5)	103	168 (9)
13.	Triangles andPolygons	42	82 (11)	115 (4)	214 (2)
14.	Circles and Concurrent Lines of Triangles	26	50 (14)	113 (6)	211 (3)
15.	Symmetry	20	35 (15)	113 (6)	172 (8)

Generally, educationists say that the chapter 'Commercial Mathematics' is being arranged in concentric method at the secondary level. As a matter of fact, it appears vice-versa. To arrange in concentric method, the interests, needs, abilities and age levels of the students are to be considered and presented in such a way that the students learn the concept ranging from simple to complex, known to unknown and easy to difficult aspects. But this is not being observed in the arrangement of the curriculum. These concepts are introduced in the VI class but not continued in the VII class. All the remaining aspects regarding the commercial mathematics are dumped in the VIII class itself without continuing in the IX and the X classes.

The solution to this problem is in the hands of the curriculum makers and textbook writers. The curriculum at the secondary level should be arranged by adopting spiral and concentric approaches rather than the topical arrangement. Hence, instead of dumping all the contents related to the secondary level in a particular class, it will be more meaningful if the contents are distributed to different classes based on the needs, interests and ability levels of students.

Table 5.18: The Learning Difficulty of VIII Class as perceived by Students and Teachers

S. No.	*Chapter Name*	*Students*		*Teachers*	
		Frequencies	*Intensity Scores*	*Frequencies*	*Intensity Scores*
1.	Real Numbers	73	98 (8.5)	121 (2)	179 (12)
2.	Commercial Mathematics	101 (1)	182 (1)	131 (1)	307 (1)
3.	Mensuration	90 (2)	139 (2)	118 (4)	248 (3)
4.	Sets	74 (5)	110 (5.5)	112 140	(15)
5.	Elementary Number Theory	61	87 (12)	111	158 (13)
6.	Exponents	81 (3)	127 (4)	114	153 (14)
7.	Polynomials	69	110 (5.5)	112	185 (11)
8.	Factorisation	79 (4)	129 (3)	111	192 (9)
9.	Linear Equations	68	105 (7)	116 (5)	219 (5)
10.	Linear Inequations	60	98 (8.5)	108	213 (6)
11.	Introduction to Geometry	57	97 (10)	113	208 (7)
12.	Straight lines	60	92 (11)	106	196 (8)
13.	Triangles and Polygons	39	69 (13)	111	231 (4)
14.	Circles and Concurrent Lines of Triangles	23	42 (14)	120 (3)	266 (2)
15.	Symmetry	16	26 (15)	114	190 (10)

From the table it can be observed that chapters 2, 3, 4, 6, and 8 are relatively more difficult for learning as per the frequencies who checked the chapters. Even from the point of the intensity of difficulty the same chapters 2, 3, 4, 6, 7 and 8 appear to be more difficult for students.

With regard to the teachers' perceptions chapters 1, 2, 3, 9 and 14 are checked as relatively more difficult for learning on the basis of frequencies, whereas chapters 2, 3, 9, 13 and 14 are the relatively more difficult for learning on the basis of intensity scores for teachers.

From the four sets of the top 5 difficulty chapters, the 2nd and 3rd chapters are considered the most difficult by students and teachers. Therefore, Commercial Mathematics and Mensuration from the VIII class textbook are posing really serious problems for students and teachers in teaching-learning mathematics.

The Investigator being a teacher educator, during her frequent visits to secondary schools had interaction with the teachers and students and observed that for covering the contents given in these two chapters alone the teachers were spending half of the academic year as these two chapters contain a large number of exercises with equal number of distinct problems. This problem can be solved probably by bringing changes in the curriculum and the textbook suitably as indicated earlier.

On the basis of the difficulty intensity scores of all the 15 chapters of the VIII class textbook on the three dimensions, namely, content difficulty, teaching difficulty and learning difficulty ranks have been assigned to students and teachers independently as presented in the table.

It may be seen from the table 5.19 that chapters 2 and 3 are found to be highly difficult in all the three dimensions of difficulty as perceived by students while the chapters 2, 3, 13 and 14 appear to be highly difficult as per the perceptions of teachers. Therefore, the chapters 'Commercial Mathematics', 'Mensuration', 'Triangles and Polygons' and 'Circles and concurrent lines of triangles' should be focussed elaborately by the teacher educators, text book writers, curriculum framers, policy makers and the authorities to set right the situation.

Table 5.19: Rank order of Difficulty Chapters in VIII Class as Perceived by Students and Teachers Content-wise, Teaching-wise, and Learning-wise

S. No.	*Chapter Name*	*Students*			*Teachers*		
		Content	*Teaching*	*Learning*	*Content*	*Teaching*	*Learning*
1.	Real Numbers	2	8	9	13	15	12
2.	Commercial Mathematics	1	1	1	1	1	1
3.	Mensuration	4	4	2	4	5	3
4.	Sets	8	2	6	15	14	15
5.	Elementary Number Theory	11	5	12	12	12	13
6.	Exponents	13	9	4	14	13	14
7.	Polynomials	9	10	5	10	11	11
8.	Factorisation	7	6	3	11	10	9
9.	Linear Equations	3	3	7	7	7	5
10.	Linear Inequations	5	13	8	5	6	6
11.	Introduction to Geometry	12	12	10	6	4	7
12.	Straight lines	6	7	11	9	9	8
13.	Triangles and Polygons	10	11	13	3	2	4
14.	Circles and Concurrent Lines of Triangles	14	14	14	2	3	2
15.	Symmetry	15	15	15	8	8	10

Content Difficulty Analysis as Perceived by Students and Teachers of IX Class

There are 11 chapters in the IX class textbook. In each chapter, the students' responses are obtained on a 3-point scale viz., less difficult, moderately difficult and highly difficult on three aspects, namely, content difficulty, teaching difficulty and learning difficulty. These responses are aggregated for total samples (students 217 and teachers 161) and presented in the following table 5.20.

It would be interesting to see the perceptions of students and teachers on the difficulty level of each chapter. The following is the description in that direction.

Arithmetic is the oldest branch of mathematics dealing with numbers. In the earlier classes pupils study natural numbers, whole numbers, integers, rational numbers and irrational numbers. In this chapter, they learn about surds, extraction of square roots of natural numbers, logarithms and mensuration.

Under the surds, types of surds, laws of radicals, comparison of surds, addition, subtraction, multiplication and division of surds, rationalisation of surds, conjugate of a surd and representation of irrational numbers on the number line are included.

The following table lists out the numerical picture regarding difficulties of students and teachers in content, teaching and learning at different levels.

Table 5.20: Frequencies and difficulty intensity scores of Chapter I

	STUDENTS					*TEACHERS*				
	L	*M*	*H*	*T*	*INT*	*L*	*M*	*H*	*T*	*INT*
C	54	91	11	156	269	20	54	59	133	305
T	33	24	9	66	108	29	58	41	128	268
L	51	26	6	83	121	19	42	78	139	337

Out of 217 students 54 (about 25%) and out of 161 teachers 20 (about 12%) teachers perceived that the contents of chapter I are difficult at the less intensity level. At the moderate level of intensity, 91 out of 217 (about 42%) students and 54 out of 161 (about 34%) teachers perceived content difficulty of chapter I. At the high intensity level, only 5 per cent of students perceived content difficulty whereas about 37 per cent of teachers noticed it in chapter I.

As far as teaching difficulty is concerned, 33 (about 15%), 24 (about 11%), and 9 (about 4%) students possessed negative attitude towards their teachers, whereas 29 (about 18%), 58 (about 36%), and 41 (about 25%) teachers perceived teaching this chapter as difficult at the low, moderate, and high intensity levels respectively.

With regard to the learning, about 38 per cent of students perceived this chapter as difficult whereas about 86 per cent of teachers viewed it as difficult for their students (on the basis of the total frequencies). In other words, when about 62 per cent of the students felt that the chapter was easy for, about 86 per cent of teachers regarded it as difficult for their students.

Even on the basis of the difficulty intensity scores it is clear that about 49 per cent to 57 per cent intensity scores are observed for students regarding the difficulty in three aspects, whereas, for the teachers the difficulty intensity scores vary from 47 per cent to 81 per cent. That means the chapter Arithmetic is moderately difficult for the students whereas it is highly difficult for teachers.

The second chapter in the textbook is Revision of Exponents and Algebraic Expressions. This chapter is a review of exponents, algebraic expressions, special products and factorisation studied by the students in the earlier classes. Hence, the students and teachers do not think that this chapter is that much difficult. The following table gives the description regarding the difficulties at different levels.

Table 5.21: Frequencies and difficulty intensity scores of Chapter II

	STUDENTS					*TEACHERS*				
	L	*M*	*H*	*T*	*INT*	*L*	*M*	*H*	*T*	*INT*
C	54	26	9	89	133	86	23	7	116	153
T	35	21	9	65	104	79	27	11	117	166
L	41	19	6	66	97	73	31	13	117	174

Out of 217 students 54 (about 25%) perceived that the contents of this chapter are difficult whereas 86 out of 161 teachers (about 53%) felt them so at the less intensity level. At the moderate level of intensity, 26 out of 217 (about 12%) of students and 23 out of 161 (about 14%) of teachers perceived content difficulty in chapter II. Of course, the difficulty at the high intensity level is negligible—only 9 out of 217 students and 7 out of 161 teachers perceived content difficulty in the chapter.

Coming to the teaching aspect, out of 217 students 35 (16%), 21(9%) and 9(4%) perceived teaching this chapter as difficult for their teachers at the low, moderate and high intensity levels whereas 79(49%), 27(17) and 11(7%) out of 161 teachers felt it difficult at all the three intensity levels respectively.

In so far as learning difficulty is concerned, 66 out of 217 (about 30%) students perceived learning this chapter as difficult whereas 117 out of 161 teachers (about 73%) thought it difficult for their students (on the basis of the total frequencies). In other words, when about 70 per cent of the students felt it easy, about 73 per cent of teachers perceived it as difficult for their students.

This shows that there is significant difference between the perceptions of students and teachers regarding content, teaching and learning. However, on the basis of the difficulty intensity scores this chapter is perceived as moderately difficult by teachers and students with a slight variation. More specifically, the difficulty intensity for students ranges from 49 per cent to 53 per cent whereas for teachers it ranges from 44 per cent to 50 per cent.

The third chapter in the text is on Square Roots of Algebraic Expressions. The contents of this chapter include the square roots of algebraic expressions and certain classes of expressions like homogeneous, symmetric and cyclic expressions and also the quadratic equations. Although the contents are a continuation from the earlier classes, the teaching and learning of this chapter is perceived as difficult both by the teachers and students on account of the abstractness of the subject.

From the table 5.22 it may be observed that 72 out of 217 students (about 33%) and 45 out of 161 (about 28%) teachers perceived that the contents of this chapter are difficult at the less intensity level. At the moderate level of intensity, 34 out of 217 students (about 16%), and 60 out of 161 teachers (about 37%) perceived content difficulty in chapter III. At the high intensity level, only 10 students (about 5%) thought it difficult whereas 25 out of 161 (about 16%) teachers felt it difficulty.

Table 5.22: Frequencies and difficulty intensity scores of Chapter III

	STUDENTS					*TEACHERS*				
	L	*M*	*H*	*T*	*INT*	*L*	*M*	*H*	*T*	*INT*
C	72	34	10	116	170	45	60	25	130	240
T	28	31	8	67	114	50	56	12	118	198
L	43	20	7	70	104	32	59	37	128	261

With regards to teaching of the chapter, 67 out of 217 students (about 30%) perceived it as difficult for their teachers (on the basis of the total responses) whereas 118 out of 161 teachers (about 73%) considered it difficult i.e., when about 70 per cent of students perceived teaching this chapter as easy for their teachers, about 73 per cent of teachers felt it otherwise.

On the basis of the total frequencies, 70 out of 217 students (about 32%) perceived learning this chapter as difficult whereas 128 out of 161 (about 80%) teachers regarded it as difficult for their students. In other words, to about 68 per cent of the students this chapter is easy, whereas to 80 per cent of the teachers it is difficult.

Even the difficulty intensity scores on the three aspects reveal that the chapter 'Square Roots of Algebraic Expressions' in IX class is felt as moderately difficult by students whereas teachers felt it as more difficult as the difficulty intensity ranges from 49 per cent to 57 per cent for students and from 56 per cent to 68 per cent for teachers.

The fourth chapter figured in the textbook is Sets. It is introduced in the 8th class itself. Since the language of sets plays a vital role in the integration of mathematics, set has been reviewed and further extended to this class also. The set operations, union, intersection and some of their properties are illustrated through examples and Venn diagrams. An attempt is made in this chapter to enable the pupil to see that the rules of algebra of sets are not very different from those of real numbers or matrices and a few applications of algebra of sets are discussed.

Table 5.23: Frequencies and difficulty intensity scores of Chapter IV

	STUDENTS					*TEACHERS*				
	L	*M*	*H*	*T*	*INT*	*L*	*M*	*H*	*T*	*INT*
C	62	13	6	81	106	104	8	1	113	123
T	33	11	4	48	67	101	10	1	112	124
L	29	11	4	44	63	101	14	0	115	129

On the basis of frequencies, at the low intensity level, out of 217 students 62 (about 29%), 33 (about 15%) and 29 (about 13%) and out of 161 teachers 104 (about 65%), 101 (about 63%) and 101 (about 63%) found difficulty in content, teaching and learning this chapter.

At the moderate intensity level, very few students and teachers perceived difficulty in chapter IV whereas at the high intensity level, the difficulties of students and teachers are at the lowest ebb.

It is observed from the table that both the teachers and students perceive teaching and learning this chapter as easy.

Surprisingly, the difficulty intensity scores also reveal that the chapter on Sets has been felt easy more by the teachers than the students because the difficulty intensity score is around 37 per cent for teachers in all the aspects whereas it varies from 44 per cent to 48 per cent for students. This may be due to familiarity of the problem situations given in the exercises.

The V chapter deals with Relations. In this chapter the idea of a relation is introduced intuitively through examples from daily life. Graphs, tree diagrams and arrow diagrams have been used as effective aids for introducing the idea of relations and their properties and for leading to the notion of a function as a relation. Hence, teaching and learning this chapter is perceived as easy by majority of teachers and students as per the table values.

Table 5.24: Frequencies and difficulty intensity scores of Chapter V

	STUDENTS					TEACHERS				
	L	*M*	*H*	*T*	*INT*	*L*	*M*	*H*	*T*	*INT*
C	60	15	8	83	114	76	32	7	115	161
T	29	11	5	45	66	72	39	4	115	162
L	27	14	5	46	70	71	36	9	116	170

The table illustrates that, out of 217 students 60 (about 28%), 29 (about 13%) and 27 (about 12%) and out of 161 teachers 76 (about 47%), 72 (about 45%) and 71 (about 40%) perceived content, teaching and learning difficulty in chapter V at the less intensity level. At the moderate level of intensity, very few students and teachers found difficulty in content, teaching and learning whereas the difficulty at high intensity level is deteriorating further.

The difficulty intensity scores obtained for the students and teachers regarding this chapter also reveal that 'Relations' is felt as difficult at less moderate level as the intensity scores vary from 46 per cent to 51 per cent for students and they are around 48 per cent for teachers.

The VI chapter in the textbook is 'Linear Equations and Inequations'. In the earlier classes pupil learns that there is a one-to-one correspondence between the points of a plane and the ordered pairs of real numbers and he finds it easy to analyse and explain various concepts of Geometry through algebraic equations. This revolutionary approach is the first significant advancement in the field of geometry since the days of Euclid. The credit for this goes to Rene Descartes (1596-1650) a French mathematician. This approach paved way to study mathematics as a unified structure. This geometry is called Analytical Geometry or Coordinate Geometry. This chapter deals with the lines that pass through given points, distance between two points, slope of a line, system of linear equations and inequations etc.

Table 5.25: Frequencies and difficulty intensity scores of Chapter VI

	STUDENTS					TEACHERS				
	L	*M*	*H*	*T*	*INT*	*L*	*M*	*H*	*T*	*INT*
C	32	53	48	133	282	43	66	19	128	232
T	24	29	21	74	144	55	57	13	125	208
L	33	23	22	78	145	34	68	23	125	239

This table gives the description of difficulties regarding content, teaching and learning chapter VI at different levels. Contrary to the above chapters, majority of the students perceived difficulty more at the moderate and high intensity levels than at to the low intensity level regarding content, teaching and learning.

32 out of 217 students (about 18%) and 43 out of 161 (about 27%) teachers perceived contents of chapter VI as difficult at the less intensity level. At the moderate level of intensity, 53 out of 217 students (about 24%) and 66 out of 161 (about 41%) teachers perceived content difficulty. At the high intensity level, 48 out of 217 (about 22%) and 19 out of 161 (about 12%) teachers felt difficulty in the contents of this chapter at high intensity level. On the basis of the total frequencies, 133 out of 217 (about 61%) students and 128 out of 161 teachers (about 80%) found that the contents of this chapter are difficult.

In the area of teaching, 24 out of 217 students (about 13%) and 55 out of 161 teachers (about 34%) perceived teaching difficulty in chapter VI at the low intensity level. At the moderate level of intensity, 29 out of 217 (about 13%) students and 57 out of 161 teachers (about 35%) considered teaching this chapter difficult. At the high intensity level, 21 out of 217 (about 10%) of students and 13 out of 161 (about 8%) of teachers regard this chapter as difficult. On the basis of the total responses, about 66 per cent of students felt it easy for their teachers in teaching, but about 78 per cent of the teachers perceived teaching this chapter as difficult.

With regards to learning, 33 out of 217 (about 15%) of students and 34 out 161 (about 21%) teachers considered this chapter difficult for their students at the less intensity level. At the moderate level of intensity, 23 out of 217 (about 11%) students and 68 out of 161 (about 42%) of teachers found learning difficulty in chapter VI. At the high intensity level, 22 out of 217 (about 10%) students and 23 out of 161 (about 14%) teachers perceived learning this chapter as difficult.

On the basis of the total responses, 78 out of 217 (about 36%) students and 125 out of 161 (about 78%) teachers viewed this chapter difficult. on the other hand, about 64 per cent of the students perceived learning this chapter as easy, about 78 per cent of teachers perceived learning this chapter as difficult for their students.

As per the difficulty intensity scores obtained on this chapter, the students perceived this chapter as a highly difficult chapter as the intensity scores range from 62 per cent to 71 per cent. Teachers also find it very difficult as the intensity scores vary from 55 per cent to 64 per cent.

This chapter is considered the most difficult chapter by majority of students since understanding the abstract concepts like inclination of a line, slope of a line and solving the systems of linear equations and inequations graphically is very difficult for both teachers and students as per the observations of the investigator.

No doubt, these can be taught meaningfully to the students by adopting Analytic Method but the teacher does not find time to teach them analytically to the students. The teacher keeps on telling the synthetic solutions, resulting in a lot of confusion among the students. For instance, to find the distance between two points on a line, which is not parallel to the axes, the teacher uses Pythagorous theorem to find the formula. But the pupil does not know why it is to be used and how it is suitable to the situation. Hence, serious thought is necessary to bring in changes in teaching – learning mathematics.

The VII chapter in the text is Matrices. Arthur Caulay (1821-1895) an English Mathematician created a new mathematical discipline called Matrices in 1858. He used Matrices to write simultaneous equations in an abridged form. James Joseph Silvester (1914-1897) another English Mathematician gave the name Matrix (plural – Matrices) to the rectangular arrangement of numbers in rows and columns.

This chapter consists of types of matrices, equality of matrices, addition of matrices, commutative and associative properties of addition of matrices, additive identity of a matrix and additive inverse of a matrix. It also deals with the multiplication of matrix by a real number, by another matrix; multiplication properties of matrices such as association and distribution; zero and unit matrix, transpose of a matrix and their properties. As it is the application of known operations in a new situation, it is perceived as easy by most of the students and teachers.

Table 5.26: Frequencies and difficulty intensity scores of Chapter VII

	STUDENTS					*TEACHERS*				
	L	*M*	*H*	*T*	*INT*	*L*	*M*	*H*	*T*	*INT*
C	55	14	7	76	104	102	15	2	119	138
T	34	12	3	49	67	98	13	4	115	136
L	35	14	6	55	81	100	15	2	117	136

The table given above has the details regarding the perceptions of students and teachers on chapter VII. At the less intensity level, out of 217 students 55 (about 25%), 34 (about 16%) and 35 (about 16%) perceived difficulty in it in content, teaching and learning respectively. Whereas out of 161 teachers 102 (about 63%), 98 (about 61%), and 100 (about 62%) experienced the same problem.

At the moderate level of intensity, very few students and teachers perceived difficulty and at the high intensity level, the difficulty is minimal percentage. It is considered the easiest chapter followed by Sets according to their perceptions.

The difficulty intensity scores obtained on this chapter reveal that as in the case of the chapter on Sets, teachers perceived it easier than the students as the intensity scores vary from 46 per cent to 49 per cent for students whereas they fall exactly at 39 per cent for teachers.

The VIII chapter in 9th class text book deals with Geometry. Up to the upper primary level, the approach is purely intuitive and the aim is to discover properties through measurements and paper foldings. In VIII class an attempt is made to present the properties clearly in a systematic way starting with undefined terms, defined terms and axioms to find new relations (called theorems) as a logical consequence of the accepted axioms. Though the approach is axiomatic, care has been taken to see that the pupils are not burdened with the unnecessary rigour of proving all the theorems.

In this class, the study is extended to areas and their applications to a few constructions, and loci and their applications to some interesting constructions. The chapter also deals with parallel lines and triangles, intercepts theorem; recall, review of chord properties in circle; arcs and angles, and cyclic quadrilateral.

Table 5.27: Frequencies and difficulty intensity scores of Chapter VIII

	STUDENTS					*TEACHERS*				
	L	*M*	*H*	*T*	*INT*	*L*	*M*	*H*	*T*	*INT*
C	32	48	33	113	227	14	44	79	137	339
T	24	35	13	72	133	19	50	58	127	293
L	25	25	13	63	114	14	34	90	138	352

This table presents a numerical picture regarding the difficulties of students and teachers in the three aspects content, teaching and learning. 32 out of 217 (about 15%) students and 14 out of 161 (about 9%) of the teachers perceived content difficulty at the low intensity level. At the moderate level of intensity 48 (about 22%) students and 44 (about 27%) teachers experienced difficulty. At the high level of intensity, 33 (about 15%) students and 79 (about 49%) teachers felt that the contents of Geometry were difficult.

In respect of teaching, 72 out of 217 (about 33%) students 127 out of 161 (about 79%) teachers perceived this chapter as difficult on the basis of the total frequencies.

As regards the learning difficulty, out of 217 students 25 (about 12%), 25 (about 12%) and 13 (about 6%) perceived learning this chapter as difficult at the low, moderate and high intensity levels respectively whereas out of 161 teachers 14 (about 9%), 34 (about 21%) and 90 (about 56 %) found it difficult for their students at the low, moderate and high intensity levels.

On the basis of the total responses, 63 out of 217 (about 29%) students 138 (about 86%) out of 161 teachers perceived learning this chapter as difficult for their students. In other words when about 71% of students found it easy, about 86 per cent of the teachers consider it difficult for their students.

This clearly shows that the students have a positive attitude towards their teachers whereas the attitude of the teachers towards their students is negative.

However, as per the difficulty intensity scores Geometry is felt as very difficult chapter by students as the intensity scores range from 60 per cent to 67 per cent whereas it is thought as highly difficult by teachers as the intensity scores range from 77 per cent to 85 per cent.

From this viewpoint it may be concluded that the teachers are more panicky about Geometry than the students. Therefore, before going to bring in any changes in the teaching-learning process, the teachers must be provided with proper counselling to develop positive attitude towards the subject, profession and students.

The IX chapter in the 9th class textbook is 'Motion Geometry'. Set and Function are the two basic concepts that have given mathematics a unified structure. A generalisation of the concept of function in geometry is given by the concept of Mapping and Transformation. Transformation is a one-to-one correspondence among all the points in a plane (or space). In motion or transformation geometry we are concerned with various types of transformations like reflection, translation, rotation and their compositions. It was Sophus Lie (1842-1899), a Norwegian Geometer and Christian Felix Klein (1849-1925) German Mathematician, who first introduced the generalised concept of function in Geometry and revealed the unified structure of mathematics. In this chapter Motion Geometry is introduced only as an alternative approach to indicate how tedious proofs could be replaced by simple proofs using Reflection, Translation and Rotation.

Table 5.28: Frequencies and difficulty intensity scores of Chapter IX

	STUDENTS					TEACHERS				
	L	*M*	*H*	*T*	*INT*	*L*	*M*	*H*	*T*	*INT*
C	23	26	38	87	189	7	32	100	139	371
T	14	16	16	46	94	11	48	74	133	329
L	16	14	15	55	99	5	28	103	136	370

The table values reveal the following details numerically regarding the difficulties of students and teachers in the three aspects, namely, content teaching and learning. When the students perceived this chapter as the 5th most difficult one, the teachers perceived it as the first most difficult chapter. To be more specific, at the less intensity level, out of 217 students 23 (about 11 per cent) and 7 out of 161 (about 4%) teachers perceived content difficulty in chapter IX. As in the case of Geometry, more number of teachers and students perceived difficulty at the moderate and the high intensity levels when compared to the less intensity level. At the moderate level of intensity, 26 out of 217 (about 12%) students and 32 out 161 (about 20%) teachers experienced content difficulty of this chapter. At the high intensity level, when only 38 out of 217 (about 18%) students perceived contents of this chapter as difficult, the maximum of 100 out of 161 (about 62%) teachers felt content difficulty in this chapter.

As regards teaching, 46 out of 217 (about 21%) students and 133 out of 161 (about 83%) teachers perceived teaching this chapter as difficult on the basis of the total frequencies.

With regard to the learning, 26 (about 12%), 14 (about 7%) and 15 (about 7%) out of 217 students and 5 (about 3%), 28 (about 17%) and 103 (about 64%) teachers out of 161 felt this chapter was difficult for their students at low, moderate and high intensity levels.

Even the intensity scores on the difficulty level of the chapter Motion Geometry point out that students perceived it as more difficult whereas teachers considered it highly difficult as the intensity scores range from 60 per cent to 72 per cent for students and 82 per cent to 91 per cent for teachers.

Apart from it, there is variation in the perceptions of the students and teachers regarding the difficulties in content, teaching and learning of chapter 9. Though the difference is significant, it need not be taken into consideration. The glaring fact is that the students were not aware of the contents in the chapter. Even then, because of the positive attitude towards the teaching and the confidence reposed in the teachers, the pupils reflected positively. But it is the teacher who knows the real difficulties in content, teaching and learning. The students are not actually in a position to see the difficulties emanating from the subject. The fact underlying here is that the teacher only could anticipate the problems of students also.

The contents in this chapter are presented with geometrical figures, which creates confusion among the students. Hence, in the beginnings these must be taught using concrete objects. Once the concept is understood by the students, these can be applied in mathematical situations.

Chapter X in the textbook is 'Statistics'. It deals with the importance of statistics—collection of statistical data—grouped and ungrouped. It also covers graphical representations, their interpretations and their applications in real life situations. In fact, pupils learn to represent numerical data by pictographs, Bar diagrams and Pie diagrams in VII class itself. In this chapter, they learn the meaning of statistics, classification of data, construction of frequency distributions (tables), cumulative frequency distributions, frequency polygon, frequency curve and cumulative frequency curves for a given data.

Table 5.29: Frequencies and difficulty intensity scores of Chapter X

	STUDENTS					*TEACHERS*				
	L	*M*	*H*	*T*	*INT*	*L*	*M*	*H*	*T*	*INT*
C	43	24	17	84	142	91	18	7	116	148
T	29	13	7	49	76	87	20	6	113	145
L	34	6	10	50	76	80	25	10	115	160

The data collected on the perceptions of the students and teachers regarding the difficulties in content, teaching and learning of this chapter elucidates the following deliberations. Both the teachers and students perceived this chapter as difficult more at the less intensity level than at the moderate and high intensity levels.

Out of 217 students 43 (about 20%), 29 (about 13%) and 34 (about 16%) and out of 161 teachers 91 (about 57%), 87 (about 54%) and 80 (about 50%) teachers perceived difficulty at the less intensity level. The difficulty does not catch hold at the moderate and high intensity levels according to the perceptions of teachers and students in all the above referred three aspects. On the basis of the total frequencies, 84 out of 217 (about 39%) students and 116 out of 161 (about 72%) teachers felt that contents of this chapter were difficult.

Regarding the teaching aspect, 49 out of 217 (about 23%) students and 113 out of 161 (about 70%) teachers perceived teaching this chapter as difficult on the basis of total frequencies. In the field of learning 50 out of 217 students (about 23%) and 115 out of 161 teachers (about 71%) considered it difficult for their students.

In other words, about 61 per cent, about 77 per cent and about 77 per cent of students perceived the contents, teaching and learning this chapter as easy, but contrary to that, about 71 per cent, 70 per cent and about 71 per cent of the teachers felt the same as difficult.

However, the difficulty intensity scores obtained on this chapter Statistics made it clear that students perceived it as moderately difficult whereas teachers felt it as a less moderately difficult chapter (as in the case of the chapters Sets and Matrices) as the intensity scores range from 51 per cent to 56 per cent for students and 43 per cent to 46 per cent for teachers. This variation is noticed because number of teachers checked the item as less difficult.

The field experiences of the investigator reveal that in this chapter, pupils find difficulty in taking scale on the X and Y-axis for constructing different graphs. They are equally confused in taking class intervals based on the variables studied. Regarding the construction of graphs, they find it difficult to take the values on X and Y-axis. They don't know why the true class limits are to be taken on the X-axis to construct Histogram whereas mid values of the class intervals on the X-axis are to be taken for constructing the Frequency Polygon. Though, pupils do not know the logic behind the construction of different graphs, they simply get it by heart for the sake of examination. In spite of the stated confusions both the teachers and pupils perceived this chapter as easy because of the monotony involved in the method of solving the problems.

Consequently, it is apt to bring in changes positively in the attitudes of the teachers towards their subject, teaching and learning.

The last chapter is on Computing. Computing is introduced in this class with a view to stimulating students and prepare them for computer programming. We are in a scientific and technological age, many industries and business concerns have introduced computers in their day to day transactions. Indian Railways have introduced computers for reservation of train journeys by the public. Big organisations like Life Insurance Corporations are using computers for their work. So many boards of examinations and universities make use of computers in processing examination results. In the launching of Satellites and sending them on the moon and other planets in particular, computers are being used extensively to control the flights. Therefore, knowledge of computing is necessary for the students.

Let us look at the following table regarding the difficulties of students and teachers in respect of content, teaching and learning this chapter.

Table 5.30: Frequencies and difficulty intensity scores of Chapter XI

	STUDENTS					*TEACHERS*				
	L	*M*	*H*	*T*	*INT*	*L*	*M*	*H*	*T*	*INT*
C	53	18	9	80	116	67	45	11	123	190
T	32	6	4	42	56	73	35	10	118	173
L	31	6	7	44	64	60	50	13	123	196

The table values reveal that majority of the students perceived this chapter as difficult at the low intensity level whereas a few students felt it so in content, teaching and learning at the moderate and the high intensity levels. Though a few teachers considered this chapter difficult at the high intensity level, a good number of teachers viewed this chapter as difficult in content, teaching and learning at the low and the moderate intensity levels.

At the less intensity level, out of 217 students 53 (about 24%), 32 (about 15%) and 31 (about 14%) and out of 161 teachers 67 (about 42%), 73 (about 45%) and 60 (about 37%) perceived this chapter as difficult in content, teaching and learning respectively. On the basis of the total responses, 80 out of 217 students (about 37%) and 123 out of 161 (about 76%) teachers regarded contents of this chapter as difficult.

Regarding teaching, 42 out of 217 (about 19%) students perceived that teaching this chapter was difficult for their teachers while 118 (about 73%) teachers experienced difficulty. In so far as the learning difficulty is concerned, 44 out of 217 students (about 20%) and 123 out of 161 (about 76%) of teachers felt that learning this chapter was difficult.

In other words, when about 63 per cent, about 81 per cent and about 80 per cent of the students perceived this chapter as easy in the content, teaching and learning respectively to a maximum of about 76 per cent, about 73 per cent and about 76% of the teachers found it difficult.

However, the difficulty intensity scores reveal that students perceived this chapter as less moderate difficult whereas teachers considered it moderately difficult as the intensity scores range from 44 per cent to 48 per cent for students and 49 per cent to 53 per cent for teachers.

The present day, information technology is wholly based on computers. So computers have become part and parcel of human life. So it has become imperative for everyone to have some basic knowledge of computers and their operations. With this object in mind, computing has been included in the school syllabus.

But surprisingly most of the schools are not provided with computers. Moreover, though it is continued in X class also in as much as there is choice provided in the public examination, the teachers opt for the other chapters, which help the students get more marks. As a result, this chapter has been neglected totally by the teachers, defeating the purpose for which it has been introduced at the school level.

Surprisingly, the students rated this chapter in the 9th place whereas the teachers placed it in the 6th place of difficulty. This is because the teachers and students concentrate only on the basic concepts and flow-charting given in the text, which is a definite question in the public examination. The flow-charting will be drawn in the text itself. The students simply mug up the steps, and reproduce them in the examinations. They don't try to learn it with logical thinking. Then what is the purpose of introducing the chapter for the students? Most of the teachers do not possess the required basic knowledge. Moreover schools are not equipped with computers. If the authorities are really serious about schools imparting computer science they should take the following steps:

The first and foremost thing is to see that orientation for the mathematics teachers is provided at least for a period of two to three weeks during the vacation to make them acquire the required skills in computing. Secondly, the computer should be installed in every school, state or central. The teachers should be trained in such a way that they impart computer knowledge to the students also to computerise their school programmes.

After having seen the perceptions of students and teachers on difficulty levels of content, teaching and learning of each chapter, it would be rather interesting to see the relative difficulty levels of different chapters as perceived by both the groups on the three kinds of difficulties.

The following table 5.31 depict the total number of subjects (frequencies) and the intensity of difficulty as expressed by the two groups on the IX class mathematics textbook.

From the table 5.31 it may be observed that chapters 1, 2, 3, 6 and 8 are the relatively more difficult as per the number of students who checked the chapters. However, as per the intensity scores of difficulty chapters 1, 3, 6, 8 and 9 stand as more difficult than the other chapters. So, the variation is in one chapter. Instead of chapter 2, chapter 9 appeared more difficult on the basis of intensity scores. It may be due to the fact that large number of students who checked chapter 2 as difficult perceived the level of difficulty as low.

Table 5.31: Table indicating the Content Difficulty for IX class as perceived by Students and Teachers

S. No.	Chapter Name	Students		Teachers	
		Frequencies	Intensity Scores	Frequencies	Intensity Scores
1.	Arithmetic	156 (1)	259 (2)	133 (3)	305 (3)
2.	Exponents and Algebraic Expressions	89 (5)	133 (7)	116	153 (8)
3.	Square roots of Algebraic Expressions	116 (3)	170 (5)	130 (4)	240 (4)
4.	Sets	81	106 (10)	113	123 (11)
5.	Relations	83	114 (9)	115	161 (7)
6.	Linear Equations and Inequations	133 (2)	282 (1)	128 (5)	232 (5)
7.	Matrices	76	104 (11)	119	138 (10)
8.	Geometry	113 (4)	227 (3)	137 (2)	339 (2)
9.	Motion Geometry	87	189 (4)	139 (1)	371 (1)
10.	Statistics	84	142 (6)	116	148 (9)
11.	Computing	80	116 (8)	123	190 (6)

An observation into the responses of teachers reveals that chapters 1, 3, 6, 8 and 9 are the relatively more difficult as per the frequencies and also difficulty intensity scores.

Thus the students and teachers in common have been facing difficulty with chapters 1, 3, 6, 8 and 9 in the IX class textbook. Therefore the chapters on Arithmetic, Square Roots of Algebraic Expression, Linear Equations and In equations, Geometry and Motion Geometry need to be re-organised keeping in view the difficulties of students and teachers.

The whole intention of mathematics education is to train the students in general skills and not in any specific solutions of problems. The transferability of skills can be best achieved when the teacher concentrates more on the general strategies rather than proceeding to synthetic computations involved in the problem even before the student visualises a clear picture with all its ramifications.

Henderson and Pingry (1953) emphasise the same very clearly when they assert that:

"Unless students study the process of solving problems as an end in it there is scant likelihood that they will learn the generalisations which will enable them to transfer their ability to solve problems to new problems as they arise."

It is very clearly stated in the assertion that problem solving is a generalisable and transferable skill.

Table 5.32: Table indicating the Teaching Difficulty for IX class as perceived by Students and Teachers

S. No.	*Chapter Name*	*Students*		*Teachers*	
		Frequencies	*Intensity Scores*	*Frequencies*	*Intensity Scores*
1.	Arithmetic	66 (4)	108 (4)	128 (2)	268 (3)
2.	Exponents and Algebraic Expressions	65 (5)	104 (5)	117	166 (7)
3.	Square roots of Algebraic Expressions	67 (3)	114 (3)	118 (5.5)	198 (5)
4.	Sets	48	67(8.5)	112	124 (11)
5.	Relations	45	66 (10)	115	162 (8)
6.	Linear Equations and in equations	74 (1)	144 (1)	125 (4)	208 (4)
7.	Matrices	49	67(8.5)	115	136 (10)
8.	Geometry	72 (2)	133 (2)	127 (3)	293 (2)
9.	Motion Geometry	46	94 (6)	133 (1)	329 (1)
10.	Statistics	49	76 (7)	113	145 (9)
11.	Computing	42	56 (11)	118 (5.5)	172 (6)

From the table it may be observed that chapters 1,2, 3, 6 and 8 are relatively more difficult for teaching as per the number of students who checked these chapters and the intensity of difficulty.

An observation into the responses of teachers reveal that chapters 1, 3, 6, 8, 9 and 11 are the relatively more difficult chapters as per the frequencies. But the intensity scores indicate that chapters 1, 3, 6, 8 and 9 are the relatively more difficult.

Out of these 3 sets of relatively difficult chapters 1, 3, 6 and 8 are the common difficult chapters both for students and teachers in teaching. Therefore, the chapters 'Arithmetic', 'Square Roots of Algebraic Expressions', 'Linear Equations and In equations' and 'Geometry' are to be revised in such a way that the contents are presented meaningfully with adequate number of illustrations.

On keen observation it comes to light that all the chapters in the IX class textbook except the chapters on Sets, Matrices and Statistics are felt relatively difficult by teachers more than students.

Table 5.33: Table indicating the Learning Difficulty for IX class as perceived by Students and Teachers

S. No.	Chapter Name	Students		Teachers	
		Frequencies	Intensity Scores	Frequencies	Intensity Scores
1.	Arithmetic	83 (1)	121 (2)	139 (1)	337 (3)
2.	Exponents and Algebraic Expressions	66 (4)	97 (6)	117	174 (7)
3.	Square roots of Algebraic Expressions	70 (3)	104 (4)	128 (4)	261 (4)
4.	Sets	44	63 (11)	115	129 (11)
5.	Relations	46	70 (9)	116	170 (8)
6.	Linear Equations and Inequations	78 (2)	145 (1)	125 (5)	239 (5)
7.	Matrices	55	81 (7)	117	136 (10)
8.	Geometry	63 (5)	114 (3)	138 (2)	352 (2)
9.	Motion Geometry	55	99 (5)	136 (3)	370 (1)
10.	Statistics	50	76 (8)	115	160 (9)
11.	Computing	44	64 (10)	123 (6)	196 (6)

From the table it can be observed that chapters 1, 2, 3, 6 and 8 are relatively more difficult in learning as per the frequencies of students. But, based on the intensity of difficulty, the chapters 1, 3, 6, 8 and 9 appear to be relatively more difficult for students in learning.

With regard to the teachers' perceptions chapters 1, 3, 6, 8 and 9 are the relatively more difficult in learning both based on the frequencies and the intensity scores. Therefore, the chapters 1, 3, 6, 8 and 9 are commonly felt as difficult by students and teachers. Thus it is essential that these chapters 'Arithmetic', 'Square Roots of Algebraic Expressions', 'Linear Equations and In equations', 'Geometry' and 'Motion geometry' are to be given precedence during the pre-service and in-service training programmes to make teaching-learning of these chapters meaningful and easy in the class room.

On the basis of intensity difficulty scores of all the 11 chapters in IX class textbook the ranks are assigned on the three dimensions namely content difficulty, teaching difficulty and learning difficulty for students and teachers independently and presented in the following table 5.34.

Motion Geometry was introduced in the X class syllabus at first instance. On account of the difficulty involved in the contents, the teachers brought to the notice of the higher authorities the difficulties they had been facing in dealing with the unit. Taking their difficulties into consideration, this unit was deleted from the syllabus. Though it was deleted from the X class at the request of the teachers for the time being, it was again introduced in IX class. Assuming for a moment that when this chapter was felt difficult for X class students, prescribing it again for the IX class students is quite ridiculous. Unfortunately, we hardly find teachers who teach this particular unit in schools. No teacher is comes forward to teach this unit as they know for certain that this particular unit is not going to be continued in X class. Furthermore, this unit is not considered important from the examination point of view. On this score also, the teachers skip it from teaching. If that is so, what is the idea in introducing the subject? Hence, the teachers must be provided with either proper orientation in this unit to enable them to teach it effectively or the unit must be deleted completely from the syllabus.

It is evident from the table 5.34 that chapters 1, 3, 6 and 8 are found to be highly difficult in all the three dimensions of difficulty as perceived by students whereas chapters 1, 3, 6, 8 and 9 are perceived as highly difficult by the teachers. Therefore, the chapters Arithmetic, Square Roots of Algebraic Expressions, Linear Equations and In-equations, Geometry and Motion Geometry should be given due priority while training the teachers during pre-service and in-service programmes to enable them transact these chapters effectively in the classroom.

Table 5.34: Rank order of Difficulty Chapters in IX Class as perceived by Students and Teachers Content-Wise, Teaching-Wise and Learning-Wise

S. No.	*Chapter Name*	*Students*			*Teachers*		
		Content	*Teaching*	*Learning*	*Content*	*Teaching*	*Learning*
1.	Arithmetic	2	4	2	3	3	3
2.	Exponents and Algebraic Expressions	7	5	6	8	7	7
3.	Square roots of Algebraic Expressions	5	3	4	4	5	4
4.	Sets	10	8	11	11	11	11
5.	Relations	9	10	9	7	8	8
6.	Linear Equations and In equations	1	1	1	5	4	5
7.	Matrices	11	9	7	10	10	10
8.	Geometry	3	2	3	2	2	2
9.	Motion Geometry	4	6	5	1	1	1
10.	Statistics	6	7	8	9	9	9
11.	Computing	8	11	10	6	6	6

Content Difficulty Analysis as Perceived by Students and Teachers of X Class

There are 12 chapters in the 10th class textbook. In each chapter, the students' responses and the teachers' responses are obtained on a 3-point scale viz., less difficult, moderately difficult and highly difficult on three aspects namely content difficulty, teaching difficulty and learning difficulty. These responses are aggregated for total samples (students 200 and teachers 161) and presented in the following tables:

It would be interesting to see the perceptions of students and teachers on the difficulty level of each chapter. The following is the description in that direction.

Table 5.35: Frequencies and intensity scores of chapter I.

	STUDENTS					TEACHERS				
	L	*M*	*H*	*T*	*INT*	*L*	*M*	*H*	*T*	*INT*
C	41	15	2	58	77	87	29	1	117	148
T	5	6	0	11	17	86	28	0	114	142
L	17	4	2	23	31	82	37	1	120	159

The first chapter in the 10th class textbook is 'Statements and Sets`. This topic has already been taught in the 8th class itself. `Statements` is the newly introduced concept to the students in X class. It deals with Connectives, Negation, Disjunction, Conjunction, Conditional or Implication, Bio-conditional or Bio-implication; converse, inverse and contrapositive of a conditional tautologies and contradictions, Algebra of statements, Quantifiers, Direct and Indirect proofs, Application of truth tables to switching networks, sets and principle of Duality.

Out of 200 Students 41 (about 20%) and 87out of 161 teachers (about 55%) perceived that the contents of this chapter as difficult at the less intensity level. At the moderate level, 15 out of 200 (about 7%) students and 29 out of 161 (about 20%) teachers felt content difficulty of chapter 1. Of course the highly difficulty level is almost negligible.

As far as teaching is concerned the students' assessment of the ability of their teachers is positive whereas the teachers do not possess positive attitude towards teaching. When only 5 and 6 students perceived teaching difficulty at low and moderate intensity levels, 86 (about 53%), and 28 (about 17%) teachers felt it at the low and moderate levels, but none perceived at the high difficulty level in teaching chapter 1.

Similarly learning this chapter is perceived as easy by majority of the students whereas about 90 per cent but 70 per cent of the teachers considered it difficult for their students.

However, the difficulty intensity as perceived by students is 44 per cent, 52 per cent and 45 per cent regarding content, teaching and learning respectively whereas it is 42 per cent, 42 per cent and 44 per cent as perceived by teachers. Therefore, it is a less difficult chapter as the difficulty intensity lies between 42 per cent to 52 per cent.

This difficulty is expressed particularly in the preparation of truth tables by majority of teachers during the field visits of the investigator.

The second chapter in X class textbook is 'Functions`. The basics of this chapter are studied by the students in the earlier classes as Sets and Relations. It deals with types of Functions, inverse of a Function, Inverse Function, Identity Function, Constant Function, Equal Functions, Composite Function and graphs of different Functions.

Table 5.36: Frequencies and intensity scores of chapter II

	STUDENTS					*TEACHERS*				
	L	*M*	*H*	*T*	*INT*	*L*	*M*	*H*	*T*	*INT*
C	37	13	5	55	78	48	62	13	123	211
T	3	7	5	15	72	63	48	9	120	186
L	20	25	5	50	85	45	59	19	123	220

From the table given above it is clear that regarding the content of this chapter, about 19 per cent, 7 per cent, and only 2 per cent of students and 03 per cent, 39 per cent and 8 per cent of teachers perceived difficult at the low, moderate and high levels of difficulty respectively.

As far as the teaching aspect is concerned very few students considered this chapter difficult for their teachers whereas about 39 per cent, 30 per cent, and 6 per cent of teachers viewed it to be difficult for students at the low, moderate and high intensity levels respectively.

As regards learning of this chapter only 50 students (25%) perceived it as difficult whereas 124 out of 161(about 75%) teachers felt it as difficult for their students. That is when 75 per cent of the students thought it easy about 75 per cent of teachers perceived learning this chapter as difficult for their students on the basis of total frequencies.

But the difficulty intensity as perceived by students regarding content, teaching and learning is 47 per cent, 71 per cent and 57 per cent respectively whereas the same is at 57 per cent, 52 per cent and 60 per cent respectively for teachers. Therefore, the chapter is moderately difficult for both students and teachers in all the aspects.

The investigator tried to draw upon her field experience as the majority of the teachers expressed their difficulty in solving problems on Bijection and Inverse Function. It amply proves the fact that, the teachers are in grave need of orientation in this particular area. Hence the teacher educators should take care of the student teachers to update the teachers' knowledge to meet the future needs.

Table 5.37: Frequencies and intensity scores of chapter III

	STUDENTS					*TEACHERS*				
	L	*M*	*H*	*T*	*INT*	*L*	*M*	*H*	*T*	*INT*
C	42	20	9	71	109	46	64	13	123	213
T	5	8	0	13	21	55	53	9	117	188
L	18	12	9	39	69	36	68	23	127	241

The third chapter dwells on Polynomials over Integers. The basics of this chapter are introduced in the VI class itself. The students study the meaning of the terms, variable, constant, monomial, binomial, polynomial, algebraic expression etc., in the VI class. In the VII class, pupils study algebraic equations in one variable, solving linear equations etc, in detail. In the VIII class, pupils study algebraic equations in two variables, addition, subtraction, multiplication of polynomials etc. In the IX class pupils study division of polynomials etc., In the X class pupils study the remainder theorem and its application in factorisation of symmetric and homogeneous expressions, solution of quadratic inequations, graphical solution of a quadratic equation, solution of quadratic inequations, mathematical induction theorem and binomial theorem etc.

As regards content of chapter III, about 21 per cent, 10 per cent and only 5 per cent of students and about 29 per cent, 40 per cent, and 8 per cent of teachers perceived difficulty at the low, moderate, and high intensity levels respectively.

With regard to teaching very few students perceived this chapter as difficult for their teachers in teaching whereas about 34 per cent, about 33 per cent and only about 6 per cent of the teachers experienced difficulty in teaching it at the low, moderate and high intensity levels.

Similarly about 80 per cent of students expressed that the chapter was easy in learning while about 79 per cent of the teachers perceived it difficult for their students as in the case of earlier chapters on the basis of total frequencies.

However, on the basis of the difficulty intensity scores, the chapter can be treated as moderately difficult as the intensity lies between 51 per cent to 63 per cent for both students and teachers regarding content, teaching and learning.

In the light of her field experience the investigator is of the opinion that this is one of the difficult chapters for majority of teachers. The reason is obvious. The concepts Mathematical Induction, Graphic method of solving the Quadratic Equations, Horner's Synthetic method etc., are new areas to the teachers, as they do not study them during their graduation. Even the presentation of the subject in the textbook is not easy since it is in Synthetic Method. Therefore, the teachers cannot understand on their own. During the B.Ed degree course the teacher educators are not bothered about the newly introduced topics like the Linear Programming, Motion Geometry, Mathematical Induction etc. They are not expected to dwell at length on Simple Interest, Compound Interest, Time and work etc., leaving aside the said newly introduced topics. They should make room for the teachers to learn the newly introduced areas. But most of them choose their lessons from Arithmetic only and quote the same examples. Even if they select the lessons from Algebra or Geometry for giving demonstrations, they form part of the basics. Thus the trainees are not really exposed to the most difficult parts of the chapter even while they do the B.Ed degree course. Hence, there is no chance for the teacher to learn the new topics. This leads to the development of negative attitude on the part of the teacher towards the subject and lack of interest in the subject.

In order to overcome the above situation, first of all, curriculum makers and textbook writers should take into consideration those teachers who are working in rural areas without any facilities to improve their academic equipment and performance. Hence, textbooks should consist of sufficient number of examples and illustrations with suitable figures to understand the subject meaningfully. Analytic approach must be adopted. For instance, take Horner's method of Synthetic division of Polynomials. Why should it be taught by Synthetic method only? Why can't it be by Analytic Method? When the teacher is supposed to adopt Analytic Method in the classroom teaching, the presentation in the textbook should also be in the Analytic Method only, if not for all the topics, at least for the topics which are new to him.

If it is not possible to prepare the textbook as stated above, the teachers should be furnished with necessary handbooks to make them understand the subject.

Table 5.38: Frequencies and intensity scores of chapter IV

	STUDENTS					*TEACHERS*				
	L	*M*	*H*	*T*	*INT*	*L*	*M*	*H*	*T*	*INT*
C	18	31	21	70	143	24	51	53	128	285
T	8	10	6	24	46	28	50	46	124	266
L	9	18	12	39	81	14	57	61	132	311

The 4th chapter in the 10th class text book deals with Linear Programming. Though it is a new technique in solving the problems, the fundamentals required for solving these problems are introduced in the 7th class itself as Linear Inequations. In the 8th class and the 9th class the students study about the solutions of linear inequations which are given in symbolic form. But in the 10th class they study the solutions of linear inequations, which are in the descriptive form.

As regards the content aspect of the chapter 'linear programming', about 9 per cent, 16 per cent and 11 per cent of students and about 15 per cent, 32 per centand 33 per cent of teachers perceived it difficult at the low, moderate, and high levels of difficulty respectively.

In so far as teaching is concerned, only a few students felt that teaching is difficult for their teachers. On the other hand, about 17 per cent, 31 per cent, and 29 per cent of teachers experienced difficulty in teaching chapter 4 at the low, moderate and high levels of difficulty respectively.

Surprisingly, about 80 per cent of the students perceived learning this chapter as easy while about 82 per cent of the teachers considered learning this chapter as difficult for their students on the basis of total frequencies. It categorically shows that the ability of the students is undermined by their teachers.

But the difficulty intensity scores regarding the content, teaching and learning the chapter clearly show that Linear Programming is highly difficult for both the students and teachers. To be more precise, the difficulty intensity as per the students' perception regarding this chapter is about 64 per cent to 69 per cent whereas the teachers perceived at about 72 per cent to 79 per cent. This variation is because more number of students checked it as moderately difficult whereas majority of teachers checked it as highly difficult.

The classroom observations made by the investigator reveal that the students and teachers experience much difficulty in dealing with the chapter linear inequations the in 9th class. The moment the target pupils enter the 10th class, almost all the targeted sections find it very difficult. The reason behind it is converting a descriptive problem into symbolic form is not taught to the students in the earlier classes and even the teachers are not able to teach them meaningfully. After this step, the same difficulty continues as in the 9th class.

This can be made easy by adopting Inductive and analytic methods with the help of suitable and simple illustrations.

Table 5.39: Frequencies and intensity scores of chapter V

	STUDENTS					*TEACHERS*				
	L	*M*	*H*	*T*	*INT*	*L*	*M*	*H*	*T*	*INT*
C	35	19	7	61	94	63	45	8	116	169
T	4	6	0	10	16	67	41	7	115	170
L	13	8	5	26	44	57	48	16	121	201

The V chapter in the X class textbook deals with Real Numbers. In fact the concept of Real Numbers is introduced in VIII class itself. In this class the students learn the operations with Real Numbers and laws of real numbers etc., The chapter continues in IX and X classes. This chapter deals with different exponential laws, the multiplication and division of radical expressions, modulus of a number, absolute value inequalities etc.

As regards content, about 18 per cent, 10 per cent, 2 per cent of students and about 39 per cent, 28 per cent, 5 per cent of teachers perceived difficulty at the low, moderate, and high levels respectively.

In so far as teaching is concerned, the students have a high positive attitude towards their teachers – only 4 students perceived teaching difficulty at the low intensity level, 6 perceived at the moderate intensity level but none perceived at the high intensity level. On the other hand about 42 per cent, 25 per cent, and 4 per cent of teachers felt difficulty in teaching chapter 5 at low, moderate, and high levels respectively.

As regards learning about 87 per cent of students considered this chapter easy and about 75 per cent of teachers regarded it as difficult for their students' learning on the basis of total frequencies.

But from the difficulty intensity scores it is clear that the students perceived Real Numbers at the moderate level of difficulty whereas the teachers perceived at the less moderate level of difficulty in all the three aspects content, teaching and learning as the difficulty intensity for students ranges from 51 per cent to 56 per cent whereas for teachers it ranges from 49 per cent to 55 per cent. The variation is due to most of the teachers checked this chapter at less difficult level.

The concept of absolute value or modulus is found very difficult for students and teachers in understanding. The reason is obvious. The way in which the definition of the said term presented in the textbook leads to confusion. Instead of giving concrete examples the abstract rules are stated in the textbook. Solving absolute value inequations is also felt very difficult by both the students and the teachers.

The sixth chapter deals with a new topic 'Progressions'. It deals with Arithmetic Progression, Geometric Progression and Harmonic Progression.

Table 5.40: Frequencies and intensity scores of chapter VI

	STUDENTS					*TEACHERS*				
	L	*M*	*H*	*T*	*INT*	*L*	*M*	*H*	*T*	*INT*
C	22	32	15	69	131	43	50	25	118	218
T	7	10	4	21	39	58	43	13	114	83
L	21	17	12	50	91	22	63	35	120	253

Based on the total frequencies, the results reveal that about 34 per cent of students and about 73 per cent of teachers perceived difficulty in the contents of the chapter.

As far as teaching difficulty is concerned, the students rated their teacher's efficiency in teaching this chapter positively. But the teachers expressed difficulty in teaching this chapter. Only 21(11%) students perceived that this chapter was difficult for teaching whereas 114 (71%) teachers considered teaching this chapter difficult (on the basis of the total frequencies).

Consequently, learning this chapter is felt easy by 75 per cent of students while about 75 per cent of teachers perceived it as difficult for their students.

But the difficulty intensity scores reveal that students and teachers are in agreement with regard to the content difficulty whereas they differ regarding the teaching and learning difficulties. That is, when students perceived more teaching difficulty for their teachers, teachers perceived more learning difficulty for their students.

However, the chapter can be treated as a very difficult chapter as the intensity scores range from 54 per cent to 70 per cent. The above variation is because more number of teachers checked the chapter at the less level of difficulty.

It is observed that solving of problems under Arithmetic Progression and Harmonic Progression is not difficult for the students and teachers. But solving problems under Geometric Progression is felt very difficult. The reason again here is that the teachers fail to adopt Analytic Method while teaching mathematics in the classroom. In fact finding solutions to problems under Geometric Progression involves critical thinking and reasoning.

Unless the teacher adopts Heuristic and Discovery approaches in the classroom during the teaching-learning process he can not do justice to the students as a Mathematics teacher. Hence, it is necessary to train the teachers during pre-service and in-service programmes to adopt these approaches in problem solving to make them fit for the teaching profession.

Chapter VII deals with Geometry. The fundamentals of Geometry start right from the V class. From there onwards the concentric arrangement of the syllabus is followed in the secondary school syllabus. The axioms and theorems are arranged based on the learning principles from simple to complex, easy to difficult and known to unknown in order to accomplish the needs of the students.

Table 5.41: Frequencies and intensity scores of chapter VII

	STUDENTS					*TEACHERS*				
	L	*M*	*H*	*T*	*INT*	*L*	*M*	*H*	*T*	*INT*
C	19	32	41	92	206	5	54	75	134	338
T	9	9	16	34	75	12	60	59	131	309
L	17	19	25	61	130	5	35	98	138	369

From the table given above it is clear that majority of students and teachers checked the chapter as difficult at the moderate and the high intensity levels but not at the low level in all the aspects namely, content, teaching and learning.

Regarding the content about 46 per cent of students and about 83 per cent of teachers perceived Geometry was difficult on the basis of the total frequencies. As regards teaching when 34(17 per cent) students revealed that teaching this chapter was difficult for their teachers, the majority of 131(81%) teachers considered that teaching this chapter was difficult. Regarding learning aspect, about 75 per cent of students perceived learning this chapter as easy and about 86 per cent of teachers felt that it was difficult for their students.

Even the intensity scores on the difficulty level of Geometry are more for both students and teachers. When about 71 per cent to 75 per cent of the intensity score is obtained for students, it ranges from 79 per cent to 89 per cent for teachers.

Even though students study Geometry right from their primary education yet they are frightened at the subject. Frankly speaking; the teachers are more frightened than the taught in this regard. The stark reality unearthed in the field visits was that majority of teachers hardly taught Geometry in secondary schools for the plain fact that the study of Geometry compels the adoption of deductive reasoning and analytic approach. But most of teachers working in secondary schools are not exposed to these approaches in teaching mathematics.

Hence the teachers should be trained to enable them to teach the Geometry effectively in the classroom during pre-service and in-service training programmes. Therefore, it is the bounden duty cast upon the curriculum makers, textbook writers, educational administrators and teacher educators to ensure that earnest steps are initiated in this direction.

During the field visits a large number of students opined that they were not taught Geometry fully in the class room. On one pretext or the other the teachers did not attempt to teach Geometry. Even if some teachers taught it, only the selected topics, which were more important from the examination point of view, were picked up. Regarding the queries relating to this the teachers say that Geometry is expected to be taught during the month of March and by that time the teachers will be busy either in conducting examinations or in revising the syllabus. In view of this backdrop they do not find time even to start the chapter in the classroom. At times, there is every likelihood of skipping this chapter. In a bid to complete the syllabus within time the teachers jump to the conclusions without imparting even the fundamentals of Geometry. The teachers should overcome these hurdles at any cost in order to establish the teaching learning process fruitful and meaningful. The responsible authorities should not pass the buck on the teachers. Anyhow a suitable strategy is to be adopted and pressed into service.

With a view to remedying the situation the policy makers and administrators should not lay stress on results. Instead emphasis should be laid on the development of thinking capacities in the students and accordingly the structure suitable for ensuring this objective is to be developed.

The VIII chapter deals with Analytical Geometry. This branch is the combination of the two branches Algebra and Geometry. It is also called as Co-ordinate geometry or Cartesian geometry. It is introduced in the VII class itself. In the beginning, it covers the basic concepts like the coordinate plane, the four quadrants, equation of a line and the coordinates in a plane etc. In the VIII class it deals with slope, slope of a line etc. In the IX class this chapter consists of the distance between two points and a mid point of a line in the coordinate plane etc., and it continues in the X class.

Table 5.42: Frequencies and intensity scores of Chapter VIII

	STUDENTS					*TEACHERS*				
	L	*M*	*H*	*T*	*INT*	*L*	*M*	*H*	*T*	*INT*
C	18	20	20	58	118	50	47	18	115	198
T	4	5	6	15	32	62	39	10	111	170
L	18	7	15	40	77	41	47	29	117	222

On the basis of the total frequencies noted in the table, it may be observed that as far as content difficulty is concerned, 29 per cent of students and about 71 per cent of teachers admitted that Analytical Geometry was difficult. As regards the teaching difficulty out of 200 students only 15(about 8%) stated that teaching this chapter was difficult for their teachers but 111(about 69%) out of 161 teachers concluded that teaching of this chapter to their students was difficult.

Similarly, when 80 per cent of the students perceived learning of this chapter as easy, about 75 per cent of the teachers reiterated that it was difficult for their students to learn it.

However, the difficulty intensity as perceived by students on this chapter lies between 64 per cent to 71 per cent whereas it ranges from 51 per cent to 63 per cent for teachers. Therefore, Analytical Geometry is perceived as highly difficult chapter by the students and moderately difficult by the teachers.

Chapter IX briefly examines the theory and practice of Trigonometry. It is a newly introduced branch in this class and continues in intermediate. It covers Trigonometric Ratios like Sine, Cosine, Tangents and their reciprocals, Sexagecimal system, Radian, Trigonometric Table Values, Trigonometric Identities like $Sin^2\theta + Cos^2\theta = 1$ etc. These topics cannot be taught in the lower classes as they involve reasoning and decision making. Owing to the difficulty level of the subject it is introduced in the X class only.

Table 5.43: Frequencies and intensity scores of Chapter IX

	STUDENTS					*TEACHERS*				
	L	*M*	*H*	*T*	*INT*	*L*	*M*	*H*	*T*	*INT*
C	16	35	62	113	272	21	62	43	126	274
T	4	1 5	12	31	70	41	58	23	122	226
L	13	24	30	67	151	14	50	70	134	324

From this table it is clear that about 8 per cent, 18 per cent and 31 per cent of students and about 13 per cent, 39 per cent and 27 per cent of teachers perceived this chapter as difficult content-wise at the low, moderate and high intensity levels respectively.

On the basis of the total frequencies, as regards teaching when about 85 per cent of students felt that teaching this chapter was easy for their teachers, about 75 per cent of teachers admitted that it was difficult for them. Consequently, about 67 per cent of students found it easy to learn whereas about 75 per cent of teachers perceived that it was difficult for their students.

As per the difficulty intensity scores, the chapter Trigonometry is considered highly difficult by both the students and teachers as the intensity scores range from 75 per cent to 80 per cent for students and 62 per cent to 81 per cent for teachers. Thus the variation observed above is because most of the students and teachers checked the chapter at the moderate and the high intensity levels.

In fact the illustrations listed in the text are not presented so well as to enable the teachers and students understand them without any problem. This is primarily because the textbook carries printer's devils .To some extent the textbook is responsible for creating confusion in the students and teachers. The errors in the textbook in respect of this particular chapter make the confusion worse confounded. The students are presumed to solve number of problems based on the concepts like angle of elevation and angle of depression. The teachers and students find difficulty even in solving the problems using trigonometric table values.

But the students find it difficult to draw a suitable figure in view of the mistaken data imbibed in the descriptive problem.

Development of the power of visualisation among the students is essential in working with such descriptive problems. Students and teachers find difficulty especially, while solving problems on Heights and Distances since, most of these problems are catch problems. They require a lot of analysis in drawing a suitable figure for the given data. These skills must be inculcated among the students by adopting the Analytic and Heuristic Approaches in the classroom. However, it is equally important to note that the teachers should be trained properly both at pre-service and in-service levels to facilitate themselves to adopt suitable methods and techniques in teaching mathematics.

The X chapter screens the topic Statistics. The fundamentals of Statistics are introduced in the VII class itself. The topics are arranged gradually from Simple to Complex and Easy to Difficult in Concentric Method. In the earlier classes this chapter covers the constructions of frequency distribution, frequency polygon etc. The present chapter consists of Mean, Median, Mode and Correlation etc. In view of the continuous customary adoption of the principles of Statistics right from the earlier classes, the teachers and students feel it more accessible to their knowledge and understanding. As a result they feel tension-free in finding out the solutions.

Table 5.44: Frequencies and intensity scores of Chapter X

	STUDENTS					TEACHERS				
	L	*M*	*H*	*T*	*INT*	*L*	*M*	*H*	*T*	*INT*
C	40	7	6	53	72	97	16	1	114	132
T	3	1	2	6	11	98	16	0	114	130
L	19	8	4	31	47	98	17	0	115	132

This table shows that about 27 per cent of students and about 71 per cent of the teachers perceived the contents of this chapter as difficult on the basis of the total frequencies. Regarding teaching, 97 per cent of students perceived teaching this chapter as easy for their teachers, whereas about 71 per cent of teachers felt it difficult. As far as learning was concerned, about 85 per cent of students considered it easy, whereas 72 per cent of the teachers regarded it as difficult for their students on the basis of total frequencies.

It is also seen clearly from the table that only at the low intensity level the teachers perceived the identical number of difficulties in content, teaching and learning. But at the moderate level very few teachers deliberated difficulty in content, teaching and learning. None perceived difficulty at the high intensity level regarding teaching and learning mathematics but one and only one perceived content difficulty at this level.

However, the difficulty intensity scores range from 45 per cent to 61 per cent for students whereas it is around 38 per cent for teachers. This indicates that Statistics is perceived as easy by the teachers whereas students felt it difficult at the moderate level.

Chapter XI deals with Matrices. The fundamentals of this chapter are introduced in the IX class itself. In the IX class it consists of types of matrices, comparison of matrices, addition, subtraction and multiplication of matrices, transpose of a matrix and laws of matrices. In the X class this chapter comprises coefficient of a matrix, inverse of a matrix, solution of system of linear equations in two variables, square matrix, singular and non-singular matrices etc.

Table 5.45: Frequencies and intensity scores of Chapter XI

	STUDENTS					TEACHERS				
	L	*M*	*H*	*T*	*INT*	*L*	*M*	*H*	*T*	*INT*
C	31	8	4	43	59	109	2	2	113	119
T	6	0	2	8	12	108	4	1	113	119
L	15	3	1	19	24	110	5	1	116	123

The responses of teachers and students regarding the difficulties in content, teaching and learning are summarised as follows:

Interestingly, the perceptions of students and teachers got struck at coincidence regarding the difficulties in content, teaching and learning both at moderate and the high intensity levels. But at the low intensity level, about 75 per cent of teachers perceived this chapter as difficult in content, teaching and learning while only 31(about 16%) students felt content difficulty, 6(3%) students found teaching difficulty and 15(about 8%) students considered that learning of this chapter was difficult at low intensity level.

Even the difficulty intensity scores on this chapter purport the same. That is for students the difficulty intensity ranges from 42 per cent to 50 per cent whereas for teachers it falls exactly at 35 per cent in all the three aspects viz., content, teaching and learning.

It may be derived from these results that the contents of Chapter XI are easy both to the teachers and students in teaching and learning at the moderate and the high intensity levels respectively. The variation is found since majority of teachers felt difficulty in teaching their students at the low intensity level.

The XII chapter in the X class textbook deals with Computing. It begins at IX class and continues in X class also.

The table 5.46 reveals that out of 200 students 32(16%) and 64(about 40%) out of 161 teachers perceived the contents of this chapter as difficult at the low intensity level.

Table 5.46: Frequencies and intensity scores of Chapter XII

	STUDENTS					*TEACHERS*				
	L	*M*	*H*	*T*	*INT*	*L*	*M*	*H*	*T*	*INT*
C	32	9	6	47	56	64	39	17	120	193
T	2	3	7	12	29	68	39	16	123	194
L	14	4	2	20	28	63	40	18	121	197

At the moderate and high intensity levels very few students perceived content difficulty in chapter 12 whereas 39 (about 24%) and 17 (about 11%) teachers felt the same at the moderate and the high intensity levels respectively.

On the basis of the total frequencies, regarding the teaching difficulty, a majority of 94 per cent of students perceived that their teachers were good at teaching this chapter, whereas about 75 per cent of teachers felt that teaching this chapter was difficult. Similarly as regards the learning difficulty, when 90 per cent of the students considered the chapter easy, about 75 per cent of teachers regarded learning it as difficult for their students.

As per the difficulty intensity scores, computing can be treated, as a moderately difficult chapter for teachers as the intensity score is about 54 per cent. But, this chapter is perceived as less moderately difficult chapter for students in content and learning whereas students perceived teaching this chapter as highly difficult as the intensity score is 81 per cent. This undoubtedly shows that the teachers faced difficulty in teaching the chapter to the students.

The reasons may be that they were not exposed to the basics of computing earlier and were not provided with any experienced hands.

With the advancement of knowledge in science and technology computer education is felt necessary to update their knowledge and to be in tune with the changing demands of the society.

The schools are ill-equipped and not provided with the facilities to install the computers. Unfortunately, most of the teachers working at Government, Zilla Parishad and Municipal Schools are not exposed to computer knowledge and so the teachers can hardly teach this chapter to the students. It is therefore imperative that the authorities concerned should provide computer facilities and also appoint qualified teachers in computer science besiding arranging short-term training programmes for in- service teachers.

After having seen the perceptions of students and teachers on difficulty levels of content, teaching and learning of each chapter, it would be rather interesting to see the relative difficulty levels of different chapters as perceived by both the groups on the three kinds of difficulties.

The following table depict the total number of subjects (frequencies) and the intensity of difficulty as expressed by the two groups on the X class mathematics textbook.

Table 5.47: Table indicating the Content Difficulty of X Class as perceived by Students and Teachers

S. No.	*Chapter Name*	*Students*		*Teachers*	
		Frequencies	*Intensity scores*	*Frequencies*	*Intensity scores*
1.	Statements and Sets	58	77 (9)	117 (8)	148 (10)
2.	Functions	55	78 (8)	123 (4.5)	211 (6)
3.	Polynomials over Integers	71 (3)	109 (6)	123 (4.5)	213 (5)
4.	Linear Programming	70 (4)	143 (3)	128 (2)	285 (2)
5.	Real Numbers	61	94 (7)	116 (9)	169 (9)
6.	Progressions	69 (5)	131 (4)	118 (7)	218 (4)
7.	Geometry	92 (2)	206 (2)	134 (1)	338 (1)
8.	Analytical Geometry	58	118 (5)	115	198 (7)
9.	Trigonometry	113 (1)	272 (1)	126 (3)	274 (3)
10.	Statistics	53	72 (10)	114	132 (11)
11.	Matrices	43	59 (11)	113	119 (12)
12.	Computing	47	56 (12)	120 (6)	193 (8)

From the table it is evident that chapters 3, 4, 6, 7 and 9 are relatively more difficult as large number of students checked these chapters. However, by considering the intensity scores, chapters 4, 6, 7, 8 and 9 stand as more difficult in contents than the other chapters for students. So the variation is in one chapter. Instead of chapter 3, chapter 8 appeared as more difficult on the basis of intensity scores. It may be so because large number of respondents who checked chapter 3 as difficult perceived the level as low.

On the other hand, the perceptions of teachers reveal that the chapters 2, 3, 4, 7 and 9 appear to be more difficult on the basis of the frequencies and chapters 3, 4, 6, 7 and 9 as more difficult chapters as per the intensity scores. Four chapters are common in both the sets and the deviation observed in one chapter, that is, chapter 2 replaced by chapter 6 is due to variation in the intensity level of difficulty as perceived by the teachers. Thus there are four sets of chapters, which are identified as more difficult in the X class textbook content wise. Out of these four sets chapters 4, 6,7 and 9 are common. In other words, chapters Linear Programming, Progressions, Geometry and Trigonometry are to be considered highly difficult content wise. Therefore, either the chapters have to be re-written or revised to suit the ability levels of students and teachers.

Similarly, an analysis of difficulties in teaching and learning as perceived by both students and teachers is presented in the following table 5.48.

From the table it may be observed that chapters 2, 4, 6, 7, 8 and 9 are the relatively more difficult as per the number of students who checked the items and as per the intensity scores of difficulty.

An observation into the responses of teachers reveal that 2, 4, 7, 9 and 12 are the relatively more difficult chapters as per the frequencies. But, based on the difficulty intensity scores, 3, 4, 7, 9 and 12 are the relatively more difficult chapters for teachers.

Out of these three sets of relatively difficult chapters 4, 7 and 9 are common. In other words, the chapters on Linear Programming, Geometry and Trigonometry are felt as highly difficult chapters by both students and teachers in teaching.

Table 5.48: Table indicating the Teaching Difficulty in X Class as perceived by Students and Teachers

S. No.	Chapter Name	Students		Teachers	
		Frequencies	*Intensity scores*	*Frequencies*	*Intensity scores*
1.	Statements and Sets	11	17 (9)	114	142 (10)
2.	Functions	15 (5.5)	32 (5.5)	120 (5)	186 (6)
3.	Polynomials over Integers	13 21	(8) 117	(6) 188	(5)
4.	Linear Programming	24 (3)	46 (3)	124 (2)	266 (2)
5.	Real Numbers	10	16 (10)	115	170 (8.5)
6.	Progressions	21 (4)	39 (4)	114	183 (7)
7.	Geometry	34 (1)	75 (1)	131 (1)	309 (1)
8.	Analytical Geometry	15 (5.5)	32 (5.5)	111	170 (8.5)
9.	Trigonometry	31 (2)	70 (2)	122 (4)	226 (3)
10.	Statistics	6	11 (12)	114	130 (11)
11.	Matrices	8	12 (11)	113	119 (12)
12.	Computing	12	29 (7)	123 (3)	194 (4)

From the table 5.49 it can be observed that chapters 2, 6, 7, 8 and 9 are relatively more difficult chapters in learning as per the frequencies of students who checked the chapters. From the point of view of the intensity of difficulty in learning, chapters 2, 4, 6, 7 and 9 appear to be relatively more difficult.

With regard to the teachers perceptions chapters 2, 3, 4, 7 and 9 are checked as relatively more difficult chapters in learning on the basis of frequencies, whereas chapters 3, 4, 6, 7 and 9 are the relatively more difficult chapters on the basis of the intensity scores for teachers.

Table 5.49: Table indicating the Learning Difficulty in X Class as perceived by Students and Teachers

S. No.	*Chapter Name*	*Students*		*Teachers*	
		Frequencies	*Intensity scores*	*Frequencies*	*Intensity scores*
1.	Statements and Sets	23	31 (10)	120	159 (10)
2.	Functions	50 (3.5)	85 (4)	123 (5)	220 (7)
3.	Polynomials over Integers	39	69 (7)	127 (4)	241 (5)
4.	Linear Programming	39	81 (5)	132 (3)	311 (3)
5.	Real Numbers	26	44 (9)	121	201 (8)
6.	Progressions	50 (3.5)	91 (3)	120	253 (4)
7.	Geometry	61 (2)	130 (2)	138 (1)	369 (1)
8.	Analytical Geometry	40 (5)	77 (6)	117	222 (6)
9.	Trigonometry	67 (1)	151 (1)	134 (2)	324 (2)
10.	Statistics	31	47 (8)	115	132 (11)
11.	Matrices	19	24 (12)	116	123 (12)
12.	Computing	20	28 (11)	121	197 (9)

From the four sets of top 5 difficulty chapters, the 4th, 6th, 7th and 9th chapters are the most difficult for learning as perceived by students and teachers. In other words, Linear programming, progressions, Geometry and Trigonometry are posing more problems in learning by students as per the perceptions of two groups. Therefore, it is suggested that these chapters are to be re-organised or re-written with more number of illustrations and examples to make them easy and interesting for the students.

On the basis of difficulty intensity scores of all the 12 chapters, on the three dimensions namely, content difficulty, teaching difficulty and learning difficulty, ranks are assigned to students and teachers independently as presented in the following table.

Table 5.50: Rank order of Difficulty Chapters in X Class as perceived by Students and Teachers Content-Wise, Teaching-wise, and Learning-wise

S. No.	*Chapter Name*	*Students*			*Teachers*		
		Content	*Teaching*	*Learning*	*Content*	*Teaching*	*Learning*
1.	Statements and Sets	9	9	10	10	10	10
2.	Functions	8	6	4	6	6	7
3.	Polynomials over Integers	6	8	7	5	5	5
4.	Linear Programming	3	3	5	2	2	3
5.	Real Numbers	7	10	9	9	9	8
6.	Progressions	4	4	3	4	7	4
7.	Geometry	2	1	2	1	1	1
8.	Analytical Geometry	5	5	6	7	8	6
9.	Trigonometry	1	2	1	3	3	2
10.	Statistics	10	12	8	11	11	11
11.	Matrices	11	11	12	12	12	12
12.	Computing	12	7	11	8	4	9

It is evident from this table that chapters 4, 6, 7 and 9 are found to be highly difficult in all the three dimensions of difficulty as perceived by students, whereas chapters 3, 4, 7 and 9 appear to be highly difficult as per the perceptions of teachers. Thus the two null hypotheses stating that 'Pupils in general do not feel studying mathematics at the secondary level is an easy task' and 'Teachers in general do not feel teaching of mathematics at the secondary level is an easy task' are accepted. Therefore, it is suggested that the chapters Polynomials over Integers, Linear programming, Progressions, Geometry and Trigonometry are to be given attention by the curriculum makers and text book writers keeping in view the problems of students and teachers. Apart from these, the teachers are to be given orientation with good number of examples so that they gain conceptual clarity and find these chapters easy. Further, some of the mathematics teachers, in general, deliver the following dialogues while introducing the new topics in the class room: "This is very tough chapter, You must be very attentive, You cannot learn easily, Be careful" etc. Of course, only to motivate students and to draw the attention and concentration of the students the teachers pass such comments in the classroom. But, these comments act negatively on students and they start avoiding such difficulties by skipping these chapters. Therefore, while providing the training to the teachers, the teacher educators should focus their attention not only on the contents and methodology but also on the development of positive attitude in teachers towards mathematics. They must be trained to develop confidence and interest in the minds of the students in learning the subject.

The main objective at this stage is to develop intuition, induction and deduction, analytical thinking and logical reasoning. Emphasis is to be laid on synthetic presentation also. It is to be remembered that learning mathematics is doing mathematics. The teacher is expected to lead the child to discover the relationships through experiments and other activities and construct for him all that is learnt. Mathematics as a formal structure makes sense to pupil only if he has a store of experiences of doing mathematics. The success of any course depends not so much on the syllabus as on the teacher and the teaching methods he employs. The teacher occupies a pivotal position on which the whole system rests. It is appropriate to reiterate that the mathematics teachers should be cautious about one thing that in the teaching-learning mathematics, the process is more important than the product. Whatever contents they teach to the students by whatever methods, the ultimate goal should be development of problem-solving abilities in the students.

In a general classroom situation the students of above average level will not be contented with the synthetic solutions figured by the teachers as they require the logic and reasoning in arriving at the solution. Even the below average students will not get satisfied with the teaching as they are not thorough with the essential previous knowledge related to the current contents. In majority of the cases the teachers fail to correlate the linkages between the essential knowledge and the present lesson which is a must for meaningful learning. Therefore, it is incumbent to train the teachers both at pre-service and at in-service levels in different skills involved in teaching viz., Skill of introduction, skill of explanation, skill of questioning and the skill of reinforcement etc. Hence, the teacher educators must lay emphasis on the micro-teaching technique during the training programme.

It is needless to say that mathematics is a logical science and the study of this science must lead the students to develop their logical thinking. But in the order of the day there is no scope for students to think logically at all. The reasons are manifold. In a way it happens that the teachers keep on telling the facts one by one in a chronological manner at a stretch and students will be interested in simply writing them down in their note books. The students find no time to think at the acquisance at all. The teacher is in a hurry to complete the syllabus and the student is forced to get by heart the transmitted reasonings without adhering to the proof. On account of the pressure inflicted by the D.E.O's and the District Collectors the teachers are in a hurry to complete the syllabus in a hurried fashion. Their target is only to complete the syllabus and obtain the cent percent results by hook or crook devoid of the assimilation of the subject by the students which is vital in teaching learning process.

Therefore, the examinations are the yardstick to help us to evaluate the students properly whether to what extent the objectives of teaching are realised. The present classroom teaching leads only to acquisition of knowledge and understanding ignoring the higher objectives such as application and skill. Teaching of mathematics becomes meaningless unless and until the students apply the acquired knowledge and understanding in solving new problems and in facing new situations adequately.

ANALYSIS OF THE PROBLEMS OF STUDENTS AND TEACHERS

Two problem check-lists-cum-problem intensity scales, one for students and the other for teachers were used for the purpose of collecting data relating to problems perceived by students and teachers while teaching-learning mathematics in our secondary schools. The frequencies on the basis of the problem checklists and the problem intensity scores obtained by the ratings of both teachers and students are analysed and appropriate discussions are presented in the following pages under two sub-sections viz. Problems as perceived by students and problems as perceived by teachers.

Analysis of Problems as perceived by Students

As explained earlier there are 67 items in the problem checklist developed by the Investigator to identify the problems related to students of VIII, IX and X classes in learning mathematics. The responses of the students were scored as explained earlier. The frequencies and intensity scores of all the items on the problem—check list meant for students in learning mathematics are presented in the table no. 5.51.

Out of 227 VIII class students as many as 135 students felt the problem of remembering different mathematical formulae. The least frequent problem (only 28 students) checked by the students is item no.36, which indicates that their teachers do not recall the previous knowledge related to the chapter while commencing the chapter. In brief, the frequencies ranged from 28 to 135 for the VIII Class students, 33 to 128 for the IX Class students, and for the X class students they ranged from 28 to 138. As per these frequencies the rank order of top 10 problems in the check list given by VIII, IX and X class students is as follows:

VIII. 2, 35, 5, 32, 21, 38, 56, 42, 14, 30.

IX. 2, 1, 38, 8, 5, 4, 56, 30, 35, 13.

X. 5, 2, 30, 38, 63, 1, 12, 13, 32, 35.

If the above numbers are arranged as per the serial number then the top 10 problems in the checklist are:

VIII. 2, 5, 14, 21, 30, 32, 35, 38, 42, and 56

IX. 1, 2, 4, 5, 8, 13, 30, 35, 38, and 56

X. 1, 2, 5, 12, 13, 30, 32, 35, 38, and 63

Table 5.51: Frequencies and Intensity scores of Problems perceived by VIII, IX, and X class Students.

Item No.	*VIII Class*		*IX Class*		*X Class*	
	Frequencies	*Intensity scores*	*Frequencies*	*Intensity scores*	*Frequencies*	*Intensity scores*
1.	79	124	123 (2)	185 (5)	100 (6)	177 (5)
2.	135 (1)	225 (1)	128 (1)	214 (2)	127 (2)	207 (3)
3.	82	146	71	137	72	128
4.	102 (11)	197 (5)	105 (6)	228 (1)	83	135
5.	128 (3)	184 (9)	107 (5)	177 (7)	138 (1)	212 (2)
6.	53	89	55	120	66	105
7.	38	64	47	98	48	72
8.	92	154	109 (4)	192 (4)	77	122
9.	58	98	66	146	72	135
10.	77	136	70	115	64	101
11.	90	144	86	139	70	116
12.	78	121	84	130	96 (8)	145

(Contd...)

Item No.	*VIII Class*		*IX Class*		*X Class*	
	Frequencies	*Intensity scores*	*Frequencies*	*Intensity scores*	*Frequencies*	*Intensity scores*
13.	88	149	96 (10)	171 (8)	95 (9.5)	166 (8)
14.	105 (9)	161	92	165	82	139
15.	62	119	40	76	51	75
16.	47	73	43	82	52	78
17.	46	78	47	86	52	85
18.	47	73	68	130	65	112
19.	99	188 (6.5)	84	194 (3)	86	168 (7)
20.	50	81	49	100	52	93
21.	117 (5)	185 (8)	93	164	98	158 (10)
22.	83	134	69	128	80	97
23.	54	88	57	97	64	104
24.	63	95	80	144	86	152
25.	28	49	41	82	39	58
26.	37	62	40	81	35	60

(Contd...)

Item No.	VIII Class		IX Class		X Class	
	Frequencies	Intensity scores	Frequencies	Intensity scores	Frequencies	Intensity scores
27.	80	115	71	127	68	104
28.	46	82	53	121	60	107
29.	101	162	77	139	86	149
30.	103 (10)	158	101 (8.5)	179 (6)	122 (3)	218 (1)
31.	39	62	60	113	61	105
32.	128 (3)	205 (4)	76	133	95 (9.5)	163 (9)
33.	41	63	45	84	38	65
34.	39	66	35	71	37	67
35.	128 (3)	212 (2)	101 (8.5)	157	92 (11)	133
36.	28	47	46	98	45	83
37.	40	61	54	107	34	60
38.	115 (6)	208 (3)	111 (3)	190	109 (4)	175 (6)
39.	40	79	52	99	29	45
40.	44	77	44	101	28	50

(Contd...)

Item No.	VIII Class		IX Class		X Class	
	Frequencies	Intensity scores	Frequencies	Intensity scores	Frequencies	Intensity scores
41.	34	47	49	94	36	62
42.	107 (8)	179 (10)	71	116	62	105
43.	44	95	47	88	44	79
44.	34	65	42	86	31	57
45.	47	80	63	132	38	58
46.	54	91	44	89	56	93
47.	53	103	47	92	41	69
48.	76	129	78	141	79	140
49.	42	85	40	81	48	77
50.	29	47	42	90	53	97
51.	36	60	39	76	40	68
52.	58	98	42	86	36	63
53.	49	91	33	68	48	93
54.	42	70	46	89	49	76

(Contd...)

Item No.	VIII Class		IX Class		X Class	
	Frequencies	*Intensity scores*	*Frequencies*	*Intensity scores*	*Frequencies*	*Intensity scores*
55.	43	75	44	80	29	48
56.	111 (7)	188 (6.5)	103 (7)	169 (9)	75	121
57.	63	120	68	119	53	89
58.	38	59	44	87	44	71
59.	44	79	39	80	41	71
60.	34	61	37	77	30	56
61.	48	86	40	83	35	63
62.	41	78	48	97	46	91
63.	55	86	59	107	102 (5)	183 (4)
64.	37	70	42	84	46	78
65.	31	57	49	107	53	96
66.	94	172	54	116	68	124
67.	71	121	92	166 (10)	78	124

The total intensity scores on each item obtained as explained earlier are arranged in the rank order. The top 10 problems as per the intensity scores given by the VIII, IX and X class students are as follows:

VIII. 2, 4, 5, 19, 21, 32, 35, 38,42 and 56

IX. 1,2, 4,5, 8, 13,19,30,56, and 67.

X. 1, 2, 5, 13,19, 21, 30, 32, 38, and 63

The frequencies and intensity scores along with the ranks of the top 10 items in the paranthesis are presented in the Table 5.52.

Problems related to mathematical formulae

- Understanding mathematical formulae is difficult.
- It is difficult to remember mathematical formulae
- Selecting the suitable formula for solving the problem is difficult.
- Deriving alternative formulae from a given formula is difficult.

These problems indicate that most of the students are facing difficulty in understanding, remembering, deriving and selecting the formulae properly in mathematics. It may be due to the dogmatic method adopted by the teacher in the classroom whereby he gives a set of formulae related to a particular topic at a time and compels the students to get by heart all the formulae at a time without any reasoning. For example, while teaching Commercial mathematics from in VIII class, teachers will write all the formulae related to profit and loss at a time on the board. Therefore, the students find it difficult to understand the mathematical formulae and unable to recall whenever required. Hence, the teachers must strictly adopt inductive method of teaching mathematics for clear understanding of the formulae whenever and wherever necessary.

Combining all the six sets of items, it may be seen that the following are the serious problems for students of VIII, IX, and X class in the study of Mathematics. Before analysing these problems item-wise, to be more clear/specific, these problems are categorized under different heads based on the type of problems such as problems related to mathematical formulae, problem- solving, textbook, homework, mathematical concepts, and Geometry. The bunches of problems are discussed in detail in the following pages:

Table 5.52: Frequencies and intensity scores of problems as perceived by students of VIII, IX, and X Class along with the ranks of top 10 items

Item No.	*VIII Class*		*IX Class*		*X Class*	
	Frequencies	*Intensity scores*	*Frequencies*	*Intensity scores*	*Frequencies*	*Intensity scores*
1.			123 (2)	185 (5)	100 (6)	177 (5)
2.	135 (1)	225 (1)	128 (1)	214 (2)	127 (2)	208 (3)
4.		197 (5)	105 (6)	228 (1)		
5.	128 (3)	184 (9)	107 (5)	177 (7)	138 (1)	212 (2)
8.			109 (4)	192 (4)		
12.					96 (8)	
13.			96 (10)	171 (8)	95 (9.5)	166 (8)
14.	105 (9)					
19.		188 (6.5)		194 (3)		168 (7)
21.	117 (5)	185 (8)			98 (7)	158 (10)
30.	103 (10)		101 (8.5)	179 (6)	123 (3)	218 (1)

(Contd...)

Item No.	VIII Class		IX Class		X Class	
	Frequencies	*Intensity scores*	*Frequencies*	*Intensity scores*	*Frequencies*	*Intensity scores*
32.	128 (3)	205 (4)			95 (9.5)	163 (9)
35.	128 (3)	212 (2)	101 (8.5)			
38.	115 (6)	208 (3)	111 (3)		109 (4)	175 (6)
42.	107 (8)	179 (10)				
56.	111 (7)	188 (6.5)	103 (7)	169 (9)		
63.					102 (5)	183 (4)
67.				166 (10)		

Thus the students are not supposed to blindly remember the formulae. They must come up to the level of deriving the formulae by applying logical thinking and reasoning. Hence, the problem of understanding and remembering the formulae as perceived by students is created by our teachers and it is not because of the students themselves.

Problems Related to Mathematical Concepts

- I do not understand the relationship between different concepts in mathematics.
- It is difficult to understand the language and symbols of mathematics.

For a clear understanding of the subject the teacher has to proceed always from known to unknown, easy to difficult and simple to complex situations or concepts. Unless the concept of Set is understood the student cannot understand the concept of Relation. Similarly, unless the concept of Relation is known the student cannot understand Function.

Further making the children to think on specific concepts by creating different practical situations in day-to-day life is very essential not only to solve the problems by themselves but also to develop analytical and critical thinking which helps them have a better conceptualisation on the given topic. If mathematics teachers do not devote at least significant amount of time on teaching of concepts thoroughly, they are bound to fail in achieving the objectives of mathematics education.

Therefore, to understand the relationship between the different concepts in mathematics the teacher has to follow the principles stated above in teaching-learning mathematics.

Problems Related to Problem Solving

- I am unable to spend more time for doing mathematics.
- I do not understand the linkage in the steps in solving a problem
- I cannot do mathematics fast.
- I commit more mistakes while solving mathematical problems.

The observations of the Investigator reveals that teachers do not pay proper and sufficient attention in making the students understand the given problem. They do not allow the students to read and analyse what is given in the problem, what is to be found out, how to establish the relationship between the known and the unknown data given in the problem, how to identify the relationship between the given data, what formula is to be selected for solving the problem etc. The teacher will simply write the steps on the board and the student notes down those steps. This leads to lack of understanding in the students. Solving problems can be made more meaningful in mathematics by adopting analytical method of teaching (not mechanical way of doing problems). Therefore the analysis part of the problem is to be made by the teacher inspiring students to think.

Students are generally committ mistakes or are unable to do the problems quickly due to fear complex. The teachers of mathematics should try to rid them of this fear complex and make them do the problems as though they are playing games. This type of sportive spirit has to be created in the students by the teachers of mathematics as the first step. Further, unless the students are thorough with the essential knowledge, they cannot solve the given problem accurately. So, to enable the students to solve the problems with speed and accuracy they must be provided with different techniques such as careful reading of the problem, clarity in writing the steps, adopting short cut methods, verification of the results and maintenance of time etc. These techniques will definitely help the students arrive at accurate results.

Problems Related to Mathematics Textbook

- There are more number of difficult topics in the mathematics text book
- The examples given in the textbook are not easy to understand.

It is true because the results obtained on the difficulty analysis of VIII, IX, and X class text books also revealed that Commercial mathematics, Geometry, Mensuration, Linear inequations, factorisation, Motion geometry, Polynomials, Trigonometry, and Linear programming,etc are perceived as most difficult chapters in content, teaching and learning by the students. The Investigator being a teacher educator with frequent interaction with the secondary school students has observed that the chapters mentioned above are perceived as difficult by the students not only because of the content difficulty but also because of the teaching in the class room. Therefore, instead of covering the syllabus by adopting the synthetic and deductive methods only, the combinations of inductive-deductive, analytic-synthetic methods of teaching help the students in meaningful understanding of the subject.

Problems Related to Homework in Mathematics

- Our mathematics teacher gives more problems for homework.
- I have no guide at home to teach mathematics.

It is true that most of the parents or members of the family are not capable of clarifying the doubts or re-teach the lessons of mathematics at home as they are not educated or they may not find time to assist their wards etc. At school the teacher is also not able to provide individual attention towards each student because of over crowded classes. Moreover, because of heavy syllabus and work load the teachers are used to give as many problems as possible to the students for homework to complete the syllabus in time. While solving the problems the students will come across some doubts. In such circumstances, if the students are not attended to properly, it may create lack of confidence, which in turn discourages the student in learning mathematics. Therefore, to overcome this problem, the mathematics teachers should develop their own strategies such as team assignments, analysing the problem before assigning homework etc. In the team assignments students must be made to exchange their knowledge among themselves for better understanding.

Problems Related to Geometry

- Drawing a figure suitable to the given theorem is difficult.
- It is difficult to suggest the suitable construction in proving the theorem.
- Geometry is very difficult for me.

The difficulty analysis of the textbook also reveals that geometry occupies the second position in the order of difficulty for X class students whereas the teachers rank it as the first one in its difficulty. The outcome of the field experience is that though IX class geometry is very lengthy, there are very difficult items given in X class geometry. This makes both teachers and students suffer in dealing with this chapter.

From the analysis of these problems, it can be concluded that the null hypothesis 'There would not be any significant problems faced by students in learning mathematics' is rejected.

The investigator has observed that very few teachers emphasise the construction part while teaching theorems in the classroom but majority of the teachers blindly follows the steps given in the textbook. This results in the creation of lot of confusion in the minds of the students. The students never tries to understand what is to be proved in the statement, what is given in the statement, whether the figure drawn is sufficient to prove the theorem, or whether any construction is required to prove the theorem etc. They never bother to connect linkage between these steps. May be, because of lack of logic or reasoning behind the steps in proving the theorem, the students find it difficult to suggest the suitable construction required for proving the theorem on their own. Therefore, it is necessary to adopt deductive reasoning and axiomatic approach while teaching geometry in the classroom for meaningful learning.

Analysis of Problems as Perceived by Teachers

As explained earlier there are 46 items in the problem check-list developed by the investigator to identify the problems of teachers in teaching the VIII, IX and X class mathematics. The responses of the teachers were scored as explained earlier.

The frequencies and intensity scores of all the items on the problem check list meant for teachers in teaching mathematics are presented in the Table 5.53.

Table 5.53: Table showing the frequencies and intensity scores of problems as perceived by teachers

Item No.	*Frequencies*	*Intensity scores*	*Item No.*	*Frequencies*	*Intensity scores*
1.	132 (1)	282 (1)	24	46	86
2.	102 (8.5)	222 (7)	25	68	124
3.	95 (11)	181	26	78	180
4.	111 (4)	228 (6)	27	51	97
5.	117 (3)	267 (3)	28	64	113
6.	65	145	29	70	145
7.	106 (5)	243 (5)	30	39	61
8.	86	165	31	48	83
9.	103 (7)	198	32	105 (6)	254 (4)
10.	67	122	33	87	190
11.	87	175	34	49	86
12.	62	122	35	45	76
13.	90	196	36	38	65
14.	76	140	37	60	111
15.	77	135	38	81	145
16.	80	149	39	33	44
17.	90	177	40	47	78
18.	85	183	41	100 (10)	220 (8)
19.	94	212 (10)	42	51	97
20.	81	185	43	80	154
21.	72	181	44	47	77
22.	102 (8.5)	216 (9)	45	91	201 (11)
23.	119 (2)	269 (2)	46	76	158

Out of 161 teachers of mathematics as many as 132 teachers felt the problem that their students were not thorough with the primary level mathematics. The least frequent problem checked by only 33 subjects is item no. 39, which indicates that if the teacher does not understand the concepts properly, he will face difficulty while teaching the same to his students. In a nutshell, the frequencies ranged from 132 to 33.

As per the frequencies of responses, the problems which obtain the top 10 ranks in the check-list given by teachers are as follows:

1, 23, 5, 4, 7, 32, 9, 2, 22, and 41. If these numbers are arranged as per the serial number given in the check-list, then, the top 10 items are as follows:

1, 2, 4, 5, 7, 9, 22, 23, 32 and 41.

As per the total intensity scores on each item obtained as explained earlier, the top 10 problems having the highest intensity scores are 1, 23, 5, 32, 7, 4, 2, 41, 22 and 19. If these numbers are arrayed as per the serial number given in the check-list, then, the top 10 items are 1, 2, 4, 5, 7, 19, 22, 23, 32 and 41. When we put these sets of problems together, we find that the most significant problems perceived by the teachers are 1, 2, 4, 5, 7, 9, 19, 22, 23, 32, and 41. Thus, it can be concluded that the null hypothesis 'There would not be any significant problems faced by teachers in teaching mathematics' is rejected.

Table 5.54: Table showing the frequencies and intensity scores of problems as perceived by teachers along with the top 11 ranks

Item No.	*Frequencies*	*Item No.*	*Intensity scores*
1.	132 (1)	1	282 (1)
2.	102 (8.5)	2	222 (7)
3.	95 (11)	4	228 (6)
4.	111 (4)	5	267 (3)
5.	117 (3)	7	243 (5)
7.	106 (5)	19	212 (10)
9.	103 (7)	22	216 (9)
22.	102 (8.5)	23	269 (2)
23.	119 (2)	32	254 (4)
32.	105 (6)	41	220 (8)
41.	100 (10)	45	201 (11)

As these problems correspond to different aspects of mathematics education, each problem may be discussed in detail in terms of finding solutions to nullify the intensity of these problems and to make mathematics education more effective.

The frequencies and intensity scores along with the ranks of the top 11 items in parenthesis are presented in the Table 5.54.

My students do not have thorough knowledge of mathematics at the primary level

In the preliminary survey conducted by the investigator it was observed that about 53 per cent of the students expressed their anguish that mathematics is a difficult subject. Even the field observation demarcates that some of the contents in the III, IV and V classes are difficult not only to students for learning but also to teachers who have not studied mathematics in their graduation in teaching some topics. Moreover, there is only one teacher to teach all the subjects at the primary level they fail to focus their attention and lay proper foundation in mathematics. The net result is that the students do not attain the minimum levels of learning mathematics at the primary school level itself. This becomes a problem for teachers to teach mathematics at the secondary level. Mathematics is a more logical subject, which requires continuity in learning. Once there is a gap in learning, one cannot learn further.

To overcome this problem the syllabus of mathematics should be thoroughly reorganised and more abstract concepts should be introduced at the higher levels. The basic concepts should be introduced to the children with more practical examples and should be taught by following activity method. Specialised teachers of mathematics should be provided at the primary level itself. If a specialised mathematics teacher is kept in charge of primary classes to teach mathematics, the gaps in learning by the children will be minimised. Keeping this requirement in view, the teacher preparation courses at the primary level (DIET/TTC) are to be reoriented towards achieving the objectives of teaching mathematics.

The students are not able to understand every problem given in the exercise unless it is worked out on the board

This is true because the problems given in the exercises of some chapters like Commercial mathematics, Mensuration, Linear programming etc are different in nature. Every teacher is expected to work out all the problems given in exercises. But, he is not able to do so for want of time. If he devotes time for doing all the exercises, he will not be able to complete the syllabus. If he fails to complete the syllabus in time, his authorities will punish him. Hence, scope should be there in the textbook to work similar problems by the students as homework.

Further, the teachers of mathematics should help the students to think analytically and critically on different related concepts whose knowledge is essential to understand the problems of different kinds. The teachers need not do every problem on the board but, he/she has to discuss the analytical part of the problem and allow the students to do the synthetic part of the problem as homework. Thus, the solution to this problem is mostly in the hands of the teacher.

Students think mathematics is a difficult subject because they are afraid of the subject

Who is creating this fear of mathematics among children? This fear complex is developed mostly by the mathematics teachers. Some teachers with the good intention of making their subject a very important subject and a few others due to their own ignorance create this kind of fear among the students. Therefore, pre-service and in-service training programmes should aim at creating a positive attitude in the minds of mathematics teachers, to make the subject interesting, joyful, creative and easy. As already submitted the subject mathematics is distinct from other subjects. It is the teacher who develops either positive or negative attitude towards the subject students. If the teacher is good at teaching the subject meaningfully then no student will think that is a difficult subject.

Students do not try to ask again to know the problems, which they do not understand

It is true that the students never try to get their doubts clarified in the classroom. The reason is students do not have access to the teacher since he is rigid and does not maintain any rapport with the students. Sometimes even if the student raises a doubt, instead of clarifying it, the teacher tries to snub him in return.

In general, every child is has the zeal to know about everything. This kind of zeal is totally killed in our classrooms. So many prejudices develop among the children. If any one raises a question, either the peer laughs at him or the teacher shouts at him and therefore the child develops an attitude not to raise any questions in future. Of course, we cannot throw the blame on the teacher too. In the over crowded classes the teacher is handicapped to answer the queries raised by the students. Individual attention exists only name sake. The class room environment is not congenial to encourage students to raise questions. Most of the teachers are not basically interested in answering the questions. They are always busy in completing the syllabus whether their transactions are really fruitful or not. This results in the creation of the problem revealed in the item.

To overcome this, there must be homogeneous group in the class, size of the class should be optimal for individual attention, the teacher should be open minded and encourage students to raise the doubts, the peer who laugh at one who raises questions should be shouted at and not the student who raises the question. The student should be encouraged to feel free to approach the teacher to get his doubts clarified.

Students do not understand some of the theorems, the riders and constructions in geometry even if they are taught effectively

There is nothing in this world which cannot be understood. But it is true that some students may not understand some theorems, riders and constructions, not because that they cannot, but because they do not possess the essential knowledge. To understand geometry properly at the secondary level, first of all, the students must be thorough with the geometry of the primary and the upper primary classes. Therefore, minimum levels of learning geometry must be achieved at every school stage by adopting axiomatic approach. To overcome the problem stated above the teacher must teach geometry for a few weeks in the beginning of the chapter to provide the essential knowledge to the students and help them to recapitulate what he was taught in the earlier classes. Further, the basics of geometry should be taught at the lower level by a proficient teacher effectively.

Students commit more mistakes while solving problems

Normally, students commit mistakes in taking down the data properly from the textbook or from the board. Often they fail to jot down the symbols as they are and inadvertently post one symbol for the other. In case of speed calculations also they commit mistakes. Hence, they cannot arrive at the right solution. Proper guidance should be given to the them by the teachers to read the problem carefully, to take down the data accurately, to use mathematical signs exactly, to maintain rough work neatly and to verify the results properly.

Covering the syllabus in time is very difficult

Because of the heavy workload or heavy syllabus, completing the syllabus in time is a problem to the teachers. The observations of the investigator is that most of the teachers opined that teaching commercial mathematics from the VIII class requires at least 3 to 4 months as there are more number of exercises with more number of problems. Similarly, in the IX class, for covering geometry they need one complete year. But, the number of periods allotted is very less and not sufficient to teach them. Hence, there is every need to re-organise the syllabus and revise the textbook to suit the abilities of learners and availability of time.

Teaching of mathematics is difficult, as there are more topics, which are above the level of students

The content difficulty has been discussed thoroughly in the previous section of this chapter. A large number of teachers perceived at least 4 to 5 chapters in each class as very difficult in all the three aspects content, teaching and learning. As stated earlier chapters like commercial mathematics, geometry, mensuration, polynomials, linear programming, motion geometry, trigonometry etc. are above the level of students, especially the average students of the Government, Zilla Parishad and Municipal schools. Therefore, teaching these topics to them becomes a major problem to the teachers.

To overcome this problem, content enrichment programmes need to be conducted for the teachers in the respective areas not only to enrich their knowledge in these areas but also to help acquire the skills of teaching effectively to the students.

Owing to the distinctness of the problems given in the exercise there is compulsion to work out each and every problem on the board

The problems given in some of the exercises are distinct in nature and so the teacher cannot give any homework to the students. If the problems given in the exercise are similar in nature then the students can solve them on their own with the help of the classroom teaching. This also helps them to have sufficient practice in solving the problems of different types. Therefore, the problem of the teacher that the teacher has to work out every problem on the board can be solved by giving similar problems in the exercise. The text book writers should take this into consideration while framing the problems in the exercises.

The parents are not evincing interest in the education of their children

Most of the parents of rural children are uneducated. They are not aware of the importance of education. Therefore, they will not pay attention the education of their children. Awareness camps should be conducted to educate those parents who do not care for the education of their children. Moreover, education has become incapable to create demand for it in the society as large number of educated people neither get employment nor can help in any production activity of their parents. In these circumstances, the illiterate parents think that education is only helping to create useless persons. Therefore, the policy makers of education and educationists should think of making education more valuable than what it is in respect of different spheres of human life. Then people will realise that education is inevitable for better human life.

It is heart rending that the teacher has no role in framing the syllabus

At last it is the teacher who has to transact the prescribed syllabus to the students in the classroom. He is the right person to decide whether the topics are suitable to the abilities, interests and needs of the students. He plays a pivotal role in constructing the curriculum. So, his views must be taken into consideration in deciding the curriculum. For example, motion geometry was introduced a few years go in the X class syllabus first. But because of the difficulty in handling the contents, it was deleted from the syllabus. Later on, again it was introduced in the IX class. The observation of the investigator is that none of the teachers is handling this chapter because of the obvious reason that when it is difficult for the X class students, how can it be easy for the IX class students. Similarly, linear programming was introduced in the X class syllabus some years go. Because of the agitation of the teachers, it was deleted from the syllabus. Later on, the teachers were provided content orientation programme in linear programming and again it was introduced in the X class syllabus. Now the teachers are able to deliver the goods from the examination point of view. In spite of it, both the students and teachers face difficulties in teaching and learning this chapter.

This is one side of the coin. The other side is that it is not possible to consult every teacher and give due importance to the suggestions given by everybody while a new curriculum is developed, with well-defined objectives. The persons in-charge of curriculum development should fulfil all the objectives and principles of a widely accepted curriculum. If suggestions given by every teacher are considered as the only principle to be kept in mind, we are going to arrive at a teacher-centred curriculum and every teacher will have his or her own curriculum. But we need to develop a child -centred curriculum. Therefore A, B, C (Articulation, Balancing and Continuity) of the curriculum are to be kept in mind as the principles of good curriculum.

The other problems perceived by the teachers are also important, but when the problems stated above are urgently attended to set right the situation in the field, the other problems having less frequency or less intensity will disappear automatically and mathematics education will become more effective at the secondary level.

ANALYSIS OF ATTITUDES OF STUDENTS AND TEACHERS TOWARDS MATHEMATICS EDUCATION

As described in the methodology chapter the attitudes of students and teachers towards mathematics are measured through attitude scales by following Likert's method of summated ratings on 5- point scale. On the basis of the responses made by the students and teachers for each item, item- wise analysis was carried out. The first sub-section describes the attitude of students and the second discloses the attitude of teachers, which are presented in the following pages:

Analysis of Attitude of Students Towards Mathematics

Out of 42 items included in the final form of attitude scale meant for students to study the student's attitude towards learning mathematics, all the items exhibited a significant trend in the response pattern as the chi-square values obtained are statistically significant at 0.01 level of probability for 4 DF. Therefore it can be concluded that the null hypothesis 'the pupils in general do not possess positive attitude towards learning mathematics' is accepted. It would be rather interesting to note the responses of students against each item to identify the specific aspects of learning mathematics, which might have created positive/negative attitudes among them in learning the subject.

The responses of the students on each item and the chi-square value obtained are presented in the following Table 5.55. *(See on next page)*

For the purpose of discussion the respondents under 'strongly agree' and 'agree' are treated as favourable and the respondents under 'strongly disagree' and 'disagree' have been treated as unfavourable towards the items. Before analysing the items, to be more specific/clear these items have been categorised under five major heads namely, favourable and unfavourable items related to students, favourable and unfavourlable items related to teachers, and items related to habits and inhibitions of students. All these items belonging to each category are analysed in detail in the following pages.

By this kind of analysis, it could be possible to list out those aspects, which are to be taken care of by the teachers of mathematics to plug out the negative predicaments in children and to create more and more enthusiasm in them to learn mathematics.

Table 5.55: Table showing the response pattern of attitudes of students towards mathematics

ITEM & S. No.	*SA*	*A*	*N*	*D*	*SD*	χ^2	*SIG at 0.01*
1.	92	83	60	56	353	494.96	**
2.	115	51	53	97	328	409.01	**
3.	103	31	62	94	354	517.23	**
4.	60	38	40	100	406	765.01	**
5.	57	37	56	79	415	801.81	**
6.	396	88	26	35	98	726.09	**
7.	110	51	51	81	351	497.80	**
8.	483	39	22	18	82	1237.54	**
9.	71	41	36	77	419	827.34	**
10.	87	41	48	100	368	574.77	**
11.	115	55	45	98	331	423.08	**
12.	51	36	53	92	412	791.67	**
13.	80	30	69	75	390	674.21	**
14.	98	61	42	87	356	515.89	**
15.	330	60	79	33	142	442.91	**
16.	86	54	40	109	355	519.18	**
17.	370	86	39	34	115	599.77	**
18.	365	86	51	44	98	557.57	**
19.	67	25	48	59	445	978.08	**
20.	107	40	75	81	341	454.73	**
21.	422	58	43	26	95	854.43	**
22.	42	57	48	86	411	781.73	**
23.	321	106	75	39	103	381.09	**
24.	127	89	57	93	278	235.13	**
25.	63	28	38	84	431	901.14	**
26.	408	83	31	26	79	786.17	**

(Contd...)

ITEM & S. No.	*SA*	*A*	*N*	*D*	*SD*	χ^2	*SIG at 0.01*
27.	430	85	30	35	64	895.95	**
28.	91	54	33	116	350	506.95	**
29.	78	35	52	96	383	644.18	**
30.	69	47	49	99	380	625.97	**
31.	52	17	36	56	483	1224.90	**
32.	68	41	43	106	386	663.34	**
33.	87	68	43	134	312	360.21	**
34.	385	111	41	25	82	672.58	**
35.	78	48	59	102	357	518.44	**
36.	300	114	65	45	120	315.98	**
37.	71	48	66	115	344	468.28	**
38.	100	55	60	123	306	329.52	**
39.	349	70	55	47	123	497.80	**
40.	67	36	75	96	370	579.03	**
41.	79	59	43	110	353	507.24	**
42.	465	62	45	11	61	1110.16	**

Favourable items relating to students:

- Mathematics develops the power of reasoning in the students (A-82%, D-11)
- Learning mathematics will be more useful in higher classes (A-81%, D-16%).
- I get my doubts clarified with my teacher whenever I come across doubts while solving problems (A-80%, D-15%)
- Life's problems can be solved easily by learning mathematics (A-77%, D-17%)
- Teaching mathematics for only one period every day is not sufficient (A-65%, D-26%)

The statements given above reflect the positive attitude of the students towards the subject. The results reveal that majority of

65 per cent to 82 per cent students possess positive attitude whereas about 11 per cent to 26 per cent of students do not possess such type of positive attitude towards mathematics.

Let us examine the items, which influence the students to develop negative attitude towards the subject.

Unfavourable items relating to mathematics

- I do not have the habit of reading the new lesson in advance before it is taught (A-34%, D-58%)
- I do not refer to other books of mathematics except my mathematics text book (A-26%, D- 67%)
- I dislike oral problems (A-25%, D-67%)
- As there were no public examinations in the earlier classes I did not do mathematics properly (A-24%, D-67%)
- I do not devote much time for practising mathematics (A-24%, D-72%)
- I leave the difficult problems given in the textbook (A-23%, D-72%)
- I do not have the habit of practising the problems at home, which are taught in the classroom (A-22%, D-72%)
- I do not have the habit of doing mathematics daily (A-21%, D-72%)
- I dislike homework in mathematics (A-20%, D-73%)
- I do mathematics only at the time of examinations (A-20%, D-71%)
- I dislike mathematics examination (A-18%, D-74%)
- I do not bother if I get poor marks in mathematics (A-18%, D- 74%)
- I get by heart mathematics (A-17%, D-76%)
- There is no relation between mathematics and real life (A-16%, D-72%)
- I do not solve problems on my own.(A-15%, D-79%)

- I copy homework from others (A-15%, D-77%)
- I do not write down properly the problems which our teacher does on the board (A-14%, D-80%)
- There is no use in learning mathematics (A-11%, D-84%)

These statements reflect the negative attitude towards mathematics. The results reveal that about 11 per cent to 34 per cent of students possess negative attitudes as they agreed or strongly agreed with the statements on different aspects of mathematics education such as problem solving, home work, oral problems, examinations in mathematics, relation of mathematics in real life etc.

The ultimate aim of teaching mathematics in schools is to develop problem-solving skills in the students to lead a better life in the society. Therefore, study of the subject should develop confidence among the students to face the challenges in life. Hence, classroom teaching should deal with more meaningful problems related to the life experiences of the students, with as many number of examples and illustrations as possible, and with adequate number of oral problems which create interest in the subject etc. For this, the curriculum must be revised keeping in view the abilities, interests and needs of the students, textbooks must be re-written suitably, and the teacher should adopt innovative methods and techniques in the teaching-learning mathematics. Also, the students must be motivated through mathematics clubs by involving them in various activities like mathematical games, puzzles, quiz competitions, fairs etc.

There are other aspects, which influence the students in developing positive/negative attitude towards mathematics. In this case, some psychological barriers, predicaments, habits and inhibitions are reflected in the attitudes of some students. Let us observe these aspects.

Items relating to psychological barriers of students

- I take mathematics lightly (A-27%)
- I am afraid of participating in mathematical competitions (A-26%)

- I solve only the easy problems and leave the difficult ones (A-25%)
- I dislike funny problems (A-23%)
- I do not worry about the mathematical problems which I cannot solve (A-21%)
- I do not bother about the progress of my fellow students in mathematics (A-18%)
- I do not discuss with my fellow students the problems, which I fail to solve (A-17%)
- I have no interest in mathematics (A-15%)
- I dislike mathematics (A-14%)

These perceptions reveal that about 14 per cent to 27 per cent of students possess negative attitude towards mathematics due to psychological characteristics. These characteristics need not be related to mathematics alone. In fact these psychological problems which are inherent in the children influence their study. Therefore, educational counselling must be provided to the students for their personality development with the help of expert counsellors. Even in the pre-service training courses these are to be discussed with due priority. Of course, the purpose of including educational psychology, sociology and philosophy in the B.Ed course is to prepare not only a good teacher but also a good counsellor. But, these are taught only for the sake of examinations without any relation to classroom situation in practical sense.

In foreign countries counselling is as important as the core subjects. Guidance services are parallel to educational services. In fact a special paper on guidance and counselling at B.Ed level, was introduced with this object only. Alas! No teacher fulfils this responsibility as a counsellor. Therefore, to bring changes in the system, first of all, the authorities should be provided with proper orientation regarding the role of the teacher in the classroom situation.

Teacher is the first person who is responsible for the development of positive/negative attitude in the students. The following items relate to the positive attitude of students towards their teachers in teaching mathematics.

Favourable items relating to the mathematics teachers

- Our mathematics teacher evinces special interest to make us understand the lesson well (A-76%, D-19%)
- Our mathematics teacher draws figures neatly on the board (A-75%, D-21%)
- Our mathematics teacher clarifies our doubts without any anger (A-75%, D-19%)

These results clearly indicate that about 75 per cent of the students are happy whereas about 20 per cent of the students are unhappy with their mathematics teachers.

Let us see the items relating to negative attitude of students towards mathematics teacher.

Unfavourable items relating to mathematics teacher

- Our teacher does not teach the problems again and again which are not understood by us (A-27%)
- Our mathematics teacher never corrects the homework (A-26%)
- Our mathematics teacher does not question us while teaching to know whether we understand the lesson or not (A-23%)
- Our mathematics teacher does not use the teaching aids to make the students understand the lesson easily (A-22%)
- Our mathematics teacher teaches well some chapters only (A-22%)
- I do not like our mathematics teacher (A-17%)
- Our mathematics teacher does not wish to teach us mathematics properly (A-14%)

From these results it is clear that about 14 per cent to 27 per cent of students possess negative attitude towards their mathematics teachers. These items mostly reflect the weaknesses/deficiencies of mathematics teachers. As these deficiencies are perceived by their students, the teachers must be careful in dealing with them in accordance with their needs and interests. As we find heterogeneous groups in the classroom, the classroom teaching must be revamped. The teacher should pay special attention to the backward students in mathematics, use the teaching aids adequately for meaningful learning of the subject, adopt formative evaluation during the teaching-learning process and finally check whether the students are able to do home work thoroughly or not. No doubt, many teachers teach some chapters in mathematics well but a good teacher should be able to teach all the chapters effectively to the students.

From the field observation it is noticed that chapters like geometry, motion geometry, analytical geometry etc. are not covered fully to the students. Even the results obtained in the earlier section reveal the same. Therefore, the teachers must be trained properly to update their knowledge and skills in dealing with the newly introduced topics.

After all it is the mathematics teacher who has to make the subject meaningful, interesting and enjoyable and easy subject to the students. Therefore, the pre-service and in-service programmes should emphasise more on the development of professional interest in the teachers, which is the basic requirement and bounden duty of every teacher to do justice to their students.

However, one thing must be taken into confidence here. Why only around 20 per cent of the students see negative characteristics in their teachers? It is because basically they possess negative attitude towards the subject. Such students search for negative elements in every aspect. Therefore, students must be guided properly to appreciate the good qualities in their teachers and to ignore the bad qualities.

Analysis of Attitudes of Teachers Towards Mathematics

Out of 43 items included in the final form of attitude scale meant for teachers to study the teachers' attitude towards teaching mathematics, all the items exhibited a significant trend in the response pattern as the Chi-square values obtained are statistically significant at 0.01 level of probability for 4 df. Hence it can be concluded that the null hypothesis 'The teachers in general do not possess positive attitudes towards teaching mathematics' is accepted. It would be rather interesting to study the responses of teachers against each item to identify the specific aspects of teaching mathematics, which might have created positive/negative attitudes in the teachers in teaching mathematics.

The responses of the teachers on each item and the chi-square values obtained for the Teachers' Attitude Scale are presented in the Table 5.56.

Table 5.56: Table showing the response pattern of attitudes of teachers towards mathematics education

ITEM & S.No.	*SA*	*A*	*N*	*D*	*SD*	χ^2 *Value*	*Sig.@* 0.01
1.	13	62	25	50	11	64.43	**
2.	88	57	10	2	4	184.12	**
3.	67	75	15	3	1	160.40	**
4.	22	47	32	47	13	28.29	**
5.	32	61	28	36	4	51.45	**
6.	30	67	32	25	7	59.09	**
7.	61	72	15	7	6	125.18	**
8.	97	40	12	10	2	188.60	**
9.	7	48	33	53	20	45.55	**
10.	21	42	34	49	15	24.93	**
11.	42	66	17	31	5	68.66	**
12.	71	64	24	2	0	140.77	**
13.	68	55	15	17	6	93.63	**
14.	8	41	35	49	28	30.15	**
15.	15	69	34	32	11	65.30	**
16.	4	11	11	51	84	146.92	**
17.	14	81	20	36	10	104.62	**
18.	33	57	28	27	16	28.66	**
19.	24	57	38	32	10	37.54	**
20.	6	28	15	72	40	82.14	**
21.	41	54	26	26	14	29.84	**
22.	67	58	17	16	3	100.09	**

(Contd...)

ITEM & S.No.	SA	A	N	D	SD	χ^2 Value	Sig.@ 0.01
23.	51	79	25	6	0	134.12	**
24.	16	68	38	31	8	67.23	**
25.	27	69	41	21	3	75.68	**
26.	20	74	37	26	4	85.49	**
27.	18	53	36	45	9	41.95	**
28.	37	69	30	20	5	70.52	**
29.	39	56	26	33	7	39.96	**
30.	76	53	13	15	4	118.35	**
31.	57	68	16	13	7	98.22	**
32.	26	59	36	29	11	38.22	**
33.	30	64	30	30	7	51.58	**
34.	25	68	36	29	3	68.66	**
35.	27	47	41	35	11	24.25	**
36.	21	59	32	42	7	48.91	**
37.	34	44	15	51	17	31.76	**
38.	20	43	38	40	20	15.80	**
39.	34	78	20	27	2	99.03	**
40.	15	45	21	59	21	44.37	**
41.	32	52	32	35	10	27.73	**
22.	35	64	26	30	6	54.31	**
43.	47	65	30	15	4	74.25	**

For the purpose of discussion, the responses under 'strongly agree' and 'agree' are treated as favourable and 'strongly disagree' and 'disagree' are treated as unfavourable towards the item. Before analysing the items, to be more specific/clear, these items are categorised under five major heads namely, favourable and unfavourable items relating to the teacher, favourable and unfavourable items relating to the textbook, and the items relating to the training and authorities. The set of items relating to each category is discussed in detail in the following pages.

By this kind of analysis it could be possible to list out those aspects which are to be taken care of by the teacher educators, educational administrators, textbook writers, curriculum makers and policy makers to plug out the negative predicaments in teachers and create greater enthusiasm to teach mathematics effectively.

Favourable Statements Relating to the Mathematics Teacher

- Without practice it is difficult to do mathematics without committing mistakes. (A- 90%, D-4%)
- A special teacher is essential for teaching mathematics at the primary level itself. (A- 85%, 7%)
- In the pre-service and in-service training programmes emphasis should be laid on the latest techniques, methods, and experiments in teaching.(A84%,D-1%)
- The teachers' Handbook is very much essential for effective teaching of mathematics. (A-83%, D-8%)
- The teacher himself should prepare the teaching aids suitably for teaching in the laboratory method. (A-58%, D-19%)
- Teaching of Geometry helps a lot to inculcate interest in the students towards mathematics. (A-52%, D-27%)

The statements reveal that about 52 per cent to 90 per cent of the mathematics teachers possess positive attitude towards mathematics as they agreed or strongly agreed with the statements.

Let us see the statements, which reflect the negative aspects of teaching mathematics.

Unfavourable Statements Relating to Mathematics Teacher

- My students are not able to do mathematics properly since they do not have understanding in fundamental concepts. (A-88%)
- Owing to the overcrowded classes, correcting the homework is another major problem for the mathematics teacher (A-80%)
- The syllabus cannot be completed if the teacher adopts the methods that are taught during the training programme (A-78%)

- It is sad that the standards of mathematics in schools are increased far above the level of students' ability to face the competition in the higher classes (A-76%)
- There is no proper recognition and encouragement for teachers who are adopting new techniques and methods in teaching mathematics (A-69%)
- The main cause for students' phobia in mathematics is Geometry only. (A- 67%)
- The students fail to understand the problems given in the textbook unless every problem is worked out on the board (A-67%)
- Analysing a problem is herculean task for the students while solving problems (A-59%)
- In view of over crowded class rooms I am unable to teach mathematics the way it ought to be taught (A-59%)
- Mathematics teacher shoulders burden rather than responsibility (A-56%)
- The present contents in the mathematics textbook fail to create interest in the students (A-52%)
- Mathematics is a difficult subject for students. (A-47%)
- The prime cause for students getting poor marks in mathematics is the teacher's teaching only (A-21%)
- It is absurd to say that thinking capacity in the student can be developed through teaching of mathematics (A-9%)

The results reveal that about 9 per cent to 88 per cent of the teachers possess negative attitude towards mathematics due to over crowded class rooms, heavy work load, standard of mathematics syllabus, below average students, and difficulty in geometry etc.

The same results are obtained from the difficulty analysis of mathematics syllabus in content, teaching-and learning in the previous sections. Geometry is commonly expressed as a difficult subject in all the three classes. Chapters like Mensuration, Motion Geometry, Linear Programming, Polynomials and Trigonometry etc. are considered the most difficult chapters by the teachers in all the three aspects namely content, teaching and learning. Low I.Q. of students, over-crowded classes, teachers' obsession with the completion of the syllabus with in the stipulated time, lack of teachers' personal attention to students all these might be the influencing factors on the teachers to develop negative attitude towards the subject, which ultimately has an adverse impact on the performance of the students. This situation can be changed by adopting the following steps.

Study of mathematics warrants practising the methods of problem solving to enable the child to understand the problem and analyse to establish the relationship between the data. For this, basically the students must be thorough with the essential basic knowledge. To meet this, student must be taught only the concepts continuously for two to three months without interruption at the beginning of the academic year. In order to make teaching-learning of mathematics more meaningful and interesting, the students must be involved in different activities such as mathematical puzzles, games, quiz competitions etc. Textbooks are to be revised or re-written to suit the needs stated above. The authorities should focus their attention on achieving minimum levels of learning in mathematics.

Favourable Items Relating to Mathematics Text Book

- Importance should be given to the comprehensive understanding of the contents by reducing the formulas and theorems in the textbook (A-76%)
- The present mathematics textbook is suitable to prepare the student to face the future competition (A-69%)
- There should be two parts in mathematics textbook — essential components and optional components (A-48%)

These statements reveal that about 48 per cent to 76 per cent of the teachers possess the positive attitude towards mathematics textbook. Now let us examine the items, which reflect the negative attitude towards the mathematics textbook.

Unfavourable Items Relating to Mathematics Text Book

- In the mathematics textbook importance is given more to the number of problems rather than to the concept formation (A-66%)

- The incomplete problems given in the textbook are posing a big problem to both students and teachers (A-60%)
- Printer's devils in the answers create difficulties for the teachers and the taught (A-58%)
- The examples given in the textbook are not sufficient to teach the problems that are given in the exercises (A-43%)
- The reasons for students' fear towards education is the present mathematics text book (A-37%)

From these statements it is clear that about 37 per cent to 66 per cent of the teachers possess negative attitude towards mathematics textbook. This may be partly true because of the enhanced curriculum and wrongly presented textbooks in mathematics.

During the British period when NCERT was not established the SSLC students could speak good English with a small text book in English whereas today with so much of syllabus and a large number of text books, even the post graduate students are not able to speak English correctly. The same is the case with mathematics. There was a time when, with limited syllabus, with small and simple textbooks, our mathematics teachers could help the students solve their real life's problems orally whereas today with heavy syllabus and voluminous textbooks, the students are unable to solve even simple problems. They depend on blind principles and written calculations mechanically. Therefore, it is not the size of the text which develops problem solving skills in the students but it is the way the contents are presented in that enables them to think effectively.

New concepts are to be included in the textbook to keep pace with the demands of the present future needs of the society. But, most of the teachers may not be aware of these concepts in mathematics. Therefore, before bringing changes in the curriculum, the teachers must be provided with orientation in these areas to equip them to deal with the subject effectively.

Amazingly, during the field visits of the investigator some remarkable truths surfaced concerning some chapters in mathematics textbook. The Motion Geometry included in the IX class syllabus was not touched upon by any one of the teachers. The computing included in the IX and the X class syllabi was not understood even by the teachers. Geometry was partially neglected by the teachers due to difficulty in teaching. Then what is the fun of introducing these chapters in the secondary school syllabus?

No doubt, the school curriculum in mathematics has been constructed to suit the objectives of teaching the subject at the school level. The evaluation should test whether the objectives of teaching the subject are achieved or not. But, the things stand on a different footing today. They test only the knowledge and understanding acquired by the student in mathematics. Therefore, teachers put the mechanical drilling in practice to make the students pass the examination. This has resulted in students getting by heart fragmental collection of dry facts. This state of affairs should go giving place to a healthy and purposeful change.

There are other aspects also which influence the teachers to develop positive/negative attitude towards mathematics. The following are statements concerning the training and the authorities in mathematics education.

Unfavourable Items Relating to the Training and the Authorities

- More time should be devoted to the demonstration of teaching skills rather than to theoretical lectures, in the pre-service training programmes (A-81%)
- The teachers are not informed in advance about the in-service training programmes (A-61%)
- In the teacher training courses innovative methods are not adopted in lieu of the general methods (A-60%)
- In view of paramount pressure from the higher authorities that every student should pass the examination, I am unable to teach mathematics as it should be taught (A-59%)
- Our authorities think about their importance and recognition and are least bothered about our problems (A-58%)
- The tenure of in-service training programme is not according to the objective of conducting it (A-58%)

- It is unfair that experienced and efficient teachers of mathematics are not involved as resource persons in the in-service training programmes (A-53%)
- In-service training classes are not conducted to the teachers on convenient days (A-52%)
- In-service training programmes are not arranged in centres having all of facilities (A-50%)
- Equal opportunities are not made available by the authorities to all the teachers to participate in the in-service training programmes (A-50%)
- It is heart-rending that the teachers ought to travel for 2 to 3 hours for attending the in-service training programmes (A-46%)
- The present in-service programmes are not catering to the needs of teachers (A-44%)
- It is of no use if the resource persons for the training programme are the subject experts from the university (A37%)
- The in-service training provided at present is not very much useful to us (A-34%)
- The experts imparting in-service training are not aware of the problems at the school level (A-30%)

From these observations it is clear that about 30 per cent to 81 per cent of the teachers are unhappy and expressed their bitterness with the authorities regarding the training programmes conducted at pre-service and in-service levels. This may be true because, most of the training programmes conducted by the D.E.O's and Dy.E.O's to the mathematics teachers lay stress only on achieving cent per cent results in X the class examinations as it is feared that there will be more number of failures in mathematics only. The authorities should plug out the loopholes in the system instead of pressurising the teachers to attain the targeted results. Instead of searching for the ways and means of getting cent per cent results, it will be useful if the authorities enquire into the causes for more number of failures in mathematics and evolve necessary remedial steps to improve the performance of students in the subject. As discussed earlier, students fail to understand certain topics as they are above their level. If the teachers are trained properly both in content and methodology to deal with these topics effectively in the classroom, this problem can be solved to some extent. In order to reap the fruits of the training programmes eminent and experienced teacher educators in their respective areas should be invited and involved as they can handle both the content and methodology parts efficiently and effectively.

DESCRIPTIVE AND DIFFERENTIAL ANALYSIS OF PROBLEM INTENSITY SCORES AND ATTITUDE SCORES AND THE INFLUENCE OF PERSONAL AND DEMOGRAPHIC VARIABLES ON DEPENDENT VARIABLES

As the problem check list-cum-problem intensity scales and attitude scales were able to provide individual scores of interval scaling level, it is proposed to study the nature of the distribution of scores with the help of descriptive statistics and to study the influence of personal and demographic variables included in the study on their problem perception and attitude towards mathematics. This section is presented under four different sub headings namely: (i) The description of the distribution of problem intensity scores of students and the influence of personal and demographic variables on these scores; (ii) The description of the distribution of problem intensity scores of teachers and the influence of personal and demographic variables on these scores; (iii) The description of the distribution of attitude scores of students and the influence of personal and demographic variables on these scores; (iv) The description of the distribution of attitude scores of teachers and the influence of personal and demographic variables on these scores.

Description of the Distribution of Problem Intensity Scores of Students

The problem intensity scores obtained through the administration of the problem check list-cum-rating scale to the students have been arranged in a systematic manner by grouping them into classes and tabulating them into frequency distribution. It may be noted that it includes the aspects relating to problems faced while learning mathematics. The analysis is carried out to know the kind of average, range and scatteredness. The different descriptive statistics such as mean, median, mode, range, quartile deviation, standard deviation, skewness and kurtosis are calculated to understand the nature of distribution. The frequency distribution and the values of descriptive statistics are set out in Table 5.57.

Table 5.57: Table showing the description of the distribution of problem intensity scores of students

Class Interval	*Frequency*	*Smoothed Frequency*	*Cumulative Frequency*
0-19	250	147.33	250
20-39	192	178.00	442
40-59	92	114.67	534
60-79	60	58.67	594
80-99	24	32.00	618
100-119	12	13.00	630
120-139	3	7.33	633
140-159	7	4.67	640
160-179	4	3.67	644

Mean	=	33.186	Range	=	178	Skewness	=	0.813
Median	=	27.00	Q.D.	=	17.767	Kurtosis	=	12.676
Mode	=	10.628	S.D.	=	30.215			

The mean problem score obtained by the sample is 33.186, which means the general intensity level of the problems of the students is far less than the average point (67×2=134) on the scale. It is even clear from the frequency distribution that there are only 11 subjects whose attitude scores are more than the mean score of the scale (134) and 630 subjects scored less than the average score of the scale. Of course, 3 subjects fall under the class interval 120-139, where the average point of the scale lies. The values of median and mode are 27.0 and 10.628 respectively which indicate that the general intensity level of problems faced by the students in learning mathematics is at a level lower than the average score. As the measures of central tendency are in the descending order, the value of mean is more than median, and it is also more than mode i.e., mode is the lowest, thus the distribution is said to be positively skewed. Of course, it is evident from the calculated value of skewness (0.813). The value of kurtosis 12.676 discloses that the distribution is platy kurtic.

The range of the distribution of problem scores is 178 (the highest score = 178 and the lowest score = 0). The quartile deviation and standard deviation are 17.767 and 30.215 respectively. These measures of dispersion reveal that the spread in the distribution is a bit away from the normal. The relationship between S.D and Q.D as it exists in the normal probability curve is 2/3. S.D=Q.D i.e., 2/3 (30.215)=20.15, it also reveals that the distribution is away from normality. However, it can be said that the distribution belongs to the family of normal curves. The graphical representation of the distribution of problem scores also indicate that the distribution follows normality with slight divergences *(see figure 5.1 on next page)*.

As the distribution of the problem intensity scores of students follows normality with marginal exceptions, it is feasible to apply all the parametric statistics in the analysis of the data.

The Influence of Personal and Demographic Variables on Problem Intensity Scores of Students

As indicated earlier, there are eight independent variables related to students to study the variations among different sub groups in the problem intensity scores and to study the significance of these differences, the 't' and 'F' ratios are calculated and presented in table-5.58 *(see on page 191)* along with mean and standard deviations.

Out of eight variables, four viz. Class, Age, Literacy Index and Father's Occupation could not significantly influence the problem intensity scores of different sub groups based on the respective variables. The remaining four variables are Sex, Locality, Management and Annual Income of the Family.

The mean problem intensity score of girl students' (38.98) is far greater than that of boys' (32.89). Therefore, it can be concluded that the girl students are more sensitive in perceiving the problems than the boy students and their intensity is also more than that of the boys. This may be because the boy students are in general extraverts and have more opportunities to interact with peer groups outside the classroom and further the parental care on the education

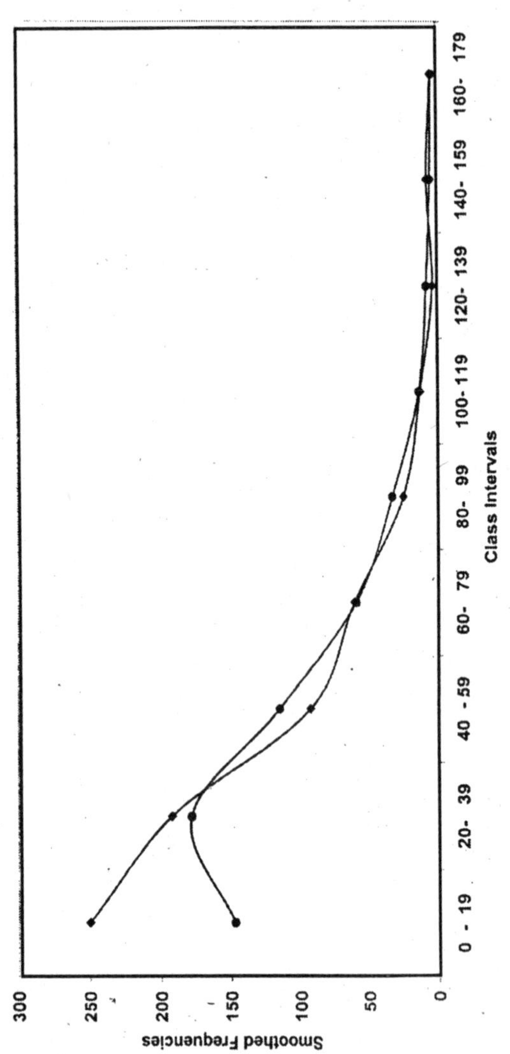

Fig. 5.1: Frequency and Smoothed Frequency Curves of Problem Intensity Scores of Students

Table 5.58: Table showing the mean and standard deviations of problem intensity scores of students and the results of t/F ratios of different sub groups

S. No.	*Variable*	*Groups*	*N*	*M*	*S.D*	*'t'/F value*
1.	CLASS	VIII	227	36.26	29.50	0.763@
		IX	217	32.79	27.77	
		X	200	35.18	33.16	
2.	SEX	BOYS	447	32.89	27.16	2.371*
		GIRLS	197	38.98	35.67	
3.	AGE	≤ 13 years	211	35.59	30.18	0.345@
		=14 years	220	35.30	30.93	
		≥ 15 years	213	33.36	29.31	
4.	LOCALITY	Urban	291	33.81	32.00	8.623**
		Semi- urban	174	28.97	20.77	t_{12}: 1.976*
		Rural	179	41.92	33.24	t_{13}: 2.61** t_{23}: 4.4**

(Contd...)

S. No.	*Variable*	*Groups*	*N*	*M*	*S.D*	*'t'/F value*
5.	MANAGEMENT	Government	183	30.51	22.04	3.354*
		Zilla parishad	231	36.77	31.43	t_{12}: 2.376* t_{13} : 0.243@
		Municipal	74	29.77	22.28	t_{14}: 2.496*
		Private	156	39.11	37.89	t_{23} : 2.112* t_{24} : 0.637@ t_{34} : 2.342*
6.	FATHERS OCCUPATION	Daily wages	123	30.93	25.21	1.2698@
		Agriculture / Business	399	35.87	30.31	
		Secured Job	122	34.98	33.76	
7.	FAMILY LITERACY INDEX	≤ 4.9	214	34.03	24.95	0.258@
		Between 4.9 to 9.9	288	35.70	31.60	
		10 & above	142	33.92	34.09	

(Contd...)

S. No.	Variable	Groups	N	M	S.D	't'/F value
8.	FAMILY ANNUAL INCOME	Upto 10000	321	32.35	25.80	3.701* t_{12}: 2.600** t_{13}: 0.372 t_{23} : 1,604@
		10000 to 50000	189	39.69	33.38	
		50000 and above	134	33.57	34.06	

Note: ** - Significant at 0.01 level.

* - Significant at 0.05 level.

@ - Not significant.

(These symbols are followed throughout.)

t_{12}: t-value between the first and second groups

t_{13}: t-value between the first and third groups

t_{14}: t-value between the first and forth groups

t_{23}: t-value between the second and third groups

t_{24}: t-value between the second and forth groups

t_{34}: t-value between the third and forth groups

of boys is relatively more and thereby the doubts of the girls may not be properly attended to. Therefore, sex is a significant factor in influencing the problem intensity scores of students in learning mathematics.

On the basis of locality, there are three groups' viz., the Urban, the Semi Urban and the Rural. The mean problem intensity score of the Rural children (41.92) is far greater than those of the Urban (33.81) and the Semi-Urban students (28.97) respectively. The calculated 'F' ratio indicates that the mean differences are significant at 0.01 level of probability for 2, 641 degrees of freedom. The 't' values between any two groups at a time also indicate that there exists significant difference in the mean problem intensity scores. Therefore, locality is a significant factor in influencing the problems of students in learning mathematics.

There are four types of schools from the point of view of their management and the problems faced by the students in these institutions exhibited significant differences. The 'F' ratio calculated was significant at 0.05 level of probability for 3 and 640 degrees of freedom. The students studying in the schools under the management of municipalities and governments experienced less intensity of problems than those studying in the schools of Zilla Parishads and Private management. Even the 't' values between any two groups except Government and municipal, Z.P. and Private schools indicate that there exists significant difference in the mean problem intensity scores. Therefore, management is a significant factor in influencing the problems of students in learning mathematics.

The annual income of the family is divided into three groups viz., low income group (upto Rs.10,000), middle income group (10,000 to 50,000) and high income group (50,000 and above). The mean problem intensity score of the middle income group (39.69) is far greater than that of the low (32.35) and the high (33.57) income groups. The calculated 'F' ratio indicates that the mean differences are significant at 0.05 level of probability for 2,641 degrees of freedom. The 't' values between the low and the middle income groups also indicates that there exists significant difference in the mean problem intensity scores of students whereas no significant difference is observed between the middle and the high income groups, and the low and high the income groups. Thus it can be concluded that annual income of the family is a significant factor in influencing the intensity of the problems faced by students in learning mathematics. This may be due to the fact that the students from high income groups will have more opportunities to refer to more number of books in mathematics, to go to tuitions and to study in better schools and therefore the intensity of problems will be less.

Thus, the null hypothesis stating that 'the personal and demographic variables of pupils would not significantly influence the intensity of problems faced by them in learning mathematics' is accepted in the case of four variables Class, Age, Father Occupation and Literacy Index whereas it is rejected in the case of the remaining four variables namely Sex, Locality, Management and Annual Income of the Family.

Description of the Distribution of Problem Intensity Scores of Teachers

The problem intensity scores obtained through the administration of the problem check list-cum-rating scale to the teachers have been arranged in a systematic manner by grouping them into classes and tabulating them into frequency distribution. It may be noted that the problem check list-cum-rating scale of teachers includes aspects relating to problems of teaching mathematics. The analysis is carried out to know the kind of average, range and scatteredness. The different descriptive statistics such as mean, median, mode, range, quartile deviation, standard deviation, skewness and kurtosis are calculated to understand the nature of distribution. The frequency distribution and the values of descriptive statistics are set out in Table 5.59. *(see on page 196)*

The mean problem intensity score obtained by the sample is 44.409 which means the general level of problem intensity of teachers in teaching mathematics is much less than the average point (46×2=92) on the scale. The values of median and mode 40.714 and 33.928 respectively also indicate the same. It is clear even from the distribution table that there are only two candidates who scored more than the average intensity score (92) and 149 teachers scored below the average intensity score and of course there are ten teachers who fall under the class interval 80-100 where the average score lies. The measures of central tendency indicates that the distribution is said to be positively skewed as mean, median and mode values in the descending order. It is evident from the calculated value of skewness i.e. 0.517. The kurtosis value obtained as 0.271 discloses that the distribution is platy kurtic.

Table 5.59: Table showing the description of the distribution of problem intensity scores of teachers

Class Interval	*Frequency*	*Smoothed Frequency*	*Cumulative Frequency*
0-20	20	26.33	20
20-40	59	40.33	79
40-60	42	43.00	121
60-80	28	26.67	149
80-100	10	13.33	159
100-120	2	4.00	161

Mean	= 44.409	Range	= 119	Skewness	= 0.517
Median	= 40.714	Q.D.	= 16.509	Kurtosis	= 0.271
Mode	= 33.928	S.D.	= 21.463		

The range of the distribution of problem scores is 119 (the highest score = 119 and the lowest score = 0). The quartile deviation and standard deviation are 16.509 and 21.463 respectively. These measures of dispersion reveal that the spread in the distribution is a bit away from the normal. The relationship between S.D and Q.D as it exists in the normal probability curve as 2/3. S.D=Q.D i.e., 2/3 (21.463)=14.31, is not observed in the distribution and it also reveals that the distribution is slightly away from normality. However, it can be said that the distribution belongs to the family of normal curves. The graphical representation of the distribution of problem scores also indicate that the distribution follows normality with slight divergences (*see fig. 5.2 on page 197*).

As the distribution of problem intensity scores of students follows normality with marginal exceptions, it is feasible to apply all the parametric statistics in the analysis of data obtained.

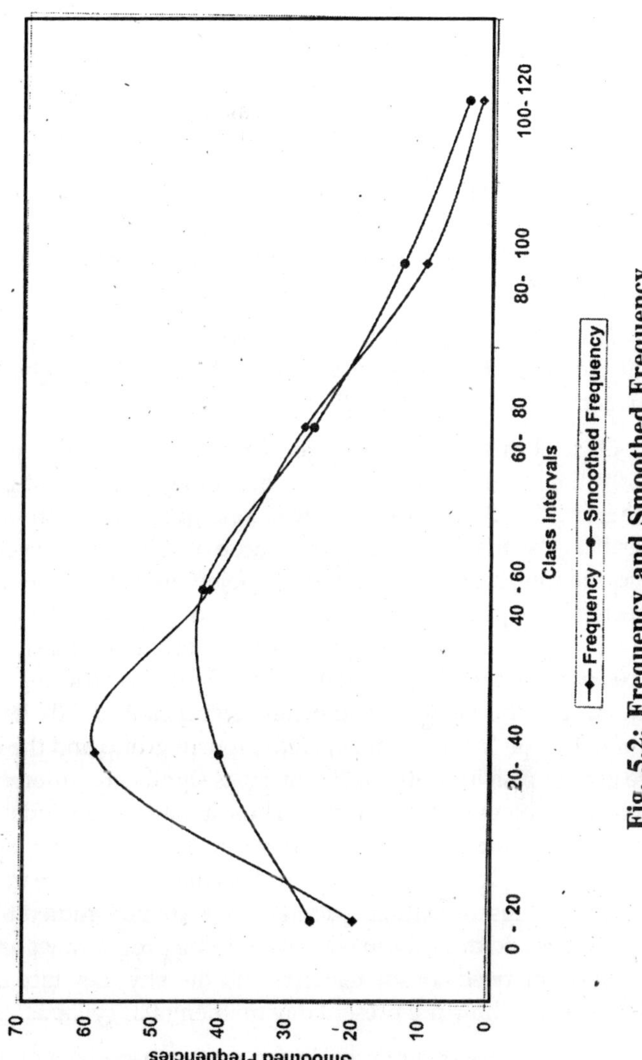

Fig. 5.2: Frequency and Smoothed Frequency Curves of Problem Intensity Scores of Teachers

The influence of personal and demographic variables on problem intensity scores of teachers

As indicated earlier, there are seven independent variables for teachers to study the variations among different sub groups in the problem intensity scores and to study the significance of these differences the 't' and 'F' ratios are calculated and presented in Table 5.60. along with means and standard deviations.

Out of seven variables, five variables viz., Sex, General Qualification, Professional Qualification, and Locality could not significantly influence the problem intensity scores of different subgroups based on the respective variables.

The remaining two variables, which could significantly influence the problem intensity scores are Age of the teachers and Management of the school.

On the basis of Age, the subjects are divided into four groups namely, the subjects from 20 to 29 years of age as the first group, those from 30 to 39 years age as the second group, those from 40 to 49 years age as the third group, and those of 50 and above years of age as the fourth group. The mean problem intensity score of the subjects of the age group of 50 years and above (63.81) is far greater than those of other three groups of teachers. From the table it can be noticed that the calculated 'F' value is 4.865 for 3 and 640 degrees of freedom and the value is statistically significant at 0.01 level of probability. The 't' values between the fourth group and the other three groups also indicate that there exists significant difference in the mean problem intensity scores. Thus, it may be concluded that the age of the teachers is a significant factor in influencing the intensity of problems faced by them. This may be because most of topics in the present mathematics textbook are not studied by the aged persons and even the in- service training programmes are not catering to the needs of the teachers and thereby they face many problems in teaching the present day mathematics syllabus.

As in the case of students, based on the management of the institutions, we may divide schools into four types and the problems faced by the teachers working there exhibited significant differences.

Table 5.60: Table showing the means and standard deviations of problem intensity scores of teachers and the results of 't'/'F' ratios of different groups

S. NO	VARIABLE	GROUPS	N	MEAN	SD	't'/'F' ratio
1.	GENDER	Male	131	45.46	22.912	0.583 @
		Female	30	42.77	22.399	
2.	AGE (in years)	20 to 29	30	40.53	23.331	4.865**
		30 to 39	77	41.97	19.740	t_{12}: 0.299@
		40 to 49	38	46.55	21.172	t_{13}: 1.100@
		50 and above	16	63.81	30.472	t_{14}: 2.67** t_{23}: 1.115@ t_{24}: 2.749** t_{34}: 2.066*
3.	GENERAL QUALIFICATION	Graduate	128	44.93	22.486	0.001@
		Postgraduate	30	45.10	24.855	
		Doctoral	3	44.67	20.551	
4.	PROFESSIONAL QUALIFICATION	Nil	5	31.80	17.167	1.849@
		B.Ed.	127	46.59	23.621	
		M.Ed.	29	40.07	18.510	

(Contd...)

S. NO.	VARIABLE	GROUPS	N	MEAN	SD	't'/'F' ratio
5.	EXPERINCE (in years)	Up to 9	96	43.38	22.292	0.806@
		10 to 19	46	45.46	20.843	
		20 to 29	17	52.65	30.522	
		30 and above	2	44.00	7.071	
6.	LOCALITY	Urban	63	40.83	22.711	1.944@
		Semi-Urban	42	45.86	23.409	
		Rural	56	48.93	21.964	
7.	MANAGEMENT	Government	23	40.43	20.079	6.013**
		Zilla parishad	70	47.89	22.702	$t_{12:}$ 1.495@
		Municipal	16	62.19	25.087	$t_{13:}$ 2.886**
		Private	52	37.71	20.074	$t_{14:}$ 0.541@
						$t_{23:}$ 2.093*
						$t_{24:}$ 2.624**
						$t_{34:}$ 3.568**

The 'F' ratio calculated was significant at 0.01 level of probability for3 and 640 degrees of freedom. Teachers working in schools under the management of municipal schools were experiencing high intensity of problems whereas private school teachers were facing less intensity of problems. The 't' values between government and municipal, zilla parishad and private, municipal and private, and lastly zilla parishad and municipal schools also indicated that there exists significant difference in the mean problem intensity scores. Thus it can be concluded that management of the school is a significant factor in influencing the intensity of problems faced by teachers in teaching mathematics. This may be because most of the students studying in municipal schools are very poor and probably they are sent to schools by their parents mainly for food and incentives. Most of them are backward in mathematics. Hence, the teachers teaching mathematics in these schools will have more difficult problems than the private school teachers, where the situation is reverse.

Thus, the null hypothesis stating that 'the personal and demographic variables of teachers would not significantly influence the intensity of problems faced by them in teaching mathematics' is accepted in the case of five variables Gender, General Qualification, Professional qualification, Experience and Locality and it is rejected in the case of the remaining two variables namely Age and Management.

Description of the Distribution of Attitude Scores of Students

The scores obtained through the administration of the attitude scale to the students have been arranged in a systematic manner by grouping them into classes and tabulating them into frequency distribution. It may be noted that the attitude scale of students includes different aspects relating to the attitudes of students in learning mathematics. The analysis is carried out to know the kind of average, range and scatteredness. The different descriptive statistics such as mean, median, mode, range, quartile deviation, standard deviation, skewness and kurtosis are calculated to understand the nature of distribution. The frequency distribution and the values of descriptive statistics are set out in Table 5.61.

Table 5.61: Table showing the description of the distribution of attitude scores of students

Class Interval	*Frequency*	*Smoothed Frequency*	*Cumulative Frequency*
40-59	8	7.67	8
60-79	15	17.33	23
80-99	29	39.33	52
100-119	74	63.67	126
120-139	88	107.33	214
140-159	160	154.33	374
160-179	215	143.33	589
180-199	55	90.00	644

Mean = 146.956	Range = 146	Skewness = -0.642
Median = 153.50	Q.D. = 21.093	Kurtosis = 0.289
Mode = 165.116	S.D. = 30.575	

The mean score obtained by the sample is 146.956 which means the general level of attitude in students in learning mathematics is far greater than the average point (42×3=126) on the scale. The values of median and mode 153.5 and 165.116 respectively have confirmed that the general level of attitude towards learning mathematics in the students is much greater. It is clear even from the distribution table that there are 430 candidates who have scored more than the average attitude score (126) and 126 subjects have scored below the average attitude score and of course there are 88 students who fall under the class interval 120 -139 where the mean attitude score lies. As the measures of central tendency are in the ascending order, mean is less than median and the median is less than mode, the distribution is said to be negatively skewed. It is evident from the calculated value of skewness i.e. -0.642. The kurtosis value obtained as 0.289 discloses that the distribution is slightly platy kurtic.

The range of the distribution of scores is 146 (the highest score = 190 and the lowest score= 44). The quartile deviation and standard deviation are 21.093 and 30.575 respectively. These measures of dispersion reveal that the spread in the distribution is normal. The relationship between S.D and Q.D as it exists in the normal probability curve as 2/3. S.D=Q.D i.e., 2/3 (30.575) =20.383, is observed in the distribution, with a negligible difference of 0.709. So it can be said that the distribution belongs to the family of normal curves. The graphical representation of the distribution of attitude scores also indicate that the distribution follows normality with slight exceptions (*see fig. 5.3 on next page*).

As the distribution of the attitude scores of students follows normality with marginal exceptions, it is feasible to apply all the parametric statistics in the analysis of data obtained.

The Influence of Personal and Demographic Variables on Attitude Scores of Students

As indicated earlier, there are eight independent variables related to students to study the variations of different sub groups in the attitude scores and to study the significance of these differences the 't' and 'F' ratios are calculated and presented in the Table 5.62 along with means and standard deviations.

From the above table it can be seen that all the personal and demographic variables included in the study would influence the attitude of students towards mathematics education significantly except the two variables viz., Age and Annual income of the family.

The six variables, which could influence the attitudes of students towards mathematics education significantly, are Class, Sex, Locality, Management, Fathers' Occupation and Family literacy index.

An observation of the table reveals that on the basis of the class, there are three groups viz., VIII, IX, and X classes and the mean attitude score of the VIII class students (149.32) is greater than that of the X class students (148.92) and it is far greater than that of the IX class students (142.26). The calculated 'F' ratio indicates that the mean differences are significant at 0.05 level of probability for 2 and 641 degrees of freedom. The 't' values between any two groups at a time indicate that there exists significant difference in the mean attitude scores of students. Thus, it can be concluded that the class is a significant factor in influencing the attitudes of students.

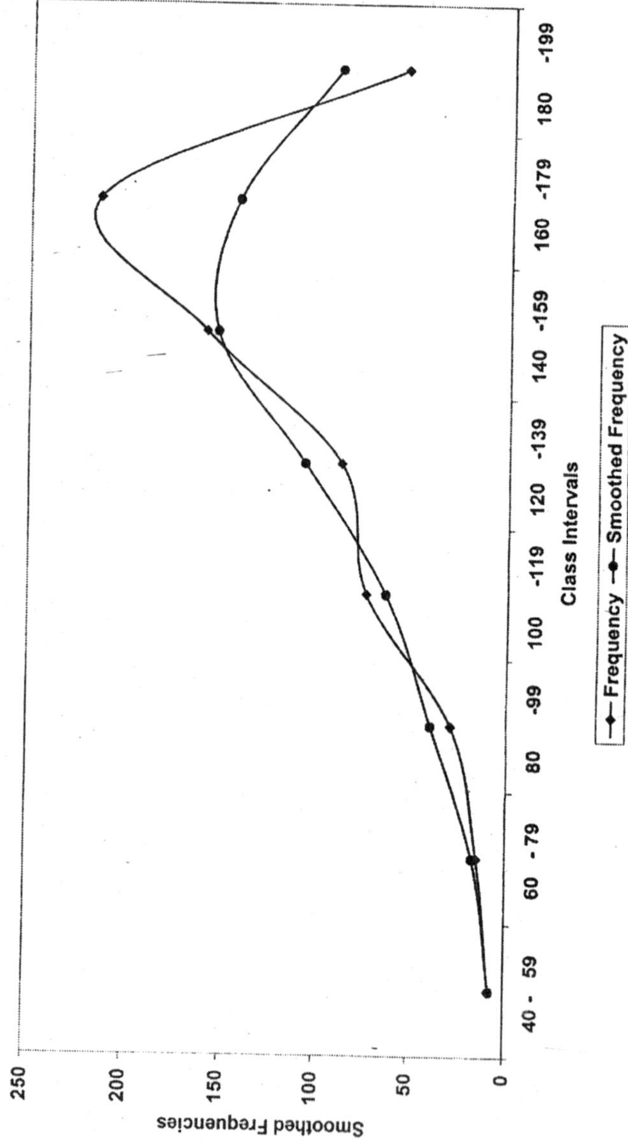

Fig. 5.3: Frequency and Smoothed Frequency Curves of Attitude Scores of Students

Table 5.62: Table showing the means and standard deviations of attitude scores of students and the results of 't'/'F' ratios of different groups

S. No.	*Variable*	*Groups*	*N*	*M*	*S.D*	*'t'/F value*
1.	CLASS	VIII	227	149.32	30.40	3.732*
		IX	217	142.26	30.99	$t_{12:}$ 2.422*
		X	200	148.92	29.10	$t_{13:}$ 0.139@ $t_{23:}$ 2.263*
2.	SEX	BOYS	447	142.86	31.64	5.085**
		GIRLS	197	155.80	24.98	
3.	AGE	≤ 13 years	211	150.16	30.43	2.840@
		=14 years	220	147.14	27.98	
		≥15 years	213	143.18	32.26	
4.	LOCALITY	Urban	291	138.59	31.99	20.727**
		Semi- urban	174	153.66	29.37	$t_{12:}$ 5.177**
		Rural	179	153.54	24.82	$t_{13:}$ 5.7** $t_{23:}$ 0.04@

(Contd…)

S. No.	*Variable*	*Groups*	*N*	*M*	*S.D*	*'t'/F value*
5.	MANAGEMENT	Government	183	149.97	33.63	25.453**
		Zilla parishad	231	151.04	26.11	$t_{12:}$ 0.353@
		Municipal	74	119.39	29.28	$t_{13:}$ 7.255**
		Private	156	149.87	25.83	$t_{14:}$ 0.031@ $t_{23:}$ 8.301** $t_{24:}$ 0.435@ $t_{34:}$ 7.653**
6.	FATHERS' OCCUPATION	Daily wages	123	140.84	35.60	6.047**
		Agriculture | Business	399	146.43	29.14	$t_{12:}$ 1.585@
		Secured Job	122	154.11	26.99	$t_{13:}$ 3.289**
						$t_{14:}$ 2.699**
7.	FAMILY LITERACY INDEX	≤ 4.9	214	142.23	31.97	5.299**
		Between 4.9 to 9.9	288	147.28	31.46	$t_{12:}$ 1.762@
						$t_{13:}$ 3.56**
		10 and above	142	152.79	23.86	$t_{14:}$ 2.019*
8.	FAMILY ANNUAL INCOME	Upto 10000	321	144.10	32.13	2.830@
		10000 to 50000	189	148.53	28.79	
		50000 and above	134	150.92	27.47	

On the basis of the responses on the attitude scale meant for students to study their attitudes towards mathematics education, the most influencing aspects are discussed in detail with the view a to nullifying the negative attitudes and encouraging positive attitude in the students towards the subject.

Further it can be said that the VIII class students are more favourable towards mathematics whereas the IX class students are less favourable and the attitudes of the X class students falls in between. This may be because teachers pay less attention to the VIII class students to concentrate more on the X class students because of the public examination. Moreover, to lessen the burden of the students at the X class and help them pass the examination the syllabus is reduced, as many topics as possible are included in the IX class. This has been clearly observed in the earlier section that IX class syllabus is more and there are number of difficult topics both for students and teachers. This may be the reason why IX class students are less favourable towards mathematics.

In a similar fashion, an observation of the attitude scores obtained by boy and girl students reveal that girl students have secured a better mean score on attitudes (155.80) when compared to their counterparts (142.86). The difference observed between the mean attitude scores is found to be significant at 0.01 level of probability for 643 degrees of freedom. Thus, sex is a significant factor in influencing the attitudes towards mathematics.

As explained earlier, the subjects are divided into three groups on the basis of locality viz., urban, semi-urban, and rural. The mean attitude scores of the semi-urban (153.66) and the rural students' (153.54) are the same whereas the mean attitude score of the urban students' (138.59) is far less than these two. The calculated 'F' ratio indicates that the mean differences are statistically significant at 0.01 level of probability for 2, 641 degrees of freedom. The 't' value obtained between the urban and the semi-urban, the urban and the rural areas also indicates that there exists a significant difference between the means. Therefore, it can be concluded that locality is a significant factor in influencing the attitudes towards mathematics.

It can further be said that the students from the rural and the semi-urban areas are more favourable towards mathematics than the urban students. This may be due to overcrowded class rooms in almost all the municipal schools in the urban areas, where the teachers cannot pay much attention to the individual student which automatically creates negative attitude towards the teacher or the subject.

As mentioned earlier, the schools under four managements, namely, Government, Zilla Parishad, Municipal and Private schools are considered to study their influence on the attitudes of students towards different aspects of mathematics education. It is observed that the mean attitude score of the students studying in Zilla Parishad schools (151.04) is far greater whereas that of those studying in municipal schools (119.39) is very less. The mean attitude scores of government (149.97) and private schools (149.87) is almost the same and a bit less than the mean score of the zilla parishad schools. The calculated 'F' value for 3, 640 degrees of freedom is statistically significant at 0.01 level of probability. The 't' values between the municipal and the other schools also indicate that there exists a significant difference in the mean attitude scores of students towards mathematics education. Thus it can be concluded that management is a significant factor in influencing the attitudes.

The above table 5.62 reveals that there are three occupational groups, namely, children of daily wage earners, agriculturists/ business people and secure job holders. The 'F' value 6.047 for 2 and 641 degrees of freedom is significant at 0.01 level of probability. The 't' value obtained between the children of secure job holders and the other two groups indicate that there exists a significant difference between the means at 0.01 level. Therefore it is clear that the occupation of the father is a significant factor in influencing the attitudes of students towards mathematics education.

The results disclose that the children of secure job holders have a more favourable attitude than the other two groups. This may be because most of the secure job holders would be educated who could solve their children's problems in learning mathematics. Naturally, this develops positive attitude in the students towards the subject.

The last variable, which could influence the attitude of students towards mathematics, is the family literacy index. The sample is divided into three groups based on the family literacy index namely, students whose family literacy index is ≤ 4, whose family literacy index is between 4.9 and 9.9 and lastly the students whose family literacy index is 10 and above. It is observed that the more the literacy index of the family, the more is the mean attitude score and the less the literacy index of the family the less is the mean attitude score of the students. The calculated 'F' value 5.299 for 2, 641 degrees of freedom is significant at 0.01 level of probability. Even the 't' values indicate that there exists a significant difference between the high literacy index group and the other two groups. Thus it is concluded that the educational level of the family is a significant factor in influencing the attitude of students towards mathematics. This may be because the educated members of the family can understand the problems of their children in studying mathematics and can clarify their doubts as far as possible. Therefore, the student develops a positive attitude towards mathematics.

Therefore, from these results it may be concluded that the null hypothesis 'the personal and demographic variables of students would not significantly influence their attitude towards learning mathematics' is accepted in the case of only two variables Age and Annual Income of the family but rejected in the case of other independent variables, namely, Class, Sex, Locality, Management, Father's Occupation and Family Literacy Index.

Naturally, the home environment will be more congenial to promote favourable attitudes towards mathematics learning when the educational background of the family and the occupation of the family are higher. Privately managed schools in the urban areas with limited number of students in the classroom will definitely provide a more congenial atmosphere than the government and municipal schools with overcrowded classrooms. The IX class textbook with the heaviest syllabus at the secondary level would definitely have a bearing on the attitudes of students towards mathematics education.

Description of the Distribution of Attitude Scores of Teachers

The scores obtained through the administration of the attitude scale to the teachers have been arranged in a systematic manner by grouping them into classes and tabulating them into frequency distribution. It may be noted that the attitude scale for teachers includes different aspects relating to attitudes of teachers in teaching mathematics. The analysis is carried out to know the kind of average, range and scatteredness. The different descriptive statistics such as mean, median, mode, range, quartile deviation, standard deviation, skewness and kurtosis are calculated to understand the nature of distribution. The frequency distribution and the values of descriptive statistics are set out in Table 5.63.

Table 5.63: Table showing the description of the distribution of attitude scores of teachers

Class Interval	*Frequency*	*Smoothed Frequency*	*Cumulative Frequency*
30-50	2	2	2
50-70	4	3	6
70-90	3	3	9
90-110	2	5.33	11
110-130	11	21.37	22
130-150	52	48.33	74
150-170	82	46.33	156
170-190	5	29	161

Mean = 145.217	Range = 144	Skewness = -0.765
Median = 151.585	Q.D. = 12.192	Kurtosis = 0.253
Mode = 157.692	S.D. = 24.987	

The mean attitude score of teachers on different aspects of mathematics education is 145.217, which is more than the average point (43×3 = 129) on the attitude scale. The values of median and mode are151.585 and 157.692 respectively. Therefore, it is confirmed that the general level of attitude towards teaching mathematics among the subjects is more. Even it is evident from the frequency distribution table that there are 139 teachers who scored more than the average point out of 161 and only 11 teachers who scored less than the average point on the scale. Of course, 11 teachers fall under the class interval 110-130, where the average point lies. Hence, it may be concluded that the teachers have a favourable attitude towards mathematics education. As the measures of central tendency are in the ascending order, the distribution is said to be negatively skewed. Of course, it is also evident from the calculated value of skewness (-0.765). The value of kurtosis 0.253 discloses that the distribution is slightly leptokurtic.

The range of the distribution of scores is 144 (the highest score = 175 and the lowest score = 31). The quartile deviation and standard deviation are 12.192 and 24.987 respectively. These measures of dispersion reveal that the spread in the distribution is not normal. The relationship between S.D and Q.D as it exists in the normal probability curve as 2/3. S.D=Q.D i.e., 2/3 (24.987) = 16.658, is not observed in the distribution. However, it can be said that the distribution belongs to the family of normal curves. The graphical representation of the distribution of attitude scores also indicates that the distribution follows normality with slight divergences (*see Fig. 5.4 on next page*).

As the distribution of the attitude scores of teachers follows normality with marginal exceptions, it is feasible to apply all the parametric statistics in the analysis of the data obtained and test the different hypotheses formulated.

The Influence of Personal and Demographic Variables on Attitude Scores of Teachers

As indicated earlier, there are seven independent variables related to teachers to study the variations among different sub groups in the attitude scores and to study the significance of these differences the 't' and 'F' ratios are calculated and presented in Table 5.64 along with means and standard deviations.

On the basis of the responses on the attitude scale meant for teachers to study the teachers attitudes towards mathematics education, the most influencing aspects are discussed in detail with the view to nullifying the negative attitudes and encouraging the positive attitude in the teachers towards the subject.

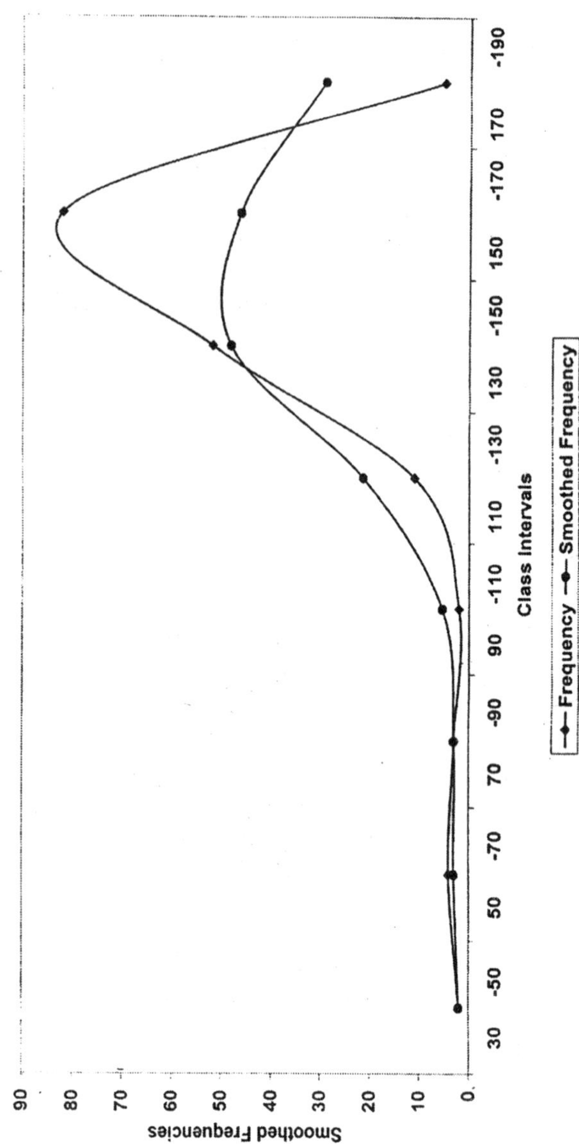

Fig. 5.4: Frequency and Smoothed Frequency Curves of Attitude Scores of Teachers

Table 5.64: Table Showing the Means and Standard deviations of Attitude scores of Teachers and the results of 't'/'F' ratios of different groups

S. No.	*VARIABLE*	*GROUPS*	*N*	*MEAN*	*SD*	*'t'/'F' ratio*
1.	GENDER	Male	131	144.95	24.384	0.654@
		Female	30	148.23	26.680	
2.	AGE (in years)	20 to 29	30	144.07	27.006	1.179@
		30 to 39	77	148.69	23.018	
		40 to 49	38	139.71	29.760	
		50 and above	16	147.19	11.119	
3.	GENERAL QUALIFICATION	Graduate	128	145.68	23.967	0.111@
		Postgraduate	30	144.47	29.349	
		Doctoral	3	151.33	8.145	
4.	PROFESSIONAL QUALIFICATION	Nil	5	149.60	8.961	0.313@
		B.Ed.	127	144.76	25.398	
		M.Ed.	29	148.34	24.066	

(Contd...)

S. No.	VARIABLE	GROUPS	N	MEAN	SD	't'/'F' ratio
5.	EXPERINCE (in years)	Up to 9	96	147.32	24.495	0.615@
		10 to 19	46	142.00	25.931	
		20 to 29	17	144.00	24.754	
		30 and above	2	156.00	1.414	
6.	LOCALITY	Urban	63	141.41	34.934	1.515@
		Semi-Urban	42	149.19	16.087	
		Rural	56	147.50	13.539	
7.	MANAGEMENT	Government	23	146.30	31.616	2.668*
		Zilla parishad	70	149.10	13.913	t_{12}: 0.412@ t_{13}: 0.988@
		Municipal	16	153.31	10.518	t_{14}: 1.022@
		Private	52	138.08	33.265	t_{23}: 1.353@ t_{24}: 2.247* t_{34}: 2.868**

From the Table 5.64 *(see table on page 213)* it is clear that all the personal and demographic variables included in the study would not influence the attitude of teachers significantly towards mathematics education except the variable management.

The 'F' ratio calculated was significant at 0.05 level of probability for 3 and 157 degrees of freedom. The teachers working in municipal and Z.P. schools exhibited more favourable attitude whereas those working in private schools showed less favourable attitude. The calculated 't' value between these, municipal Z.P. and private schools indicate that there exists significant difference between the means. Therefore, it can be concluded that management is a significant factor in influencing the teachers' attitude towards mathematics.

Generally, the teachers working in municipal schools do not teach all the topics given in the prescribed textbook, as most of the students are backward in mathematics. Therefore, it is enough if the teachers concentrate on the select and easy topics to see that every student passes the examination. Thus, most of the time they concentrate on drilling the students from the examination point of view. Hence, these teachers may not know the difficult topics given in the textbook. All these aspects are responsible for the development of positive attitude towards mathematics.

But, the situation is different with the teachers working in private schools. The management of these schools put compulsion on them to drill the students, to conduct tests, to correct and to clarify students' doubts – all these constitute a laborious task for them. Moreover, in most of these schools, the teachers are not fully qualified and therefore they may have difficulty in handling the subject, which naturally develops negative attitudes in the teachers towards mathematics.

Hence, from this discussion it may be concluded that the null hypothesis 'the personal and demographic variables of teachers would not significantly influence their attitude towards teaching mathematics' is accepted in the case of only six variables, namely, Gender, Age, General Qualification, Professional Qualification, Experience and locality but rejected in the case of only one independent variable, namely, Management.

CONCLUSION

Most of the important findings in the item analysis, description of problem scores and attitude scores and testing the descriptive hypotheses, the influence of personal and demographic variables on testing the statistical hypotheses are summarised along with other aspects in the subsequent chapter, the Summing up.

6

Summary and Conclusions

SUMMARY

This chapter is a summing up of the study including the sub-topics such as introduction, statement of the problem, significance of the study, objectives, hypotheses, variables of the study, development of tools, selection of the sample, collection of data and their analysis and conclusions.

Introduction

The development of a country is primarily determined by the quality of its human resources, which depends on the level of knowledge, skills and attitudes. Therefore, creating the right minds through the right process of education acquires the top-most priority.

The aim of education is to develop the human mind. The child who is trained to think creatively finds himself not only a better acquirer of knowledge, but also a better user and producer of new knowledge. If thinking skills are properly developed at this stage, acquisition of knowledge of a more complex nature will not be a difficult thing to him at all.

For an individual, career and financial prospects depend heavily on how much mathematics he has learnt. Modern science and technology depends increasingly upon mathematics. Consequently, from social and scientific points of view there has developed a growing interest in how one learns mathematics, how one thinks through the analysis of the mathematical problem.

In many occupations such as Accountancy, Banking, Shop-keeping business, Tailoring, Carpentry, Taxation, Insurance, Postal Jobs etc., by which the needs of man are fulfilled, indirect or direct use of Mathematics is made. It has become the basis of the world's entire business and commercial system. Thus the use of Mathematics is felt at each and every step, every minute and every moment of man's life.

Mathematics occupies an important place in the school curriculum. Thus the Education Commission setup in 1964 recommended that it should be taught as a compulsory subject of general education up to class X. Since general education envisages Mathematics for all, the selection of content should be relevant to the practical needs of everyday life. Hence the load of Mathematics curriculum should be realistic.

Hence in the study of mathematics the emphasis should be more on the development of a general problem-solving ability rather than on finding a solution to a particular problem.

"Of all the different factors which influence the quality of education and its contribution to the national development, the quality, competence and character of teachers are undoubtedly the most significant. Nothing is more important than securing a sufficient supply of high quality recruits to the teaching profession, providing them with the best possible professional preparation and creating satisfactory conditions of work in which they can be fully effective."

—*Indian Education Commission, 1966, (P. 46)*

But, many changes are being made in the mathematics curriculum. There are certain new topics included in the present curriculum, with which the teachers are not familiar. Even in other topics, there could be some points about which the teachers have some doubts. Heavy syllabus is one of the severe problems of both teachers and students in mathematics. The authorities insist on the completion of the syllabus with in the stipulated time frame, and also expect cent per cent results in the subject, which is a hard task for the teachers.

To enable the teachers to handle the difficult topics effectively, they must be provided with self-learning materials like teachers' handbooks etc. To help students understand the more abstract concepts easily and meaningfully, schools must be provided with necessary audio- visual aids like models, charts, and different types of boards etc.

But no teacher's guides are available in mathematics. Individual teachers are left completely to their resources. They even do not read the textbooks. Textbooks are used for their collection of problems.

It has been observed that the teacher in a mathematics class room presents solutions to problems giving little scope for the students to attempt to learn any skill individually or independently. Most times, teachers resort to the synthetic process of displaying the solution of a problem, ignoring the analytical thinking that has to be cultivated in the process in the students.

Therefore many pupils find the subject very difficult and uninteresting. Naturally their performance is poor and unsatisfactory. At present there is a great hue and cry against lack of interest in general and the number of failures in particular in Mathematics.

Generally teachers at the secondary level feel that over crowded classrooms, heavy syllabus, non-academic activities etc., are the causes for ineffective teaching in the classroom. Especially, they blame the teachers working at the primary level. They express that students who are entering the secondary schools are not thorough with the primary level mathematics. They lack even the knowledge of four fundamental operations, etc. Is this blame thrown by secondary school teachers of mathematics on primary school teachers justified? What are the real causes for these problems? How to overcome them? How to achieve the objectives of teaching mathematics at the secondary school level?, these are the areas to be investigated.

Statement of the Problem

The problem for the present investigation is "An Investigation into the Problems Relating to Teaching-Learning Mathematics at Secondary Level."

Significance of the Study

Also, there is some criticism of mathematics as:

" It is too remote from life to interest the student".

"Mathematics has outlived its usefulness as a subject of secondary school instruction".

There are negative comments like

"Mathematics is completely taught on theoretical grounds

"It is more abstract in its nature".

"Teaching is confined to the classroom and not related to pupil's life".

What are the causes for this situation? How to overcome this situation in the study of mathematics? In these circumstances, how to develop positive attitudes in teachers and students?

To address all these questions, and to make the teaching-learning of Mathematics effective and purposeful, this research work is undertaken.

Hence an attempt has been made in this study to identify the difficulties in content, teaching and learning mathematics, to identify the problems faced by students in learning the subject and the problems of teachers in teaching it, and to know the attitudes of students towards learning it and attitudes of teachers towards teaching it as perceived by both students and teachers and to suggest suitable strategies for improving the situation.

Objectives of the Study

The main objectives of the study were:

1. To identify the difficulty areas in secondary level mathematics as perceived by the pupils and teachers.
2. To identify the problems faced by the pupils in learning mathematics and by the teachers in teaching mathematics.
3. To study the attitudes of pupils towards learning mathematics and of teachers towards teaching the subject.
4. To study the variations in the problems and attitudes of pupils of different sub groups depending upon their personal and demographic variables.

5. To study the variations in the problems and attitudes of teachers of different sub groups depending upon their personal and demographic variables.

6. To suggest the suitable strategies for the improvement of teaching-learning mathematics at the secondary level.

Hypotheses of the Study

To realise these objectives, the following descriptive and statistical hypotheses have been formulated for the purpose of testing. The hypotheses formulated are in null-form as they are akin to statistical testing.

1. The pupils in general do not feel studying mathematics at the secondary level an easy task.

2. The teachers in general do not feel that the teaching of mathematics at the Secondary level is an easy and pleasant job.

3. There would not be any significant problems faced by students in learning mathematics.

4. There would not be any significant problems faced by teachers in teaching mathematics.

5. The pupils in general do not possess positive attitudes towards learning mathematics.

6. The teachers in general do not possess positive attitudes towards teaching mathematics.

7. The personal and demographic variables of pupils would not significantly influence the intensity of problems faced by them in learning mathematics.

8. The personal and demographic variables of teachers do not significantly influence the intensity of problems faced by them in teaching mathematics.

9. The personal and demographic variables of students do not significantly influence their attitudes toward learning mathematics.

10. The personal and demographic variables of teachers do not significantly influence their attitudes toward teaching mathematics.

Variables included in the Study

As the present study is an investigation into the problems relating to teaching-learning mathematics at the secondary level on the basis of the difficulties (in content, teaching and learning), problems, and attitudes of students and teachers, the dependent variables are as follows:

Dependent Variables

1. Difficulty level of different chapters (in content, teaching and learning) as perceived by students and teachers in secondary level mathematics.
2. Problems of teachers and students in teaching and learning mathematics respectively.
3. Attitudes of students and teachers towards mathematics education.

Independent Variables

The independent variables considered in the investigation are two kinds, namely, student related personal and demographic variables and teacher related personal and demographic variables. The student related independent variables are: Class, sex, age, locality, management of the school, father's occupation, family literacy index, and annual income of the family etc. The teacher related independent variables are: Sex, age, educational qualifications general, and ii) professional, experience, locality, and management of the school etc.

Methods of Investigation

The present study is a survey. The various procedures adopted in the construction and standardisation of data gathering instruments to measure different variables included in the study and the methods followed in the selection of the samples, collection of data, scoring and analysis are as follows:

Construction of the Instruments

The investigator has developed the tools for the study as given below:

1. Rating Scales to measure the Difficulty level of the Chapters included in the textbooks of VIII, IX and X classes for students and teachers to know the difficulty areas in secondary level mathematics both for students and teachers;

2. Problem check list-cum -Rating scales with 46 items for teachers and 67 items for students to know their problems in teaching and learning mathematics at secondary level;

3. Five point attitude scales with 43 items for teachers and 42 items for students to know their attitudes towards mathematics education.

These tools have been developed following all the steps included in the construction of rating scales, Problem check lists, and attitude scales viz., collection of items from different sources, preparation of item pool, scrutiny of the items by the experts, preparation of pilot form, pilot study, item analysis, selection of items for final study, establishment of reliability and validity etc, as described in the IV chapter. To collect the relevant information regarding the personal and demographic variables, carefully worded personal data sheets have been incorporated in the first page of rating scales meant for identifying the difficulty chapters for students and teachers.

Selection of the Sample

A two stage random sampling technique was employed for the selection of the sample. At first stage 80 schools were selected at random in total from three districts namely.,Chitttoor, Kadapa, and Nellore, which are covered by Sri Venkateswara University. At the second stage, 8 to 10 students were selected at random from each one of these selected schools to make the first sub sample of students equal to 644. Cluster sampling technique was followed to select the second sub sample of 161 teachers from all the above selected schools taking all the available mathematics teachers.

Collection of the Data

For collecting the data, the Investigator personally visited all the 80 schools and with the permission of the Head Masters of the schools, the self-explanatory instruments developed by the Investigator were administered to 644 students and 161 teachers. The students were given instructions and motivated to respond genuinely to all the items given in the data gathering tools.

Scoring of the Responses

As the instruments used in this investigation were rating scales, problem check list-cum-rating scales and attitude scales, they were scored by giving the following weightages. Rating scales were scored on a 3-point scale by giving weightages 3, 2 and 1 to the three alternatives viz., maximum extent, moderate extent and least extent respectively.

The problems were scored on a 3-point scale by giving weightages 1, 2 and 3 to the three alternatives viz, least extent, moderate extent and maximum extent. The grand total (frequencies and intensity scores) to each individual on the entire scale was obtained by adding the weightages on all the items.

The attitude scales were scored on a 5-point scale by giving weightages 5, 4, 3, 2 and 1 in the case of positive items and 1, 2, 3, 4, and 5 in the case of negative items respectively. The grand total to each individual on the entire scale was obtained by adding the weightages on all the statements.

Analysis of the Data

As the data collected through the different statements in the tool from different subjects are basically qualitative in nature, item-wise analysis was carried out to identify the specific deficiencies in different aspects of teaching and learning mathematics in secondary schools. Statistics such as frequencies, percentages and chi-square were employed to make the description more precise.

The total scores (problem intensity scores and attitude scores) obtained by all subjects on all the variables were computed. The data were carefully analysed employing appropriate statistical techniques. The obtained numerical results were interpreted numerically to draw conclusions and thereby educational implications.

MAJOR FINDINGS AND CONCLUSIONS

The analysis chapter (Chapter-V) has four sections viz., difficulty analysis of chapters for students and teachers, analysis of problems in teaching and learning mathematics, analysis of attitudes of students and teachers towards mathematics and finally description of the distribution of problem intensity and attitude scores of students and teachers and the influence of personal and demographic variables on them.

1. On the basis of the difficulty analysis of chapters from the VIII, IX, and X classes, the most difficulty chapters are as follows:
   - It has been found that in the VIII class text book the chapters 'commercial mathematics' and 'mensuration' are the most difficult chapters for the students whereas for the teachers along with the above two chapters 'triangles and polygons', and 'circles and concurrent lines of triangles' are the relatively most difficult chapters.
   - It has been found that in the IX class text book five chapters namely, 'arithmetic, square roots of algebraic expressions, linear equations and inequations, geometry and motion geometry' are the relatively most difficult chapters for both the teachers and students.
   - Similarly, in the X class text book the chapters namely 'linear programming, progressions, geometry and trigonometry are felt relatively most difficult chapters for students and teachers. Also, instead of progressions teachers feel polynomials over integers as the fourth most difficult chapter.
2. The problems related to students in learning mathematics are categorised under five major heads. On the basis of the analysis of problem intensity of students in learning mathematics, the most severe problems are the following:
   - It has been found that students are facing problems relating to mathematical formulae in understanding, in remembering, in deriving and in selecting suitably while solving the problems.

- Students are facing problems in understanding the mathematical language, symbols and relation between different concepts in mathematics.
- Students are not able to spend more time for doing mathematics, understand the linkage between the steps in solving a problem, do the mathematics fast; and they also commit number of mistakes while solving problems in mathematics. Students also feel that there are more number of difficult topics in the mathematics textbook, and the examples given in it are not easy to understand.
- Students are facing problems related to homework in mathematics as their mathematics teachers give more number of problems for homework and they have nobody at home to help them in solving problems.
- Students are facing problems relating to geometry in drawing the suitable figure and in suggesting the suitable construction for proving the theorem.

3. On the basis of the analysis of multifaceted problem intensity of teachers in teaching mathematics, the most serious problems are the following:

    - Students do not have the knowledge of the primary level mathematics; they are not able to understand the problems unless every problem given in the exercise is worked out on the board; they think mathematics is difficult because they are afraid of it; they do not try to ask the teachers to teach them again the problems which they do not understand; they do not understand some of the theorems, riders and constructions in geometry even if they are taught effectively; they commit more mistakes while solving problems; covering the syllabus in time is very difficult; teaching of mathematics is difficult as there are a large number of topics which are above the level of students; distinctness of the problems is given in the exercises; parents are not showing any interest towards the education of their children; and the teacher is not taken into confidence in constructing the curriculum in mathematics.

4. Based on the analysis of attitudes of students towards learning mathematics, the following are the quite disturbing aspects:

   - It is found that the most important aspects which create negative attitude in the students with regard to mathematics are: They dislike oral problems, they do not have the habit of studying new lessons in advance before they are started, they did not do mathematics properly in the earlier classes, they do not have the habit of practicing the problems, which are taught in the classroom, they leave difficult problems given in text book, they do not have the habit of doing mathematics daily, they do not refer to other books related to mathematics except the prescribed text book, and they do not spend much time practicing mathematics.
   - Similarly it is found that the areas which create the negative attitude in the students are: Neglecting the subject, doing only easy problems and leaving the difficult ones, disliking funny problems, not worrying about the problems which they cannot solve, and afraid of participating in mathematical competitions etc, out of fear.
   - Teacher- related aspects resulting in negative attitude in students are: Teacher does not teach the problems which are difficult to the students again and again, teacher does not use teaching aids, teacher never corrects the home work, teacher does not questions while teaching to know whether students are able to understand or not, teacher teaches well some chapters only.

5. The analysis of the attitudes of teachers towards mathematics education reveals the most serious aspects as the following:

   - It has been found that the most important aspects which create negative attitude in the teachers with regard to teaching of mathematics are: The cause for students' phobia in mathematics is geometry only, students fail to understand the problems given in the textbook unless every problem is worked out on the board, the syllabus can not be completed if the teacher adopts the methods that are taught during the training programme, correcting homework is not possible due to overcrowded classrooms, standard in mathematics is increased far above the level of the student's understanding ability, there is no proper recognition and encouragement for teachers who adopt new methods and techniques, and students do not have the basic knowledge of fundamental concepts.

- The most important aspects which create negative attitude among the teachers with regard to mathematics textbook are: The examples given in the textbook are not sufficient to teach the problems given in the exercises, printer's devils in the answers are alarming, prominence is given to number of problems rather than to the presentation of the concepts, incomplete problems, and students are afraid of mathematics textbook.

- Similarly difficult aspects found with regard to training are mere theoritical explanations are given in the training classes, experienced and efficient teachers are not involved as resource persons, teachers are subjected to great pressure by the authorities to achieve cent per cent results in the examinations, duration of the in-service training programmes is not fixed in accordance with the realisation of the objectives of the programmme, discovery approaches are adopted, higher authorities are least bothered about the teachers' problems, teachers are not informed in advance about the in-service programmes, in-service classes are not conducted on convenient days etc.

6. The influence of personal and demographic variables on the problems faced by students and teachers in teaching and learning mathematics reveals the following:

   - It has been found that the independent variables viz., Sex, Locality, Management and Annual income of the family could significantly influence the intensity of the problems faced by them whereas the variables viz., Class, Age, Literacy index of the family and Father's occupation could not influence the intensity of problems faced by them.

- The independent variables namely, Age and Management could influence the intensity of the problems faced by teachers in teaching mathematics whereas the remaining variables viz., Sex, General qualification, Professional qualification, Experience, and Locality could not influence the problems of teachers significantly.

7. On the basis of the influence of personal and demographic variables, the attitudes of students and teachers towards mathematics education are the following:

   - Class, Sex, Locality, Management, Father's occupation, and Literacy index of the family are the variables which could influence the attitudes of students towards mathematics significantly whereas the remaining variables—Age and Annual income of the family could not influence the attitudes of students towards the subject.
   - All the personal and demographic variables except the variable, Management of the school could not influence the attitudes of teachers towards mathematics education.

The major findings of this study clearly point to the imperative need of plugging the loopholes in the areas discussed, to make mathematics education at the Secondary school level effective, easy, purposeful, enjoyable and rewarding.

7

Educational Implications of the Study, Limitations and Suggestions for Further Research

This chapter discusses the educational implications of the study, which probably help improve teaching-learning mathematics at the secondary level. Further the conclusions arrived at would lead to develop favourable attitude towards mathematics education in the students and teachers. Of course, the other section of the chapter presents the limitation of the study and offers suggestions for further research.

EDUCATIONAL IMPLICATIONS OF THE STUDY

From the previous chapter it is evident that both teachers and students felt difficulty with a few chapters included in the mathematics textbooks of the VIII, IX, and X classes. It might be mostly because the organisation and presentation of the content in those chapters was not appropriately suited to the ability levels of the children or it could be because of abstractness and heaviness in terms of both concepts and exercises. Therefore it is suggested that the curriculum experts and the textbook writers should be reoriented to bring suitable changes in the textbooks. There should be an open invitation by the state authorities to all the sections of the society to suggest suitable and viable modifications in the prescribed textbooks. Hasty decisions of deleting certain portions of the syllabus, and some problems in the exercises for examination purpose will not do at all. Further, it is suggested that the teachers of mathematics should come forward with constructive ideas to make the presentation of abstract chapters more concrete so that it would become easy for teachers to teach and for students to learn them. Whenever, the curriculum is revised by the authorities, it would be rather essential to plan in-service training programmes to the teachers and to introduce novel ideas, methods and improvisations relevant to the local needs to deal with the new elements of revised curriculum effectively.

It is also found in the study that there are very severe problems faced by the students and teachers. These problems again relate to content (curriculum in the textbook) and the method of teaching and learning. To have an effective teaching learning process, the pre-requisites are efficient and committed teachers, congenial physical atmosphere in the institution and the most required academic amenities such as black board, chalk, and teaching aids (charts, models etc.). The pre-service training to prepare teachers should aim at producing committed teachers in general and mathematics teachers in particular. It is necessary to overhaul teacher education programmes thoroughly. Even after the establishment of the NCTE, a statutory body to control the quality of teacher education, the scenario of teacher education in the country has been bleak. Unusual expansion at the expense of consolidation has been observed in most of the states. The quality and commitment of teachers produced from these institutions has become a big question with no answer. Establishing a teacher education institution is being treated as the most lucrative enterprise through which one can make abundant profits. With the kind of teachers that these big business centres produce, even if we have congenial atmosphere and good academic inputs, it would not be possible to ensure quality in our school education and more so in mathematics education. Further, there are no minimum facilities in most of the secondary schools to teach mathematics effectively.

The most significant problems faced by both students and teachers originate at the primary level, as there are no specialist teachers to teach them the basic concepts of mathematics. The children are subjected to confusion than clarity over the basic concepts and fundamental operations of arithmetic. Mathematics teaching is not related to life. Students are taught abstract principles by most of the teachers. Further, they create fear about mathematics in the early stages while teaching the four fundamental operations—Addition, Subtraction, Multiplication and Division. Play way, activity oriented methods, reasoning and analytical thinking are not practised and promoted appropriately by our teachers at the primary level. Multi-grade teaching and teaching of multiple subjects by a single teacher in most of the primary schools and non-availability of specialist teachers also contribute to inefficient teaching of mathematics.

Education is supposed to develop positive attitude towards any positive aspect. Knowledge of mathematics is definitely a positive aspect. But both teachers and students expressed many negative attitudes or less favourable attitudes towards different issues of mathematics education. This kind of situation is to be averted. The teacher educators working in the field of mathematics education, who prepare/train teachers of mathematics should be capable of creating positive attitude in the prospective teachers of mathematics. Once the teacher is positive towards mathematics, he can device different methods to develop positive attitudes in children towards the subject.

Thus, it is necessary to bring appropriate changes in our curriculum and mathematics textbooks. The powers that should strengthen both pre-service and in-service training programmes to produce efficient and committed teachers of mathematics, provide minimum infrastructural and academic requirements in the schools to teach mathematics effectively, appoint specialist teachers of mathematics at the primary level, design more para-mathematical activities as curricular inputs, and eliminate the fear of mathematics in children, etc for ensuring the quality school education to all the children upto collective level (say 10th class). Beyond this collective level, the programmes of education are selective and those who want to specialise in the area of mathematics and related branches must be competitive with sound knowledge of mathematics. Then only the comment made by Radhakrishna in University Education Commission that 'the weakest link in Indian Education is the Secondary Education' can be nullified.

"Education should be a pleasure but not the pressure"

LIMITATIONS OF THE STUDY AND SUGGESTIONS FOR FURTHER RESEARCH

1. The present investigation is limited to mathematics education only. This kind of research on different school subjects can be planned to plug the week areas in the respective subjects.

2. The present investigation was carried out only on 161 teachers and 644 students covering only 3 districts (S. V. University area). Other districts in Andhra Pradesh and other parts of the country may be covered by prospective research scholars.

3. In the present investigation, preliminary survey is conducted on a limited sample covering primary children, teachers and parents. A comprehensive study on this area may yield more fruitful results, which may throw light on mathematics education at the primary level.

4. The tools used for measuring the difficulties, problems and attitudes of teachers and students in teaching and learning mathematics are made by the investigator and are not standardised because of the paucity of time. Therefore it is suggested that standardised tools should be developed for repeated use by different researchers keeping in view the existing conditions in school mathematics.

5. The effect of limited personal and demographic variables is taken up for study in this research work. To get more information about the study other personal and demographic variables may be studied.

6. The variables difficulties, problems and attitudes alone are studied. Other variables may also be studied to improve the situation further.

Bibliography

Aggarwal, J.C. (1999). Principles, Methods and Techniques of Teaching. Vikas Publishing House, Masjid Road, Jangpura, New Delhi, pp. 16-17, 42, 55, 245.

Aggarwal, J.C. (2000). Essentials of Educational Technology:Teaching Learning, Vikas Publishing House, Masjid Road, Jangpura, New Delhi, pp. 62.

Alfred S. Posamentier, Hope J. Hartman and Constanze Kaiser (1998). Tips for the Mathematics Teacher-Research Based Strategies to Help Students Learn, Corwin Press, A Sage Publications Company, California, pp. 9-11.

Allpana Trehaan. (2000). Total Quality in Management Education, Implementing the Operative Schemata Through Effective Learning System. *University News*, 38(23), June 5, pp. 1-5.

Alvi, Mohammad Sarwar. (1986). Effects of Individualised Instruction on Achievement and Aptitude in General Mathematics in the Ninth Grade. *Dissertation Abstracts International* (UMI), Vol. (9), March 1987.

Arora, G.L, Raj Rani and Saroj Pandey. (2000). DPEP CALLING, pp. 32-35. April-July, pp. 32-35.

Ausubel, D. (1960). The Use of Advance Organisers in the Learning and Retention of Meaningful Verbal Learning. *Journal of Educational Psychology*, 51, 267-272.

Barbara Anthony and Bryce B.Hudgins. (1978). Problem-Solving Processes of Fifth Grade Arithmetic Pupils, *Journal of Educational Research*, Vol. 72, Nov/Dec, pp. 63-67.

Barting, G.O. (1981). Second Year Book of the Department of Elementary School Principles, pp. 411-21. (Mohan, K., A Diognostic Study of Errors Comitted by Pupils of VII Standard in Fractions, Unpublished M. Ed., Dissertation in Education, S.V. University, India.

Behr, A.N. (1973). Achievement, Aptitude and Attitude in Mathematics. *Two-Year College Mathematics Journal*, 4, 72-74.

Beryl, G.M. (1981). Parental Involvement and Children's Mathematics Achievement. *Dissertation Abstracts International*, 5049-A.

Bhatia, Kusum. (1992). Identification and Remedy of Difficulties in Learning Fractions with Programmed Instructional Material, *Indian Educational Review*, Vol. 27, No. 3, pp. 102-106.

Bhattacharya, M. (1986). An Investigation into the Learning Disabilities Developed by Secondary School Students in the Area of Equation-Sums in Algebra, Ph.D Thesis in Education, University of Kalyani in India.

Brain Bolt and David Hobbs. (2001). Mathematical Projects, Cambridge University Press, Trumpington Street, Cambridge, U.K.

Buch, M.B. (1979). Second Survey of Research in Education, p. 280. New Delhi: S. Chand and Company Ltd.

Buch, M.B. (1991). Fourth Survey of Research in Education, New Delhi, NCERT, p. 693.

Callahan, W.J. (1971). Adolescent Attitudes Toward Mathematics. *Mathematics Teacher*, 64 (8), 751-755.

Chase. (1960). The Position of Certain Variables in the Prediction of Problem-Solving in Arithmetic. *Journal of Educational Research*, 54: 9-14.

Chel, Madan Mohan, D. (1990). Diagnosis and Remediation of Under Achievement in Compulsory Mathematics of Madhyamic Examination in West Bengal. Ph.D. Thesis in Education, Sc. University of Calcutta, India.

Dandapani, C. (1992). Dimensions of Effective Teaching of Mathematics, Ph.D. Thesis in Education, Annamalai University, India.

Desai, H.G. (1973). The Attitudes to Mathematics of High School Students of Saurashtra – A Field Study, Dept. of Education Saurashtra University., (UGC financed).

Desai, H.G. (1979). Under-Achievement Syndrome Among High Ability High School Boys. In M.B. Buch (Ed.) *Second Survey of Research in Education*, Baroda, p. 579.

Deshmukh, Veena. (1988). Some Temperamental Correlates of Mathematics Learning, Ph. D., Thesis in Education, Nagpur University, India.

Dutta, Anima. (1990). Learning Disabilities in the Reasoning Power of the Students in Geometry – Diagnosis and Prevention, Ph.D., Thesis in Education, University of Kalyani, India.

Ediger, Dr. Marlow. (1981). Reporting Pupil Progress in Arithmetic Achievement. *Indian Education*, Vol. X, No. 11, Feb, pp. 37-39.

Ediger, Dr. Marlow. (1997). Democratic Supervision in the School Setting. *Experiments in Education*, Vol. XXV, No. 12, Dec, pp. 23-27.

Ediger, Dr. Marlow. (1999). Parents, the Teacher and Mathematics, *Experiments in Education*, Vol. XXVII, No. 6, June, pp. 93-103.

Edward, A. L. (1969). Techniques of Attitude Scale Construction. A Textbook, Vakils, Feffer and Simons Pvt. Ltd., Bombay, pp. 151-155.

Edward, A.L. & Kilpatrick, F.P. (1948). Technique for the Construction of Attitude Scale. *Journal of Applied Psychology*, Vol. 32, pp. 374-383.

Felsenthal, H. M. (1969). Sex Differences in Teacher-pupil Interaction and Their Relationship with Teacher Attitudes and Pupil Reading Achievement. *Dissertation Abstracts International*, Vol. 30, No. 10, p. 3711-A.

Fennema, Elizebeth and Sherman, Julia. (1976). Instruments Designed to Measure Attitude Towards the Learning Mathematics by Females and Males. *Journal of Research in Mathematics Education*. 7:5, 324-326.

Foong, P.Y. (1987). Anxiety and Mathematics Performance in Female Secondary School Students. *Singapore Journal of Education*. 8:2, 22-31.

Fraser, E. (1959) Home Environment and School. London, University of London, Ltd.

Gakhar Dr. S.C. (1982). A Study of Acquisition of Mathematical Concepts Among 8th Graders of Different Types of Schools, *Experiments in Education*, Vol. X, Nc. 9, pp. 164-167.

Gakhar, Dr. S.C. (1983). An Enquiry into the Relationship of Mathematical Concepts Learning of 8th Graders and School Structure Variables of Size, Teacher-Pupils Ratio and Expenditure. Experiments in Education, Vol. XI, No. 2, April, pp. 25-29.

Gakhar, Dr. S.C. (1986). Home Variables as Determinants of Mathematical Concepts Learning. *Experiments in Education* Vol. XIV, No. 6, August, pp. 97-102.

Gakhar, S.C. and Kiran Saini. (1991). A Study of the Effect of Teacher's Qualification, Experience and In-service Training Upon the Students' Achievement in Mathematics, *The Educational Review*, Vol. XCVII, No.10.

Garrett, H.E. (1973). Statistics in Psychology and Education, A Textbook, Vikils, Feffer and Simons Ltd. Bombay-1, pp. 215, 337-370.

Gomathi Mani, Dr. (1983). Motivation Through Mathematical Games, *Experiments in Education*, Vol. XI, No. 3, April, pp. 39-41.

Gorden and Will, B. (1978). A Profile of High and Low Achievers in Mathematics Among Sixth Grade Students. *Dissertation Abstract International*. Vol. 38 (8). p. 4639A.

Government of India, Department of Education. (1992). National Policy on Education-1986 (with Modifications Undertaken in 1992), New Delhi, Ministry of Human Resource Development, pp. 6-7.

Government of Andhra Pradesh, (1996). Mathematics Text Book, VIII Class, Hyderabad.

Government of Andhra Pradesh (1997). Mathematics Text Book, IX Class, Hyderabad.

Government of Andhra Pradesh, (1998). Mathematics Text Book, X Class, Hyderabad.

Grewal, Dr. S. S. and Kirpal Kaur. (1981). Achievement – Motivation and Anxiety as Related to Academic Success in Mathematics. *Experiments in Education*, Vol. VIII, No. 12, Feb, pp. 221-223.

Gupta, R. C. (1972). Backwardness in Mathematics and Basic Arithmetic Skills, *A Survey of Research in Education*, 1, 282.

Gupta, V. K. (1995). Readings in Science and Mathematics Education, The Associated Publishers, Kacha Bazar, Ambala Cantt, 133001(India).

Harneek Dr. S. Kaile and Manjit Kumar, (1990). Achievement Motivation in Relation to Over- and Under-Achievement in Science and Mathematics. *Experiments in Education*, Vol XVIII No. 4, pp. 111-114.

Hazelbaker and Deborah Jean, (1997). A Comparative Study of Examining the Effects of Alternative Methods of Teaching Mathematics on Mathematics Achievement and Attitude Towards Mathematics; Comparing the Lecture—Cooperative Learning Method to the Computer Assisted Method, *Dissertation Abstracts International*, Vol. 58, No. 8, p. 3053. Head, John. (1981). Personality and the Learning of Mathematics. Educational Studies in Mathematics. 12, 339-350.

Helen L. Burz and Kit Marshall. (1996). Performance-Based Curriculum for Mathematics, Corwin Press, Inc, A Sage Publications Company, Thousand Oaks, California.

Hilton, T.L., and Berglund, G.W. (1974). Sex Differences in Mathematics Achievement: A Longitudinal Study. *Journal of Educational Research*, 67, 231-237.

Hiroshi Isero, (2003), Positive Attitude for Learning, Perspectives, January, Vol. 19, No. 1, pp. 10-12.

Hukum Singh. (2000). Status of Mathematics Education, *Journal of Indian Education*, February, pp. 35-42.

Husen, T. (1967). International Study of Achievement in Mathematics—Comparison of 12 Countries, Sex Bias in Education, 59-59.

Husten, T. (1967). International Study of Achievement in Mathematics: A Comparison of 12 Countries. New York: John Willey and Sons.

I.G.N.O.W. (1998). Indira Gandhi National Open University, Nature, Objectives and Approaches to Teaching of Mathematics, ES-342, Reaching of Mathematics, November, pp. 7-15.

Iyer, R.K. (1977). Some Factors Related to Underachievement in Mathematics of Secondary School Students. Unpublished Ph.D. Thesis in Education, University of Kerala, India.

Iyer, K.K. (1986). Some Factors Related to Underachievement in Mathematics of Secondary School Students. In M. B. Buch (Ed.) *Third Survey of Research in Education*, New Delhi, NCERT, p. 668.

Jackson and Jeanetha Williams. (1977). Factors Affecting Students' Learning of New Mathematics Concepts in Three Nashville Area—Remedial and Developmental Studies Mathematics Programmes, *Dissertation Abstracts International*, Vol. 58, No. 8, 3053.

Jain, D.K. (1988). A Study of Significant Correlates of High School Failures in Mathematics and English with Special Reference to Jammu Division, In M. B. Buch, *A Survey of Research in Education*, p. 652.

Jain, S.L. and Burad, G.L. (1988). Low Results in Mathematics at Secondary Examinations in Rajasthan, Independent Study, Udipur, State Institute of Educational Research and Training.

James T.F.Poon. and T J Ng. (1991). Students' Perceptions of Mathematics and Design and Technology. *Experiments in Education*, Vol. XIX, No. 9, September, pp. 239-248.

Justin Paul. (2000). Towards Academic Excellence, University News, 38(23), June 5, pp. 7-8.

Kapoor.J.N. (1986). Problem Solving in Mathematics, Indian Institute of Technology, Delhi, UGC, *Mathematical Education*, Quarterly, October/December, pp. 46-51.

Kapoor, J.N. (1990). Some Aspects of Mathematics Education in India, Arya Book Depot, Karol Bagh, Delhi, pp. 46-51.

Kapoor, J.N. (1993). Some Aspects of School Mathematics, Arya Book Depot, Karol Bagh, New Delhi, pp. 15-16, 79-83.

Kapoor, J.N. (2002). Mathematics Enjoyment for the Millions, Arya Book Depot, Karol Bagh, Delhi.

Kasat, B.S. (1991). In-depth Study of Causes of Large Failures in Mathematics at S.S.C. Examination of Marathi Medium High School Students in Palghar Tahsil, M. Phil., Dissertation in Education, Indian Institute of Education, Pune, India.

Kerenha Krupalini. T. (1992). An Investigation into the Extent of Use of Multi-media in Teaching Mathematics in a Few High Schools of Bangalore South District, Department of Extension Services, R.V. Teachers College, Jaya Nagar, Bangalore.

Khalid, Mohd Nasir, Factors Affecting Mathematics Achievement in Malaysian Schools, *Dissertation Abstracts International*, Vol. 58, No. 7, p. 3449, 1997.

Kirkire, P.L. (1981). Analysing the Impact of Objective-based Lesson Plans on the Classroom Verbal Interaction on Pupil Achievement in Mathematics. Unpublished Ph.D. Thesis, Indore University.

Krishnamurthy, S. (2000). Achievement in History As Related to Academic Achievement Motivation, *Experiments in Education*, Vol. XXVIII, No. 3, pp. 47- 52.

Kumar, M. (1985). Language Ability and Acquisition of Mathematics Concepts at Primary School Level. *Experiments in Education*, Vol. XIII, No. 5, pp. 81-84.

Lalthanhawla. (1983). An Investigatin into the Causes of Failure in Science and Mathematics in High School Certificate Examination in Mizoram, Aizwal: North Eastern Hill University Campus, Unpublished M.Ed. Dissertation.

Lalithamma, K. N. (1975). Some Factors Affecting Achievement of Secondary School Pupils in Mathematics, *Second Survey of Educational Research*, 2, 349.

Leder. Gilah. (1980). Bright Girls, Mathematics and Fear of Success. *Educational Studies in Mathematics*. 11, 411-422.

Lovell, K. (1961). The Growth of Basic Mathematical and Scientific Concepts in Children. London: London University Press.

Lynwood, Wren, F. (1960). A Survey of Research in the Teaching of Secondary School Algebra, 1935 As Cited in Chester W, Harris (Ed), *Encyclopaedia of Educational Research*, Third Edition.

Maharashtra State Bureau of Textbook Production and Curriculum Research. (1974). A Survey of Primary Teachers' Qualifications—Their Opinions Regarding Mathematics and Science Syllabi, Pune, India.

Mainka, G.K (1983). Acquisition of Concepts in Mathmatics of Pupils at Primary Level and its Relation to Some Personal and Environmental Variables of the Pupils, Ph.D. Thesis in Education, Bombay University, Bombay, India.

Marshall, P.S. (1984). Sex Differences in Children's Mathematics Achievement—Solving Computations and Story Problems. *Journal of Educational Psychology*, 76, 2, 194- 204.

Menon, S.K. (1987). A Comparative Study of Personality Characteristics of Over Achievers and Under Achievers of High Ability. In M.B. Buch Ibid, p. 674.

McIntosh, W. (1986). The Effect of Imagery Generation on Science Rule Learning, *Journal of Research in Science Teaching*, 23(1), 1-9.

Michael J.Zimmermann and Julius M. Sassenrath. (1978). Improvement in Arithmetic and Reading and Discovery Learning in Mathematics, *Educational Reserch Quarterly*, Vol. 3, No. 1, Spring, pp. 27-33.

Microsoft® Encarta® Encyclopaedia. © 1993-2001 Microsoft Corporation. All Rights Reserved.

Miyan, Mohammad. (1982). A Study to Examine the Effectiveness of the Methods of Teaching Mathematics in Developing Mathematics Creativity. Ph. D. Thesis, Jamia Millia Islamia.

Mohapatra, P.C. (1990). A Critical Appraisal of the Secondary School Mathematics Curriculum of Orissa, Ph. D. Thesis in Education, Utkal University, Orissa, India.

Morris, Janet (1981). Mathematics Anxiety: Teaching to Avoid It. *The Mathematics Teacher*. 74:6, 413-417.

Mrinalini, T. (2000). Teacher Self-Appraisal Technique, Feed Back from the Students, *University News*, 38(24), June 12, pp. 1-5.

Nagalakshmi, R.S. (1995). Construction of a Problem-solving Ability Test in Mathematics for Secondary Students and Study of Problem-Solving Abilities of X class in Twin Cities of Hyderabad, Ph.D. Dissertation, Osmania University.

Nair, A.S. (1981). Some Socio-Familial Variables Causing Underachievement in Secondary School Mathematics. *Journal of Educational Research and Extension*, 18 (2): 10-14.

National Policy on Education (1986). Ministry of Human Resource Development. New Delhi, Government of India (Department of Education).

N. C. E.R T. (1970). 'The National Board of School Textbooks': *Report of the Second Meeting , New Delhi*, N.C.E.R.T.

N.C.E.R.T. (1975). The Curriculum for the Ten Year School—A Framework. New Delhi, India.

Newcomb, T. M., Murphy, G. and Others (1937). Experimental Social Psychology. New York: Harper and Brothers, Revised Edition.

Newman, S.R. (1984). Children's Achievement and Self-evaluation in Mathematics. A Longitudinal Study, *Journal of Educational Psychology*, 76, 5, 857-873.

Nickerson, R.S., Perkins, D.N., and Smith, E.E. (1985).The Teaching of Thinking. Hillsdale, NJ: Lawrence Eelbaum.

Nilima Kumari, (1991). A Study of Relationship Between Socio-Economic Status and Conservation of Number and Substance in Delhi School Children. In M.B. Buch *Ibid*, p. 693.

Padma, M.S. and Chakrabarty, Parijat. (1990). Attitude of High School Students Towards Computer Education. *Journal of All India Association for Educational Research*. Bhubaneshwar, 3: 17-21.

Patel, A.D. (1977). Development and Tryout of Auto-Instructional Programmes in Some Units of Geometry for Class VIII and to Study Its Effectiveness in the Context of Different Variables, Ph.D. Edu., SPU.

Patel Dr. R.S. (1997). An Investigation into the Causes of Under-achievement in Mathematics of VIII Grade Pupils Having High Numerical Ability, Experiments in Education, Vol. XXV, No. 12, Dec, pp. 239-243.

Patel, C.B. (1975). To Develop Auto-Instructional Programmes in Geometry for Std. IX and to Find Out Their Effectiveness in Relation to Different Variables.,Ph.D. Edu., Gujarat University.

Patil, B. (1966). Some Factors Associated with Achievement in High School Mathematics, *Journal of the College of Education*, Karnataka University, V, 1, 18-20.

Pattison, P and Grieve, N. (1984). Do Spatial Skills Contribute to Sex Differences Contribute to Sex Differences in Different Types of Mathematical Problems, *Journal of Educational Psychology*, 76, 4, 678-689.

Peterson A.D.C. (1986). Techniques of Teaching, Education and Research Division, *UGC Mathematical Education Quarterly*, October/December.

Philips, Robert. Bass, Jr. Racher. (1970). Attitude as Related to Student Attitude and Achievement in Elementary School Mathematics, *Dissertation Abstracts International*, Vol. 30, p. 4316.

Pillai, K.K. (1970). A Survey of Teaching Mathematics in Secondary Schools in Kerala, *First Survey of Research in Education*, 292.

Purkait, B.R. (2002) Principles and Practices of Education, New Central Book Agency, Chintamoni Das Lane, Calcutta, pp. 222-229.

Rajendra Mishra. (1980). A Study of Attitudes Towards Mathematics of Secondary School Students. (Thesis Submitted to Patna University 1978), *Indian Educational Review*, pp. 91-94.

Rajasekhara, C.L. (1979). A Study of the Problems Faced by the Primary School Teachers in Teaching New Mathematics, Unpublished M.Ed. Dissertation, Bangalore University, Bangalore, India.

Rajendra Prasad, T.J. (1975). A Study of the Responding Behaviours of Junior High School Mathematics Teachers in Problem-solving in Real and Simulated Classroom Situations, Illinois.

Rajput, A.S. (1984). Study of Academic Achievement of Students in Mathematics in Relation to Their Intelligence, Acievement Motivation, and Socio-Economic Status, Ph.D. Thesis in Education, University of Punjab, India.

Ram D. Singh, Sudarshan P. Ahluwalia and Sunil K. Verma. (1994). A Study of Attitude of High School Students Towards Mathematics. *Experiments in Education*, Vol. XIII No. 10, October, pp. 207-215.

Raths, James. (1967). Studying Teaching, Prentice Hall, Inc., Englewood Cliffs, New Jersey.

Report. (1966). Education Commission, India, Ministry of Education, Mathematics, pp. 199-396.

Raymont, T. (1960). The Principles of Education, Orient Longmans, Mount Road Madras.

Reiss, K., and Albrecht, A. (1994). Unterscheiden Sich Madchen Und Jungen Beim Geometrielernen Mit Und Ohne Computer? [Is there a Difference Between Girls and Boys Concerning Learning of Geometry with and without Computer?]. *Mathematica Didactica*, 17(1) 90-105.

Dr. Rita Sinha Dasgupta. (1997). Emerging Trends in Science and Mathematics, *Education at the Dawn of New Millennium*, pp. 25-32.

Rosaly, A. (1992). The Relationship Between Attitude of Students Towards Mathematics and Achievement, M.Phil., Dissertation in Education, Madurai Kamaraj University, India.

Samant, B.B. (1944). A Survey of Teaching of Mathematics in Secondary Schools with Special Reference to Bombay Province, *First Survey of Research in Education*, 297.

Santhanam, M.R. (1972). Sex Differences Across Some Behavioural Dimensions of Teachers in Teaching Mathematics, *The Mathematics Education*, March, p. 57.

Dr. Santhamma Raju and Sree Prakash. (1996). Mathematical Aptitude in Relation to Socio-Familial Variables, *Experiments in Education*, Vol. XXIV No. 1, Jan, pp. 13-18.

Sarla Rajput and Mamta Agarwal (1998). How Well are Teachers Aware About Continuous Evaluation, *Indian Educational Review*, Vol. 33, No. 1, January, pp. 132-142.

Sax and Ottina.(1958). The Arithmetic Achievement of Pupils Differing in Experience, *California Journal of Educational Research*, 9: 15-9.

Shakuntala Devi, (2002). Figuring—The Joy of Number, Orient Paperbacks Madrasa Road, Kashmere Gate, Delhi.

Shakuntala Devi, (2002). Mathability: Awaken the Math Genius in Your Child, Orient Paperbacks Madrasa Road, Kashmere Gate, Delhi.

Schunert, J. (1951).The Association of Mathematical Achievement with Certain Factors in the Teacher, in the Teaching, in the Pupil and in the School, *Journal of Experimental Education*, XIX, 3, 219-238, March.

Seshagiri Rao D. (1981). Teaching the Slow-Learners in Mathematics, *Indian Education Journal of the AIFEA*, Vol. XI, No. 4, July, pp. 29-31.

Shah, P.A. (1992). A Critical Evaluation of Mathematics Syllabi Introduced in the Schools of Gujarat State, Ph.D. Thesis in Education, Gujarat University, India

Sharma, K.K. (1977). The Effect of Different Techniques of Feedback Upon the Attainment of Teaching Skills Related to Stimulus Variation, Reinforcement, Silence and Non-Verbal Cues in the Student Teachers'. Unpublished Doctoral Thesis, M.S. University of Baroda.

Sharon Wilhelm and Douglas M. Brooks. (1980). The Relationshnip Between Pupil Attitudes Toward Mathematics and Parental Attitudes Toward Mathematics, *Educational Research Quarterly*, Vol. 5, No. 2, Summer, pp. 8-16.

Shashi Kala. S.M. (1985). An Investigation into the Learning Difficulties in Algebraic Factorisation at VIII Standard in Some Selected Schools of Bangalore City and Try Out of a Remedial Approach, Department of Extension Services, R.V. Teachers College, Jaya Nagar, Bangalore.

Shiva Prasanna T.D. (1993). A Study of Problems of Mathematics Teachers in Bangalore City in Teaching Mathematics at Secondary Level, Department of Extension Services, R.V. Teachers College, Jaya Nagar, Bangalore.

Shukla, S. (1981). Identification of Major Skills Involved in Mathematics Teaching at Secondary School Stage, Ph.D. Thesis in Education, Banaras Hindu University, Varanasi, India.

Singh Chauhan C.P. (1978). Mathematics Education and Cognitive Factors, *Indian Educational Review*, July, pp. 86-91.

Singh (Dr.) R.D. and Verma (Dr.) S.C. (1992). Mathematics As a Function of Intelligence, Sex and Age: A Study of Attitudes of High School Students. *Indian Educational Review*. January, pp. 47-55.

Sinha, D.K. (1976). Evalution of Curricular Materials in New Mathematics, Jad. U., (NCERT Financed)

Sinha, R. (1996). Science and Mathematics Education for 21st Century, *Paper Presented at Visva Bharati University*, Santiniketan.

Sinha, R. (1997). Mathematics and Modern Civilisation, *Journal of Centre of Pedagogical Studies in Mathematics*.

Sloan, F.A. and Pate R. (1969). Teacher Pupil Interaction Differences Between School Mathematics Study Group and Traditional Mathematics, Oklahoma University, Norman, Oklahoma.

Smith, R.L. (1985). Presentational Behaviours and Student Achievement in Mathematics, *The Journal of Educational Research*, 78, 5, 292-298.

Srivastava, J.P. (1992). A Study of Learning Outcomes in Terms of Objectives in Mathematics, Independent Study, Meerut University, India.

Sudha R. Sinha. (1980). Effect of School System on the Competence of Secondary School Students. *Indian Educational Review*, January, pp. 62-77.

Sudheer Kumar (2000). Teaching of Mathematics, Anmol Publications Pvt. Ltd., Ansari Road, Darya Ganj, New Delhi, pp. 170-171.

Dr. Sumangala V. (1995). Some Psychological Variables Discriminating Between High and Low Achievers in Mathematics, *Experiments in Education*, Vol. XXIII, No. 10 and 11, Oct/Nov, pp. 165-174.

Sumangala, V. (1998). Effect of Tutoring at Home on Acievement in Mathematics of Secondary School Pupils, *Experiments in Education*, September, Vol. 26, No. 9, pp. 155-158.

Sundararajan, Dr. S. and Dhandapani, Mr. B.(1991). Attitude of the Higher Secondary Students of the Pondicherry Territory Towards the Study of Mathematics and Their Achievement in It. *Experiments in Education*, Vol. XIX, No. 9, September, pp. 249-260.

Dr. Suneel Sumar Singh, Shaheen Malik and Dr. A.K. Singh (2003). Achievement Difference Class II Students in Maths, with Regard to Area, Gender, and Social Groups, during B.A.S. and M.A.S. in Gonda District. *The Educational Review*, March, Vol. 46, No. 3 pp. 55-57.

Supples and Ginsberg. (1962). Experimental Studies of Mathematical Concept Formation in Young Children. *Science Education*, 46:230-40.

Supples and Macknight.(1961). Sets and Numbers in Grade One.1959-60, *Arithmetic Teach*, 9: 96-97.

Dr. Thilaka Suresh and C. Geetha, (2003). Mathematics and Anxiety Among High School Students. *The Educational Review*, January, Vol. 46, No. 1, pp. 11-13.

Thomas, K.J. (1991). A Study of Attitude Towards and Achievement in Mathematics Among Secondary School Students in Aizawl Town. Aizwal: North Eastern Hill State. Unpublished M.A. (Education) Dissertation.

UNESCO. (1983). *Science for All*, Bangkok.

Upinder Dhar. (2000). "Managing Educational Services", With Special Reference to Management Education in India. *University News*, 38(20), May 15, pp. 8-9.

Vani R.H. (1992). A Study to Identify the Essential Competencies in Teaching Mathematics as Perceived by Secondary School Teachers, Department of Extension Services, R.V. Teachers College, Jaya Nagar, Bangalore.

Vasanthi, R.(1991). Mathematical Learning Disabilities in Relation to Certain Psychological, Social and Educational Factors, Ph.D. Thesis in Education, University of Madras, India.

Vasanthi, Dr. R. and Bamalalithambika. (1997). Interest of the High School Students in Mathematics., *Experiments in Education*, Vol. XXV, No. 4, April, pp. 76-82.

Vijayalakshmi, Ch.(1982). Application of Action Research in Teaching Mathematics, *Indian Education Journal*, Vol XII, No. 1 and 2, April/May, pp. 52-55.

Vijayalakshmi, Dr. G. (1992). Problems of Physical Science Teachers. *Experiments in Education*, Vol. XX, No. 2, Feb, pp. 35-39.

Vijay Kumar Dubey.(1992). Factorial Nature of Numerical Aptitude and Its Bearing on Mathematical Learning., *Indian Educational Review*, July, pp. 80-87.

Virginia, R.H.(1982). Assessing Pupil Attitudes Towards Mathematics Grades 4-6, Educational Resources Information Center, 18, 7.

Vygotsky, L. (1978). Mind in Society. Cambridge, MA: Harvard University Press.

Wanchoo, V.N. and Sharma, H.L. (1974). Survey and Development of Research in Science and Mathematics Education, NCERT, New Delhi.

Whimbey, A., and Lochhead, J.(1982). Problem Solving and Comprehension. Philadelphia, PA: Franklin Institute Press.

Whyburn, Lucille, S. (1970). Student Oriented Teaching—The Moore Method, *American Mathematical Monthly*, April.

Wilson, John W. (1967). The Role of Structure in Verbal Problem-Solving, *The Arithmetic Teacher*, 14, December.

Yadav and Chhangur Prasad. (1988). A Study of the Attitude of Teachers Towards New Mathematics in Secondary Schools of Uttar Pradesh, Ph.D., Thesis in Education, Patna University, India.

Yasui, Roy Yoshio. (1967). An Analysis of Algebraic Achievement and Mathematics Attitude Between the Modern and Traditional Programmers in the Senior High School. Document Resumes: ERIC. *Research in Education*, 6, (12): 80.

Zook, K.B., and Divesta, F.J.(1989). Effects of Overt, Controlled Verbalisation and Goal-specific Search on Acquisition of Procedural Knowledge in Problem Solving. *Journal of Educational Psychology*, 81(2), 220-225.

Index

W

Z

❑❑❑